AF505907

Education, Training and Labour Market Outcomes in Europe

Education, Training and Labour Market Outcomes in Europe

Edited by

Daniele Checchi
Università degli Studi di Milano

and

Claudio Lucifora
Università Cattolica, Milano

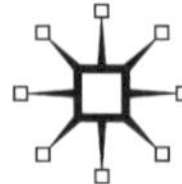

First published 2004 by
PALGRAVE MACMILLAN
Houndmills, Basingstoke, Hampshire RG21 6XS and
175 Fifth Avenue, New York, N. Y. 10010
Companies and representatives throughout the world

PALGRAVE MACMILLAN is the global academic imprint of the Palgrave Macmillan division of St. Martin's Press, LLC, and of Palgrave Macmillan Ltd. Macmillan® is a registered trademark in the United States, United Kingdom and other countries. Palgrave is a registered trademark in the European Union and other countries.

ISBN 1–4039–2080–X

This book is printed on paper suitable for recycling and made from fully managed and sustained forest sources.

A catalogue record for this book is available from the British Library.

Library of Congress Cataloging-in-Publication Data
Education, training and labour market outcomes in Europe/edited by Daniele Checchi, Claudio Lucifora.
     p. cm.
  Includes bibliographical references and index.
  ISBN 1–4039–2080–X (cloth)
    1. Education–Economic aspects–Europe–Cross-cultural studies–Congresses. 2. Private schools–Sociological aspects–Europe–Cross-cultural studies–Congresses. 3. Labor market–Europe–Cross-cultural studies–Congresses. I. Checchi, Daniele. II. Lucifora, Claudio.
LC67.E9E39 2003
306.43'094–dc21   2003055269

10   9   8   7   6   5   4   3   2   1
13 12 11 10 09 08 07 06 05 04

Printed and bound in Great Britain by
Antony Rowe Ltd, Chippenham and Eastbourne

Contents

Notes on the Contributors

Paolo Barbieri is Assistant Professor of Economic Sociology, Department of Sociology and Social Research, University of Milano-Bicocca, Milan, Italy.

Giuseppe Bertola is Professor of Economics, Department of Economics, University of Turin, Italy, and Istituto Universitario Europeo, Florence, Italy.

Gianna Boero is Associate Professor of Econometrics, Department of Economics, University of Cagliari, Italy, and Department of Economics, University of Warwick, UK.

Giorgio Brunello is Professor of Economics, Department of Economics, University of Padua, Italy.

Daniele Checchi is Professor of Economics, Department of Economics, University of Milan, Italy.

Gianni De Fraja is Professor of Economics, Department of Economics, University of York (UK).

Claudio Lucifora is Professor of Economics, Department of Economics, Catholic University of Milan.

Abigail McKnight is Senior Researcher, CASE, London School of Economics, London, UK.

Robin Naylor is Professor of Economics, Department of Economics, University of Warwick, UK.

Stefani Scherer is Senior Researcher at the Mannheim Centre for European Social Research (MZES), University of Mannheim, Germany, and the Department of Sociology and Social Research, University of Milan-Bicocca, Milan, Italy.

Peter J. Sloane is Professor of Economics and Director of the Centre for Economic Research, University of Swansea at Wales, UK.

Jeremy Smith is Professor of Economics, Department of Economics, University of Warwick, UK.

Alan Wagner is Professor and Chair, Department of Educational Administration and Policy Studies, School of Education, University at Albany, State University of New York.

Gregory Wurzburg is Principal Administrator, Education and Training Division, Directorate for Education, Employment, Labour and Social Affairs, Organisation for Economic Co-operation and Development, Paris, France.

Part I
Education Quality

1
Education, Training and Labour Market Outcomes

Daniele Checchi and Claudio Lucifora

Education and training have been at the forefront of public policy discussions and government policy making in most European countries in recent decades. A significant number of educational reforms have been implemented and others are pending. One of the reasons for this continuous attention to education and education policies is the strategic importance that the accumulation of knowledge has gained in the functioning of modern economies. Investment in human capital, in the form of education and work-based training, has proved a powerful way of improving individuals' employability, wages and lifetime earnings. At the macroeconomic level there is evidence that investment in education is crucial for countries' economic growth, productivity and competitiveness.

However, despite the ongoing debate on education and the generally shared view among researchers and government policy makers that education does matter for economic performance, on a number of important issues little is known at both the theoretical and the empirical level. For example do high-growth countries owe their performance to large investments in education, or is it that their high growth rates permit them to spend more on education? Are highly qualified individuals really more productive, or simply sorted into more productive jobs because of their relatively high qualifications? What does the coexistence of private and state schools imply for growth, social equality and social mobility? At the heart of these questions lie more fundamental economic questions, such as what determines the quality and efficiency of education systems? How do state–private schooling systems develop and how do they compete when they coexist? How can the education system be financed in an imperfect and incomplete market? How do education and training correlate in the population?

This volume takes a fresh look at the traditional debate on education, training and labour market outcomes. The following chapters, which were originally presented as papers at a conference on 'Education, Training and Labour Market Outcomes in Europe' at the Università Cattolica del Sacro Cuore on 16–17 November 2001, address two extensively debated issues: the role of private education, and the impact of education on labour market outcomes.

On the first issue, the theoretical literature claims that the existence of private education allows parents to choose the optimal amount of education needed to accord with the expected income of their offspring. In the political debate this claim corresponds to a plea for greater freedom of choice for all, especially when (as in the case of Italy) private institutions are mostly religious ones. However two interconnected factors should be distinguished: quantity and quality. Private institutions can tailor their services to the demands of parents (extracurricular activities, shortening/lengthening school hours and so on), and in principle they can improve the quality of teaching they offer as they are said to be more efficiently organised. Therefore from a social welfare perspective there are two good reasons to promote the creation of private schools. However two of the chapters in this volume raise some concerns about this conclusion.

In Chapter 3 DeFraia highlights a fact that is often neglected in the Italian debate but is very important in the UK one, namely that an important characteristic of the market for education is that the price is not the main strategic variable for providers. In many cases institutions face substantial unsatisfied demand at the price charged for attendance, and the allocation of places to applicants is made via some or other administrative mechanism, the most common of which is a quality threshold: only students whose potential (usually measured by past performance) is above a certain level are granted admission. But this mechanism opens the possibility of a (self-) segregated educational system, whose impact in terms of inequality can only be attenuated by a suitable voucher or scholarship system. The mere presence of fee-charging supplier, of education when free education is provided by the state suggests the existence of better-quality education. However empirically testing this proposition is not straightforward because self-sorting of students prevents direct comparisons of achievements. Students who attend private schools generally come from richer families and often have a better socioeconomic background.

In Chapter 4 Bertola and Checchi focus on the problem of self-selection in the choice of private schooling, and measure the net impact of attendance at private schools on academic performance. The main finding is that private schooling has a negative effect on tertiary academic performance, but, that private institutions do play a positive remedial role in improving the ability of less able children from rich families. Not surprisingly, Italian Catholic private schools play a different role from that of their American counterparts, which have traditionally catered to relatively poor students. The authors also draw attention to another fact that is typically overlooked in the Anglo-American literature but is crucial to the analysis of education systems in continental Europe. When the education system is stratified – that is, when there are separate vocational and generalist schools – families and children can self-sort themselves along this dimension instead of according to the private – public divide. In the case of Italy there is considerable evidence that children from richer families are overrepresented in high schools (*licei A*) and under-represented in technical schools (*istituti tecnici*). With this divide, families that want a better schooling environment for their children do not need to pay the price of private education since select high schools are publicly available at no cost. Students who attend high schools are typically oriented towards a subsequent university degree, and the peer effect works in the same direction. Conversely students in technical schools tend to come from a social environment that is more work-oriented. In this situation private institutions cannot offer a select environment, as it is already available, and therefore they offer more specialist products such as a religious orientation and/or support for less able students. With regard to the recent introduction in Italy of a voucher system to fund private schooling, given the abovementioned opportunity for social self-selection a significant change in family choices cannot be expected with such a system. As a consequence, the efficiency gains are likely to be limited and making school financing conditional on quality assessment would be more effective.

The second issue dealt with in this book is the labour market outcomes of education. Theoretical models of school choice are based on the assumption that better-quality education is recognised in the labour market. Thus students from better schools and/or with a better school performance should have better prospects in terms of earnings and/or employ ability. This raises two related concerns: how do we define the 'quality' of education, and what are the actual consequences of education in the labour market? In Chapter 2 Wagner and Wurzburg address the first of these questions in a comparative perspective. According to their analysis, quality in formal education systems cannot be evaluated just by means of the usual criteria for judging the academic proficiency of students against internal standards – it also needs to be evaluated in terms of how well individuals are equipped to engage in learning as adults. This in turn depends on the capacity of education systems to be inclusive and to sustain quality consistently, but Wagner and Wurzburg's empirical analysis of OECD countries shows that the mean level of quality in education systems appears to be independent of their degree of inclusiveness.

With regard to the recognition of educational quality in the labour market in Chapter 6, Boero, McKnight, Naylor and Smith compare the Italian and UK university systems. They show that secondary school qualifications have a strong bearing on performance at university in both countries but that, unlike in the UK, the earnings of Italian university graduates are largely unrelated to measured educational performance. This can be partially explained by the differences between the education systems in the two countries. Unlike in the UK, in Italy tertiary education is a lengthy process, and the longer the time spent at university the more negative the effect on performance and subsequent pay. Similarly, students in Italy who move to a university outside their home region generally perform less well than students who do not, while the opposite is true in the UK. But this may also have something to do with differences between the national labour markets. If we think of the labour market as consisting of (formally or informally) queuing lists for better jobs (see Thurow, 1975), then the return to educational qualifications materialises as long as better jobs become available. But this in turn depends on the employment strategies of firms, labour turnover and more generally on what affects the average tenure of jobs. Unlike in the UK, the Italian labour market has always been fettered by excessive protection, and the reduced importance of educational credentials could be connected to this. Nowadays most of the newly created jobs are in non-traditional employment sectors, which are characterised by wage flexibility and greater dispersion of earnings. In a context of pure competition, this should mean higher returns from educational qualifications, as long as all jobs are all alike. However if the returns from rent-seeking activities (see Murphy *et al.*, 1990) are higher than those obtained from productive activity, the *status quo* is likely to be maintained.

Thus UK and Italian students face rather different prospects. The former know in advance that a good academic performance will result in improved earnings and career opportunities, and therefore they will try to achieve a first-class degree, while the latter know that job opportunities are barely related to academic performance, and therefore the opportunity costs are low and there is little incentive to achieve a good degree. This could also explain the lower participation rate in tertiary education in Italy (see also Breen *et al.*, 1998).

In Chapter 8 Brunello investigates training incidence in 11 European countries and finds a positive relationship between educational attainment and subsequent training. He shows that this is related to labour market institutions (wage compression, minimum wages and employment protection), and suggests that even where educational achievements are not immediately reflected in the wage structure, they can prove useful in individuals' careers, both within and outside the firm. As a consequence further education in countries such as Italy, where the monetary returns are low, is still a rational choice when considered in relation to lifelong earning.

References

Breen, R., Iannelli, C. and Shavit, Y. (1998) 'Occupational returns to education in Italy: a consideration of rational action theory of university attendance', European University Institute, Florence.
Murphy, K., Shleifer, A. and Vishny, R. (1990) 'The allocation of talent: implication for growth', *Quarterly Journal of Economics*, May, pp. 503–30.
Thurow, L. (1975) *Generating Inequalities* (New York: Basic Books).

2
Redefining Education Quality: Lessons from an International Perspective[1]

Gregory Wurzburg and Alan Wagner

Introduction

Quality – in terms of its definition and measurement – is subjective. Moreover the implications of judgements about quality can be variable or ambiguous in that education policy serves the multiple objectives of reproducing and transmitting social and cultural values and tradition, as well as cognitive development. Assessments of education quality sometimes have unclear implications for policy because the governance of education varies across political jurisdictions; implications are controversial because of the stakes involved, including the institutional stakes of providers.

However the debate on education quality appears to be in a state of flux because of three interrelated developments: the economic stakes have increased and become starker; participation in education has risen; and the space in which learning occurs and the circle of actors with stakes in the provision and outcome of education has widened. At the same time there has been a shift in the preoccupations of these stakeholders – decision makers responsible for a broad range of policies, learners and their families, and social partners – away from education inputs and towards education outputs and outcomes. Because of these developments the debate on education quality needs to take into account two new criteria against which education systems are judged: inclusiveness and systemic capacity to sustain quality.

This chapter briefly surveys the developments that have influenced the education quality debate, and the reasons for introducing additional criteria. It then discusses where countries stand with respect to these additional criteria, and the implications of this. In so doing the chapter adopts an international comparative perspective.

Developments that have influenced the quality debate

As stated above, three developments have influenced views on the definition and evaluation of education quality. The following discussion summarises these developments from the international perspective of the Organisation for Economic Co-operation and Development.[2]

Rising economic stakes

Labour and skills have long been seen as important determinants of economic performance. In 1776 Adam Smith argued in *The Wealth of Nations* that the division of labour was the key to productivity and that education contributed to specialisation. From the 1950s a substantial body of theoretical and empirical literature on human capital began to emerge. At the microeconomic level it focused on the relationship between investment in human capital in the form of formal education, and then on work-based training. It tended to support the view that education and training had a powerful impact on employability, wages and lifetime earnings. Subsequent empirical studies demonstrated a strong positive relationship between early formal education (including tertiary studies before entry into the labour market) and later participation in various forms of further education and training. At the macroeconomic level researchers found strong empirical evidence of a positive relationship between investment in formal education, and economic growth, productivity and competitiveness. In both the microeconomic and macroeconomic literature there were recurring questions about causality and the real contribution of education to various measures of performance. Are highly qualified individuals really more productive, or simply sorted into employment because of their relatively high qualifications? Do high-growth countries owe their economic performance to a large investment in education, or is it that their high growth rates permit them to spend more on education? Overall, by the end of the 1980s it was generally agreed by researchers and government policy makers that education did matter for economic performance.[3]

In the early 1990s, however, there was a marked shift in perceptions about the relationship between human capital investment, public education policy and private training on the one hand, and economic performance on the other. The economic restructuring that followed the oil shocks of the 1970s and the stagflation of the late 1970s and early 1980s brought far-reaching changes in the economies and societies of industrialised countries. The shift started as a decline in traditional manufacturing output and jobs and an increase in service provision and employment. Low-skill jobs disappeared more quickly than high-skill jobs emerged. To an extent the changes were pushed by shifts in relative factor prices (including the cost of energy and low- and unskilled labour), but some of the strongest forces were the growth of information and computer-based technology (ICT) and the liberalisation of trade and direct investment.[4]

These developments, summed up as the 'transition to the knowledge society', raised the premium on knowledge and know-how and focused the attention of policy makers and stakeholders on policies and institutional arrangements that would influenced the level, distribution and quality of investment in human capital. They also prompted concern about the impact of these policies and institutional arrangements on the flow of knowledge and know-how, for two reasons:

- Long-term unemployment was suffered disproportionately by poorly qualified adults. These were people who had entered the labour market with adequate qualifications but then found themselves jobless and underqualified for new employment as entire industrial sectors restructured or collapsed.
- It was becoming apparent that, as the pace of innovation and economic restructuring picked up, even those with qualifications had to take steps to upgrade and update their knowledge and know-how.

Regardless of whether the importance of education and training had changed, by the late 1990s education and training policy were increasingly perceived by macroeconomic policy makers, trade unions and employers as key instruments in national strategies for growth, welfare and competitiveness. While this point of view did not deny the non-economic goals and values of national education systems, they certainly sharpened concern about the quality and accessibility of education.[5]

Rising participation rates

The economic developments in the OECD member countries did not occur in a vacuum. As economies evolved away from primary industries and manufacturing and incomes rose, social aspirations rose too, as did educational attainment. There was a sharp increase in participation in tertiary education in the US immediately after the end of the Second World War, and that trend spread throughout the OECD countries, with participation and completion rates in upper-secondary and tertiary education rising steadily. One can see the magnitude of this by comparing the educational attainment of younger and older persons (OECD, 2001a, ch. 2, 2001b). Taking the OECD countries as a whole in 1999:

- People aged 25–34 were 60 per cent more likely to have completed upper-secondary education than 55–64 year olds.
- The same group of younger persons was 78 per cent more likely to have acquired an academic tertiary qualification and 80 per cent more likely to have acquired a technical tertiary qualification.
- The increase in participation was more dramatic among women – younger women were nearly 150 per cent more likely than older women to have a tertiary qualification.

This trend was supported in part by policies to increase expenditure on education. But it was also driven by a growing social demand for education, which was in turn fed by rising standards of living, higher expectations among young people and their parents, and the call for better opportunities for girls and young women. High levels of youth unemployment during the 1980s drove home the point that skill requirements were edging up. The slack labour markets also lowered the opportunity cost of young persons who wished to pursue further study by robbing many of them of the option of gainful employment. Finally, the substantial earnings gains associated with higher education and the high, and in some countries rising, internal rates of return on higher education also stimulated increased participation in higher education (see OECD, 1997a, 1998b).

More recently, increased participation was endorsed when OECD ministers committed themselves to making lifelong learning a reality for all. When setting targets, education and labour ministers alike pushed for near universal completion of upper-secondary education or its equivalent (completion of an apprenticeship programme leading to a recognised qualification) and increased participation in tertiary education. By the end of the 1990s the profile of the pupil and student population had been transformed and was in terms of academic ability, career aspirations, preferred programmes of study and learning needs.

A shift in focus away from education inputs and towards outputs and outcomes

As human capital came to be seen as a more decisive influence on economic and social outcomes and as participation in education increased, a shift in perceptions about how to influence education and the larger process of human capital development was inevitable. Perhaps the clearest manifestation of this was the 'lifelong learning' mandate, which was endorsed at the international and European levels by OECD education and labour ministers and the European Commission respectively.[6] It stressed the importance of individuals learning throughout their lives in the full spectrum of settings (ranging from formal education to the workplace, the home and other informal and non-formal settings).

In putting the focus on the learner, stressing the need for all persons to engage in lifelong learning and emphasising the diverse settings in which learning could take place, the commitment to lifelong learning was accompanied by shift in focus away from education inputs and towards education outputs and outcomes. This too was inevitable because when the institutional arrangements for human resource development extended beyond the formal education system, inputs to the formal system were no longer the only instrument for change. What the learner knew was more important than how the learner learned what he or she knew. And what the learner could do was as important as what the learner knew.

The shift in focus away from inputs to the formal education process was not the result of the lifelong learning mandate alone. There was growing concern in the education community about the quality of education, defined in terms of the curriculum and outputs such as academic performance (OECD, 1989a). The availability of statistics and indicators on output and outcomes provided empirical support for the shift in focus. Publication by the OECD of international statistics on educational attainment enabled international evaluations of quality to take better account of the labour market outcomes associated with different education inputs (OECD, 1989b). The shift in focus both supported and was supported by the International Adult Literacy Survey, the first results of which were published in 1995. The survey provided internationally comparable evidence of education outputs, learning outcomes, as measured by literacy scales, and the labour market outcomes associated with different educational attainment and literacy levels (OECD and Statistics Canada, 1995).

Finally, in an attempt to focus even more narrowly on the outputs and outcomes of the formal education sector, in the late 1990s more than 30 countries agreed to undertake a new international survey of education output and outcomes. The OECD's new Programme for International Student Assessment (PISA) takes a broad approach to the definition of assessments, rather than drawing on definitions that are limited to specific curricula or are specified solely in terms of subject-matter knowledge (OECD, 2000c). Its purpose is to provide a basis for judging how well schools are helping young people to acquire and use the knowledge needed to function properly in today's economy and society. It also will provide the basis for evaluating the relative efficacy of policies and institutional arrangements in different countries in overcoming the effects of family social background of other contextual factors that influence education output and outcomes.

Conclusions: a changed standard for evaluating education quality

The developments outlined have changed the roles and functioning of education systems, enlarged the circle of actors who have stakes in the quality of human capital, and changed people's views on and expectations of the processes, institutions and policies involved in human capital formation. In this context, quality in formal education systems cannot be evaluated just by means of the usual criteria for judging students' academic proficiency against internal standards. It also needs to be evaluated in terms of how well it equips individuals in a society to engage in learning as adults. This in turn depends on the capacity of education systems to be inclusive and consistently sustain quality. There is also value in evaluating countries in a comparative international context, since in a world that is increasingly characterised by global markets for education as well as labour, the benchmark against which countries should be judged is the performance of other countries. The following sections compare the quality of national education systems according to these general criteria, using a number of indicators.

The inclusiveness of education systems

In societies that attach social and economic importance to learning, 'inclusiveness' is a crucial criterion for evaluating the quality of education systems: *ceteris paribus*, the more accessible that education is the better. The long-standing policy of eight to ten years of compulsory education has provided the foundation for completion rates in upper-secondary education in most industrialised countries to creep past 85 per cent. Now that countries are pursuing policies to make lifelong learning a reality for all, and as the social and economic demand for education continues to increase, inclusiveness is assuming greater importance as a criterion for judging education at all levels, from preschool onwards. The following discussion compares education systems by considering evidence on enrolment in preschool, upper-secondary and tertiary education.

A prerequisite for lifelong learning is a sound foundation in basic educational competences. There is ample evidence that, on average, children are more likely to underperform in compulsory education if they enter school poorly prepared to learn (OECD, 1999a, ch. 2; 2001c, pp. 34–43). Students do badly in tertiary studies if they lack critical analytical and drafting skills (OECD, 1998b). Adults who are unable to read can hardly learn on the job, benefit from further training (OECD and Statistics Canada, 2000) or overcome the risk of social exclusion in a knowledge-based society (US Department of Education and OECD, 1999). Further learning by the adult population is associated with better jobs and working conditions, and with improved enterprise performance (OECD, 1997b; 1999b, chs 3, 4).

'Foundation' in this context, then, refers not to basic skills but to a continuity of learning that extends into the first stage of tertiary education. In different ways, country quality assessments already reflect linkage and continuity across levels. Denmark's Centre for Quality Assurance and Evaluation of Higher Education, now called the Danish Institute of Evaluation (EVA), had its mandate extended to undertake a systematic and mandatory evaluation of teaching and learning at all levels of education. New Zealand's Qualification Framework, on which unit standards for all levels of education are placed, provides comprehensive coverage of learning standards, if not full coverage of how units are linked in terms of progress. Progression and continuity within and across all stages of education is the focus of Ireland's new Qualifications Authority (QA), an umbrella body that oversees awards committees and individual higher and further education institutions. Its guiding principle is 'the facilitation of access, progression, transfer and mobility' (Langford, 1999). These and other countries make use of different measures of progression (or lack of progression), linkages and recognition, but mostly not in ways that fully embrace 'foundation' learning (including foundation learning for adults who have not acquired competences). Within and among countries, however, quality in terms of the breadth and extent of education can be at least partly gauged by the degree of participation in a range of learning activities.

Drawing on available evidence, the indicators presented below enable a partial assessment of where countries stand in respect of inclusiveness of access to education for school-aged children and youths and learning opportunities for adults.

Early childhood education and care

There is no doubt about the importance of early childhood experiences for the cognitive, behavioural and social development of children and the development of a sound foundation for lifelong learning. Disadvantages at this stage of life can hinder later learning. But what this implies for policy depends on societal views about the respective roles of society and of the family. Some countries opt for policies that reinforce the role of the family by making it easier for working parents to withdraw from the workforce to care for their children at home. This reduces the need for institutional places for early childhood education and care (ECEC). Conversely some countries put considerable emphasis on the creation of ECEC programmes for children whose parents work, while other countries remain neutral in this regard.

Evaluating inclusiveness at this level would ideally take account of the availability of home and institutional child care, as well as the comparative quality of such care. A more limited and pragmatic approach is to review the existing range of international indicators on ECEC and to interpret such data with due regard to other considerations, such as evidence of whether parents are likely to be able to assume full-time child-care responsibilities. One such indicator is the proportion of three-year-olds in pre school education. Figure 2.1 shows that in 1998 there was a large variation among OECD countries with regard to the provision of learning opportunities for three-year-olds, ranging from over 90 per cent in France, Belgium (the Flemish community) and Italy to less than 5 per cent in Ireland and Turkey. The OECD thematic review on early childhood education and care suggests that there are limitations to this particular indicator. For example in Australia and some other countries there are numerous facilities for care outside the institutional providers whose enrolments are captured in the statistics. Countries that have opted to encourage ECEC activities within the family do not show high participation rates on this measure. Despite these limitations, much of the variation in Figure 2.1 reflects real differences in policies and priorities. For example the differing participation rates are partly a reflection of policy choices on the allocation of financial resources. Those countries in which more than 50 per cent of three-year-olds take part in organised, centre-based programmes typically spend more than 0.5 per cent of GDP on pre school

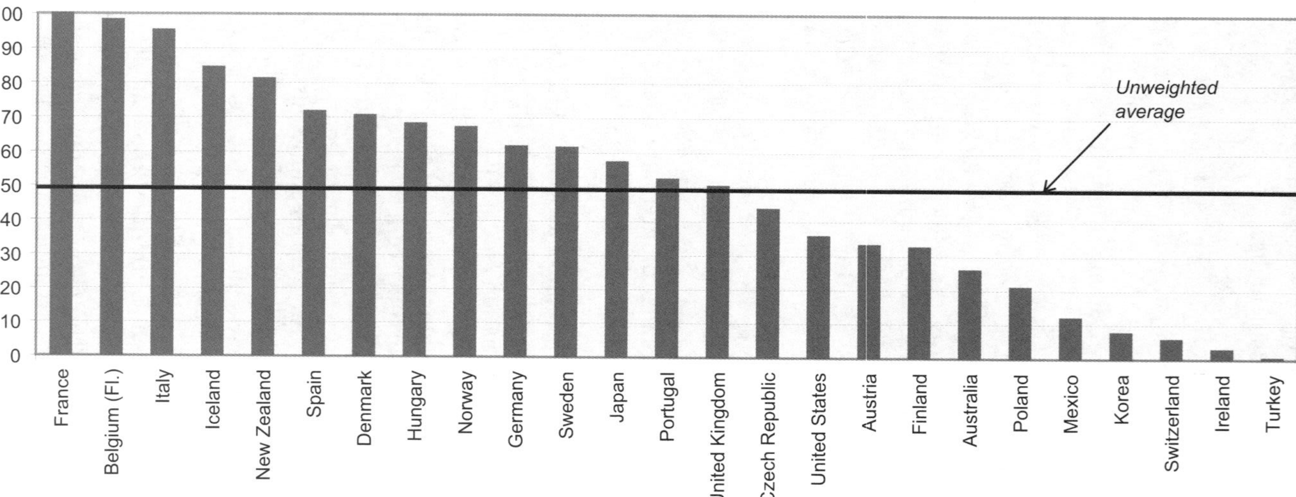

*The data refer to participation in organised, centre-based instruction programmes for children between the age of three and compulsory school age. Programmes organised as day care, play groups and home-based structured and developmental activities are not included. *Source*: OECD (2000a).

Figure 2.1 Participation in preschool education, OECD countries, 1998 (per cent)*

education, for example France spends 0.7 per cent and Denmark 1.1 per cent.

What does all this evidence imply for the quality of education? First, probably more than in any other area of learning, it is difficult to discern a 'quality norm' for best or good practice. The variation across countries in participation rates and overall spending appears to reflect a high degree of differentiation in policies. The OECD's reviews of early childhood education and care have found considerable variation across countries with respect to the age of eligibility for publicly provided programmes and the extent to which they are targeted or universal. Countries also differ with respect to the degree that such services are centrally administered and regulated, and the extent to which ancillary policies such as provisions for parental leave are related to ECEC policies (OECD, 1999a ch. 2, 2001c, pp. 48–61). In Europe, countries differ in the nature of the institutions that provide ECEC. Nearly all but the Nordic countries provide nurseries/day-care/play groups for children up to the age of 3, the Nordic countries focus on non-school, education-oriented programmes, and Spain has school-based programmes that begin at less than six months. Individual arrangements become less diverse within and across countries from the age of three, when participation in some countries rises markedly. Three fourths of all EU countries rely entirely or partly on schools, and half rely on mixtures of two or more forms of provision (European Commission, 2000, pp. 43–63).

In sum it appears that the quality of ECEC, defined in terms of its inclusiveness, varies considerably. One likely explanation of this is cost. Estimates suggest that, for most countries for which data are available, the capacity of facilities will have to increase substantially above the 1995 base (for example by more than 20 per cent) if the participation rate of all children below the age of six in 2005 is to reach the levels found in the countries with the highest participation rates. Switzerland, Finland and Turkey, for example, would need to increase their capacity by 100 per cent or more to achieve these levels (OECD, 1999a, ch. 1, fig. 1.2).

Upper-secondary education and training

Inclusiveness at the upper-secondary level is crucial. Recent OECD research suggests that, on average, completion of upper-secondary education or the acquisition of a recognised apprenticeship certificate is the minimum requirement for successful entry into the labour market and continuing employment (OECD, 1998b, 2000a; OECD and Statistics Canada, 2000).

The OECD member countries are now achieving high completion rates for upper-secondary education. In 1998 in three quarters of member countries, 70 per cent or more of 25–29 year-olds had completed upper-secondary education (Figure 2.2). In the Czech Republic, Norway and Korea the figure was more than 90 per cent. Figure 2.2 illustrates the substantial progress made over time by comparing the attainment levels of 25–29 year olds in 1998 with those of 50–54 year-olds who had left school two to three decades previously. Some of the most dramatic improvements occurred in countries where educational attainment had been very low, such as Spain and Portugal. By 1998 Australia, France, Korea and Finland had almost caught up with the countries with the highest upper-secondary completion rates.

Tertiary education

As completion of upper-secondary education has become near-universal in the OECD countries, it could be argued that tertiary education should also be judged on the basis of inclusiveness. However unlike appropriate benchmarks are not as evident as in upper-secondary education. The most obvious indicator is the proportion of the population with tertiary qualifications. This measure varies marked by among countries, ranging from up to 15 per cent of adults aged 25–64 in Austria, the Czech Republic, Hungary, Italy and Portugal to more than 30 per cent in Canada, Japan and the US (OECD, 2000a, p. 33). One can estimate the trend in enrolment by comparing the proportion of 30–34 year-olds with tertiary qualifications with the proportion of 50–54 year-olds with similar qualifications. As can be seen in Figure 2.3, the attainment rate had risen in all countries by 1998 but there was a marked difference between countries in terms of how quickly they were catching up with the leaders. Greece, Iceland, Korea and Spain had more than doubled their rates, and of these Iceland and Korea had experienced such a large growth in attainment rates that they had risen above the OECD average. For most countries with available data, the proportion of 30–34 year olds with tertiary qualifications lagged behind those in the leading countries and showed little evidence of catching up. In a few cases the gap had actually widened.

As many countries pursued policies to expand participation in tertiary education in the 1980s and 1990s, another useful measure of quality is the balance between academic versus more applied and technical streams of study in tertiary education. The logic for evaluating quality on this basis is that it measures the capacity of systems to provide a more diverse programme of studies to match the diversity of students' preferences and abilities, which is likely to increase as parti-

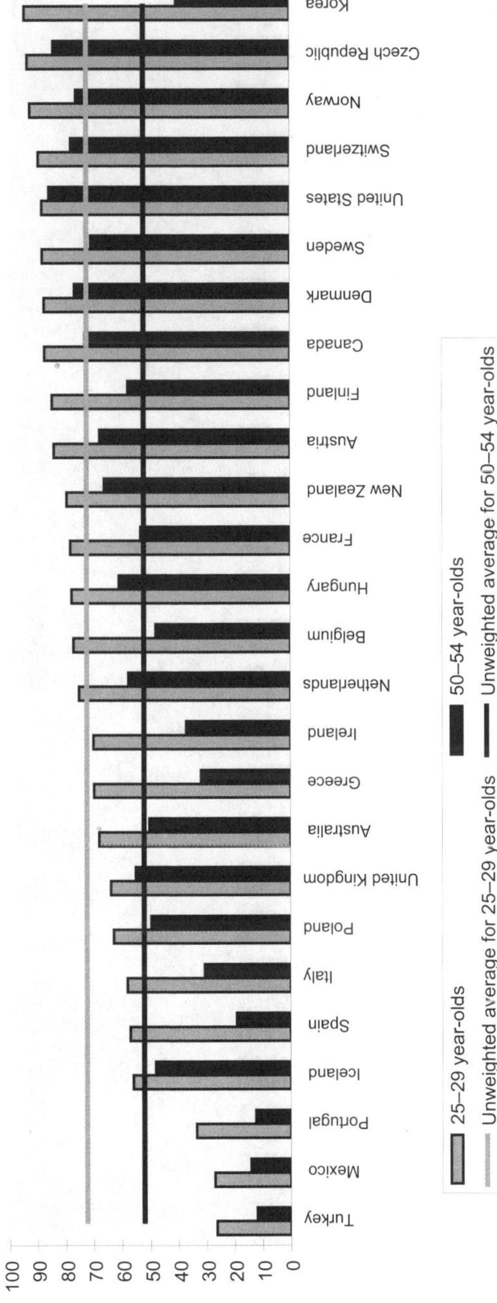

Source: OECD Labour Force Survey database (2000).

Figure 2.2 Percentage of 25–29 year-olds and 50–54 year-olds with upper-secondary education, OECD countries, 1998

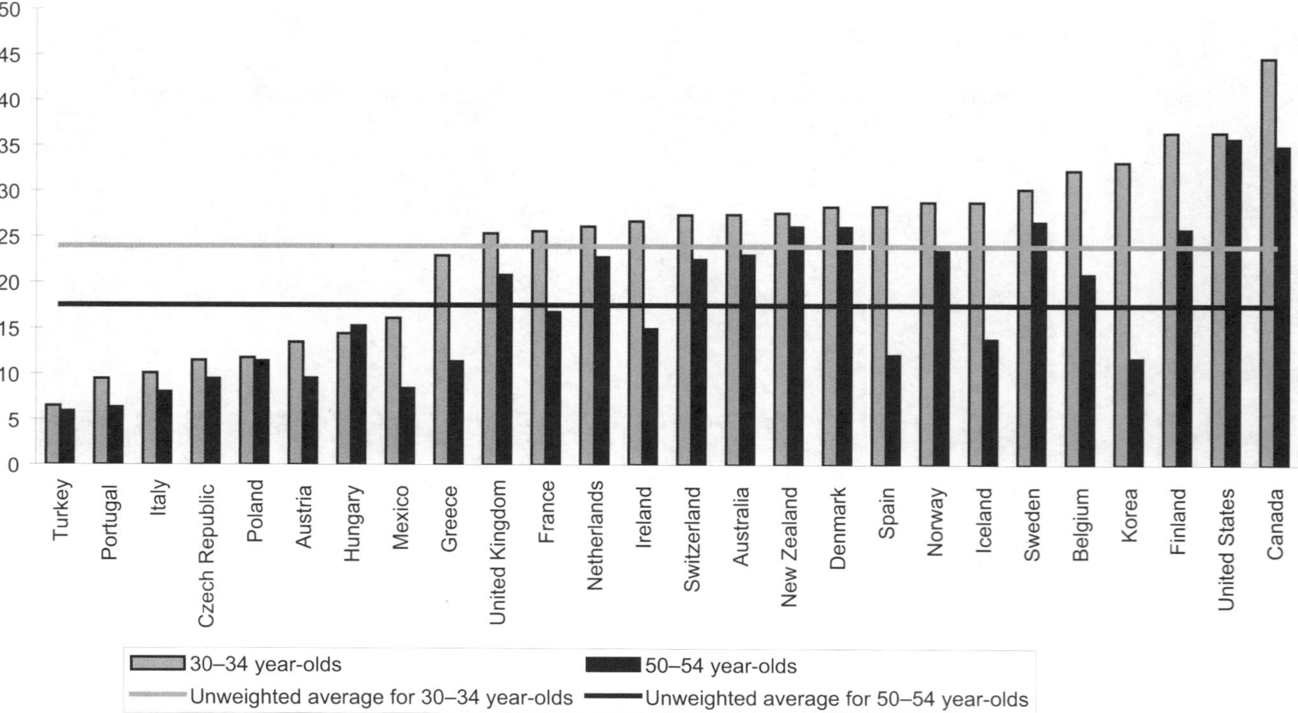

Source: OECD Labour Force Survey database, 2000.

Figure 2.3 Tertiary qualifications, OECD countries, 1998 (per cent)

cipation becomes more broad-based. Many countries' higher attainment rates are due to the expansion of tertiary education outside university-based studies. In Austria, the Czech Republic, Denmark and Finland – all of which have a relatively low proportion of unversity graduates and have shown little sign of change – alternatives to university studies are now being offered. Austria and Switzerland have introduced the equivalent of Polytechnics (called *Fachhochschulen*) and Finland has set up similar institutions, AMKs, to attract young persons who might otherwise not pursue tertiary education. The Finnish AMKs, from a very small base in the early 1990s, are expected eventually to account for more than two thirds of all tertiary-level enrolment. There is also growing diversity within the traditional sector. For example universities are offering more professionally oriented study programmes, including the French *instituts universitaires professionalisés* and the new bachelors' degrees in European universities, and private tertiary education establishments have been set up in Portugal, Mexico, Japan and Korea, and to a lesser extent in France and Germany (see OECD, 1998b). New cross-curricula and cross-border cooperations and links, (for example the introduction of technical and further education institutes within universities in Australia or dual degree programmes offered by private colleges and training schools in Japan), are other examples of diversity in provision.

Continuing education and training

One of the most important consequences of the emergence of the 'knowledge society' has been to force education systems to pay more attention to adults. The pace and nature of structural and technological change have made it necessary for adults to update and/or upgrade their knowledge, skills and competences. 'Once-and-for-all' education and training has become less and less adequate as a basis for continued employment. Many adults are handicapped by their low educational qualifications, and others who were adequately qualified when they left school have witnessed their occupations being transformed or disappearing altogether. On average, better-educated adults earn more and are less likely to be unemployed, and in this regard completion of upper-secondary education appears to be particularly important.[7] It is claimed that the pace and skill-bias of technological change have made it necessary for adults to advance their knowledge and skills, whether by returning to formal education and training, participating in structured further education and training, or undertaking non-formal learning through on-the-job training, peer-coaching or self-directed learning (Ernst & Young Center for Business Innovation and OECD, 1997; OECD and Statistics Canada, 2000; OECD, 2000c). It is also argued that in the knowledge society, continuous learning is needed if adults are to stay active outside working life (OECD, 1996, 1997b).

In two important ways these developments have changed the 'rules of the game' when it comes to judging education quality. First, they have increased the importance attached to adult participation in existing systems – this means a new role for education systems or enlargement of an existing role. Second, it embraces a more functional view of learning that extends beyond the actual (and feasible) reach of formal education to include the workplace, community and labour market training programmes, for example.

The upshot is that the criteria for assessing quality are more ambitious and the mechanisms for ensuring accountability are less certain. When judging participation in the range of extra-educational learning settings, the best one can hope for is that the usual agents of education policy and provision will influence quality though the part they play in enabling access. This calls for a rethinking of policies, perhaps using partially financing providers to promote and support cooperation and recognition. When education quality, in the form of adult participation in a broad array of learning opportunities, is absent, the consequences for policy and action are unclear. The discussion below addresses the issue of quality in adult learning by duly focusing on adult enrolment in formal education institutions.

Despite the widely held view that continuing education and training are important, there is only limited public provision of adult education and labour market training programmes. Adult education typically comprises just a small slice of total education provision under the auspices of ministries of education. Some of this takes the form of remedial education for adults with limited basic skills, plus vocational and non-vocational courses, usually up to the equivalent of secondary level, and adult enrolment in initial formal education, including tertiary education.

What can be said about formal education systems' capacity to accommodate the learning needs of adults? One way of assessing this is to examine the adult share of total enrolments in formal education. As can be seen in Figure 2.4, there are appreciable differences between countries. The share accounted for by individuals aged 35 and over is less than 2 per cent of total enrolments in more than half the countries for which data are available. This suggests that, for whatever reason, formal education systems are either not encouraging or not facilitating participation by

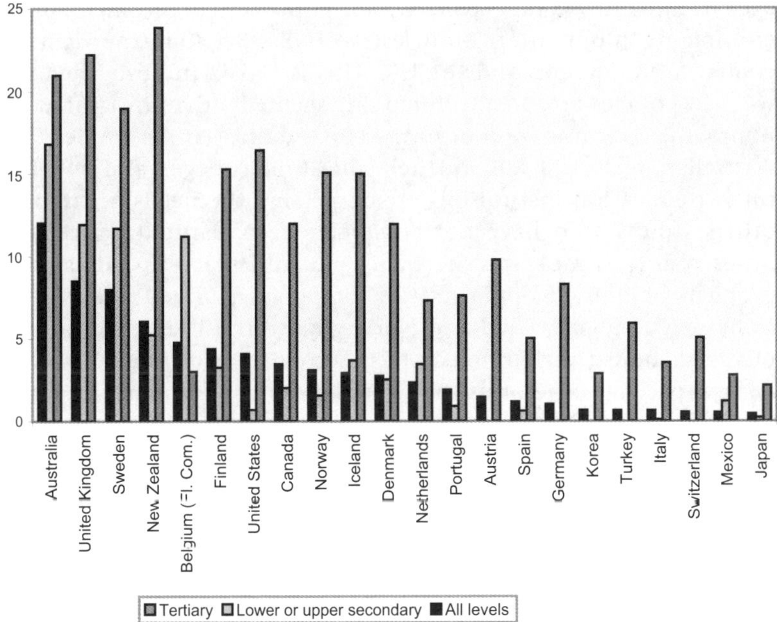

*Percentage of enrolled adults aged 35 and over
Source: OECD Education database.

Figure 2.4 Adult share in formal education by educational level, OECD countries, 1998 (per cent)*

adults. However this is not universal. In Australia, the UK, Sweden and New Zealand, 35-year-olds account for 6 per cent or more of total enrolments. Adult enrolments in formal education are concentrated in tertiary institutions. In several countries such institutions are being urged to extend their offerings for adults to degree as well as non-degree programmes. Provisions for adults are seen both as a response to adult demand and, more pragmatically, as a means to maintain enrolments in the face of a decline in the size of youth enrolments and secure revenues. This has long been the practice in countries such as Canada, New Zealand, the UK and the US, and it is now being adopted in other countries as well. Provision often takes the form of short industry-focused programmes and part-time and distance study options.[8]

There is a recognised need for increased learning options below the teritary level for adults with low educational attainment and literacy levels, but institutional responses have been limited. Persons aged 35 and older comprise more than 11 per cent of secondary level enrolments in only four countries: Australia, Belgium (the Flemish community), Sweden and the UK. This is linked in fairly obvious ways to policies and institutional arrangements that are geared to improving learning opportunities for adults. For example The Australian technical and further education colleges and the UK further education institutions are addressing the needs of, among others, adults who have not completed secondary education. In other countries measures are being put into place to redress the problem of limited opportunities for pooly qualified adults. For example in August 2000 the Norwegian authorities gave poorly qualified adults the right to complete secondary education as part of a larger package of reforms that would also include credits for non-formal learning. But the programme has not yet been implemented (details of how and where the education will be financed and pro-vided are under negotiation), so it is too early to know how many adults will take up the right to return to formal education.

Another facet of education for adults that should not be overlooked is the training provided by labour authorities, usually to teach new skills to the unemployed or at-risk individuals. On average the OECD countries spend about 0.2 per cent of their GDP on this (OECD, 2000d, pp. 223–30 and table 2.A in the statistical annex). However such train-ing is usually subordinate to the goal of employment placement and expenditure tends to be countercyclical (ibid.) Courses are typically of short duration and attendance is sometimes linked to eligibility for unemployment benefit (ibid., ch. 4).

In a number of OECD countries these training programmes serve substantially more than the unemployed: in a third of the countries for which data are available, employed workers account for nearly 50 per cent of all enrolments. In Belgium, Denmark, Portugal and Ireland such enrolments constitute an appreciable share of total adult educa-tion and training. In Portugal in 1998, for example, the percentage of employed people who took part in training programmes amounted to 9.3 per cent of the total labour force. In the same year an estimated 14 per cent of adults participated in continuing education and training (ibid., tables 2.A, 2.B, statistical annex). While this suggests that such training programmes are a significant source of educational oppor-tunity for adults, it is difficult to judge their quality.

Private educational organisations offer courses in relatively narrowly defined areas, such as foreign languages, computer and software skills and certain business skills. While the available data suggest that participation in such programmes is substantial and growing rapidly (Adelman, 2000), the data are too limited to allow a national, let alone an international, analysis of coverage and quality. It might be argued that such courses are of only marginal relevance to a discussion of education quality, but as they are an important element of the opportunities available to individual adult learners and of the learning environment in which education providers operate, they will merit attention in the future.

This section has reviewed evidence on the quality of education, as judged by the criterion of inclusiveness. This evidence suggests that in most countries the primary, secondary and tertiary education sectors are achieving relatively high participation rates, especially in the case of upper-secondary education. The picture is much less clear – and perhaps less satisfactory – with regard to learning in early childhood and adulthood.

The ability to deliver satisfactory education outputs and outcomes

The impact of increased participation in learning activities is either nullified or reduced if education systems and other institutional arrangements for human resource development cannot consistently sustain the quality of learning outcomes. The following subsections examine evidence on the average quality of outcomes and the degree of inclusiveness in formal education and on the relationship between quality and the degree of variance in the outputs and outcomes of formal and informal education systems.

Quality of education outcomes from the formal system

As formal education systems (as well as other institutional learning facilities have become more inclusive the spectrum of students' abilities and learning needs has broadened (OECD, 1989a), prompting concern about the quality of provision. The response has been to adapt curricula to increase the choices available to students (see OECD, 2001a, ch. 3) and to implement policies and processes to improve or maintain performance. In many countries these policies have been backed by governance and financing arrangements that allow for autonomy in educational establishments. The approaches include the setting of common standards, more frequent and/or more detailed inspections, external reviews (often involving independent, non-school inputs, perspectives and judgements) and performance indicators. In tertiary education, quality assurance through self-evaluation has been complemented and extended by quality assessments of the following items:

- Setting standards. In the UK the forerunner of the Quality Assurance Agency (QAA) undertook to develop and define 'graduateness' or what all higher education graduates should be expected to know and be able to do. That work evolved into the benchmarking of 'threshold standards' for individual fields of study.
- Linking standards to qualifications. More recently the QAA has developed a framework to facilitate 'public understanding of the achievements represented by higher education qualifications' (Quality Assurance Agency for Higher Education, 2001). The generic qualification descriptors complement the subject benchmark statements and programme specifications. Ireland's new Qualifications Authority combines processes concerned with quality with those for qualifications.
- Assessing student learning. The results of final sencondary-school examinations are used in France, Germany, the Czech Republic and elsewhere. Other countries obtain some indication of quality from levels of performance in tertiary education entrance examinations. In addition to student assessments at different stages of education, Mexico and Brazil have introduced (exit examinations for tertiary graduates in order to gauge quality. In the late 1990s Australia's minister of education proposed such a measure to demonstrate the quality of his country's higher education system.
- Assessing labour market outcomes. The US and Australia include in their assessments of the quality and performance of tertiary education consideration of the employment experiences of new graduates (Department of Education, Training and Youth Affairs, 1998; National Center for Public Policy and Higher Education, 2000; Smith *et al.*, 2000). This reflects both the greater importance attached to labour market outcomes and the growing availability of data and information.
- Benchmarking education performance. The Netherlands and the US among others, have produced reports that benchmark education performance, in the Dutch case as part of a broad review of the competitiveness of the Dutch economy (Netherlands Ministry of Economic Affairs, 1995). In the (school levels between kindergarten and 12th grade) US independent assessments have been conducted to benchmark K-12 and higher education (National Center for Public Policy

and Higher Education, 2000). Ireland's Higher Education Agency has been given the task of establishing benchmarks against which Irish higher education can be assessed in order to gauge Ireland's performance relative to the top quarter of OECD countries.

These initiatives reveal a trend towards stricter quality assurance and assessment, although the approaches require refinement and the measures are limited and uneven.

There are two ways of determining whether countries' education systems are inclusive and able to sustain quality. The first is to compare countries according to inclusiveness (proxied by the percentage of 25–29 year-olds who have completed upper-secondary education) and quality of outcomes (proxied by the mean literacy levels of people who have completed upper-secondary education and no more) (Figure 2.5). The literacy (quality) measure is based on the mean results of the 'document scale' of the International Adult Literacy Survey (IALS).[9] There is a fairly strong positive correlation (0.42) between the degree of inclusiveness of education systems and the quality of educational outcomes. This implies that there is not necessarily a trade-off between quality and inclusive-

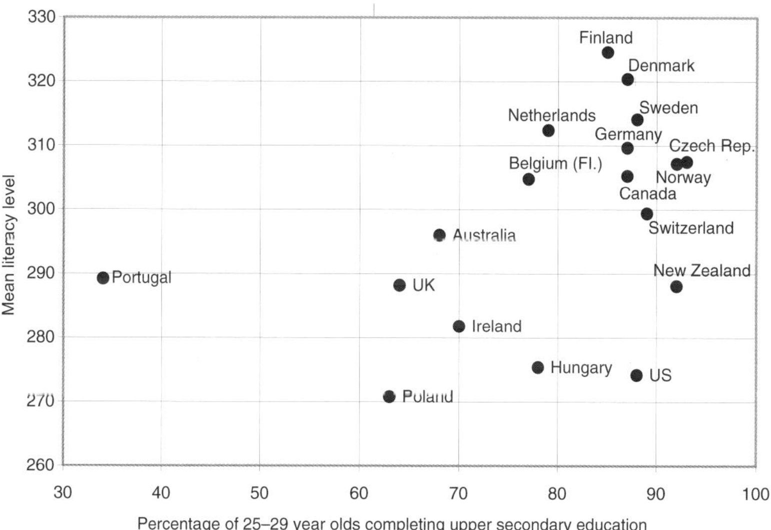

*Selected OECD countries, upper secondary completion and literacy levels
Sources: OECD, Education database and IALS.

Figure 2.5 Inclusiveness versus quality, 1994–98*

ness. However among the group of countries with highly inclusive education systems (levels of educational attainment above 85 per cent), quality varies widely, with New Zealand and the US faring poorly and Denmark, Finland and Sweden doing comparatively well.

The second approach is to look at the relationship between the mean quality of the output of national systems and variance around that mean, to see if, for example, higher mean values for quality are possible only by increasing the spread between stronger and weaker performers. This approach uses three types of data: data on the quality of education output in terms of the achievement scores of students after eight years of education, as measured by the Third International Mathematics and Science Study (TIMSS):- 1999 (this was a follow up to a study conducted in 1995) data on the quality of education outcomes in terms of mean literacy scores on the document scale of the International Adult Literacy survey (1994–96); and data on the achievement of 15 year-olds in respect of reading, mathematical and scientific literacy, as measured by Programme for International Student Assessment (PISA) in 2000. Figure 2.6 presents the TIMSS results for mathematics and science. The results show that not only is there no trade-off between mean quality and variance, but that the relationship is strongly negative (the correlation coefficient for science is –0.51 and for mathematics –0.58).

Figure 2.7 shows the relationship between outcomes in the form of literacy levels of individuals who have completed upper-secondary education and no more on the one hand, and variance on the other. In countries where the literacy levels of upper-secondary completers are higher, the variance in outcomes is smaller. This confirms that higher-quality outcomes are strongly associated with low levels of variance in those outcomes (correlation coefficient 0.68). Figure 2.8 presents the mean literacy scores of 15 year-olds with regard to retrieval of information, interpretation of text and reflection and evaluation (OECD, 2001d, pp. 34–7). Here the relationship between mean quality and variance is less pronounced than in Figures 2.6 and 2.7. However the results support the finding that high mean levels of quality are consistent with a relatively small degree of variation in quality (even when controlling for socioeconomic status, although this is not done in Figure 2.8).

Before considering the implications of these data, it is important to note that they have certain shortcomings that limit the inferences that can be drawn.

- Because the data are cross-sectional it is impossible to evaluate what happens over time within countries when policy pushes are made

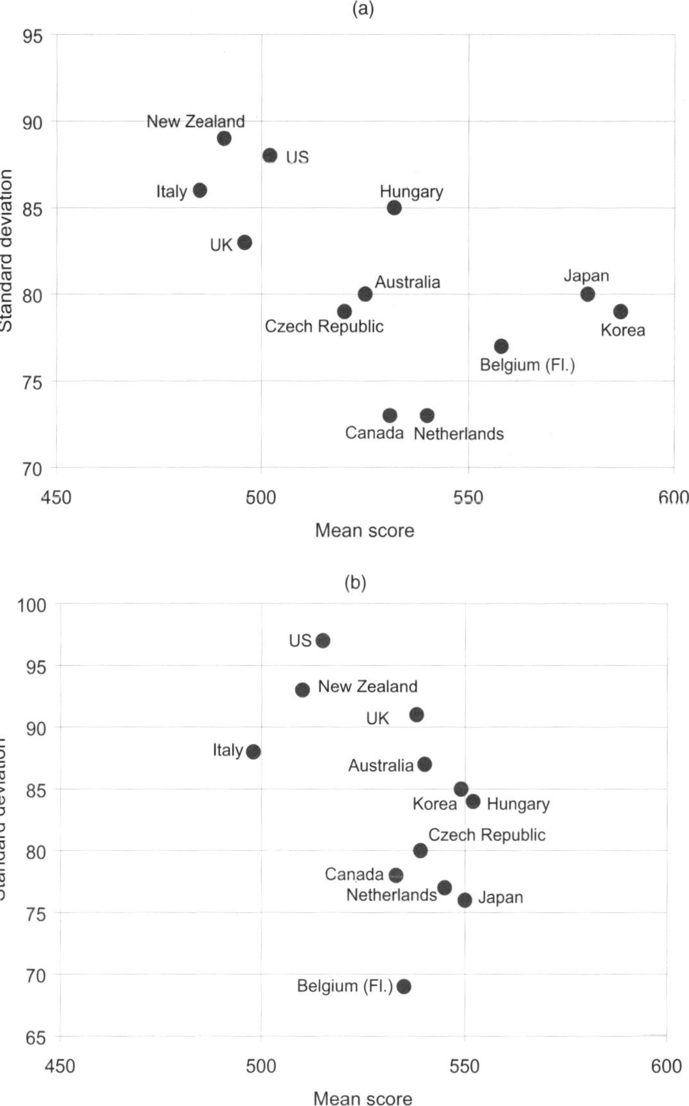

*Mean scores and standard deviations for eighth grade. In the case of Belgium, the UK and the Netherlands; the guidelines for sample participation rates were met only after replacement schools were included.
Source: OECD (2001b).

Figure 2.6 Levels and consistency of quality outcomes, OECD countries, 1999: (a) mathematics achievement, (b) science achievement*

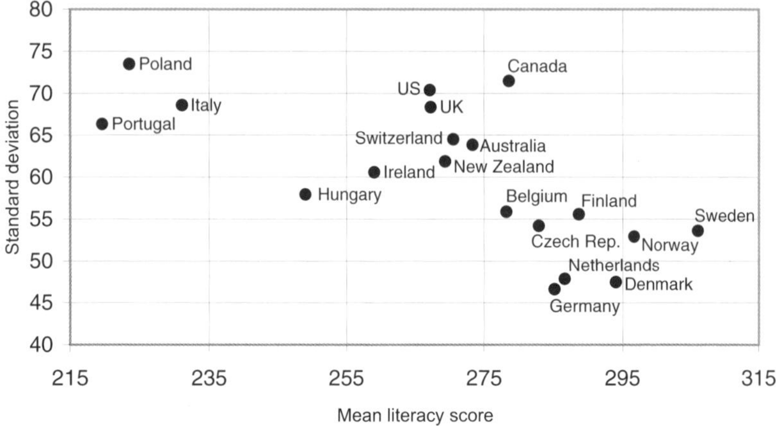

*Mean scores and standard deviations, as measured on the document scale of the International Adult Literacy Survey.
Source: IALS.

Figure 2.7 Levels and consistency of quality of outcomes: variance in quality versus inclusiveness, OECD countries, 1994–98*

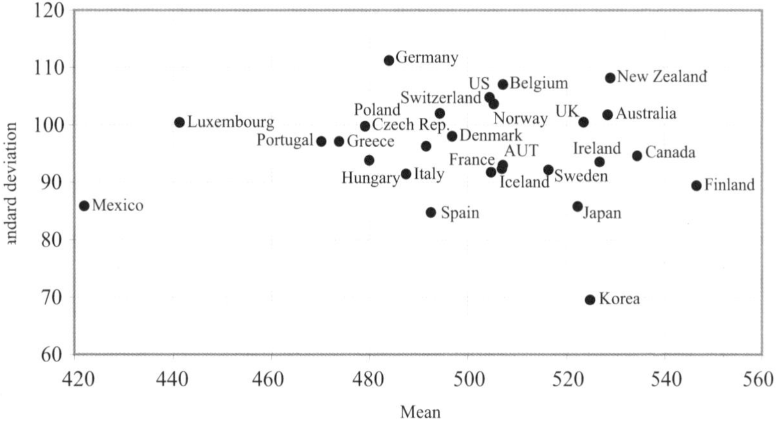

Source: PISA.

Figure 2.8 Variation in student performance on the combined reading literacy scale, OECD countries

for education systems to become more inclusive and or raise quality standards.

- The data for Figures 2.6 and 2.7 are highly aggregated. Therefore it is not possible to control for differences between countries in terms of, say socioeconomic composition or resources invested in education.
- The data used in Figures 2.6 and 2.7 relate to the education system as a whole, and not to subunits such as individual schools or regional school districts; hence they mask potentially important variations within countries.
- For the reasons outlined in the second and third points, the data provide no clues over the determinants of observed country routing.

Despite these caveats, the results show that these are considerable differences between countries. Among the countries covered by all the data, Belgium (Flemish), Canada and the Netherlands have been fairly consistent in achieving above-average levels of inclusiveness, above-average levels of quality and below-average levels of variance in output and outcomes. In contrast New Zealand and the US have a high degree of inclusiveness (but not the highest), mediocre to low levels of quality (whether measured in terms of literacy or achievement in maths and science) and a high degree of variability in the quality of output and outcomes. Among the countries for which only literacy data are available (Figures 2.5 and 2.7), the Nordic countries, the Czech Republic and Germany can be added to those which are performing well.

Perhaps the most important implication to emerge from this analysis is that it appears that at least some countries are successfully addressing 'the long-standing question . . . of reconciling excellence of provision with equality of opportunity for all citizens to gain access to good education and training', which was uppermost in the minds of OECD education ministers when they met in January 1992 (OECD, 1989a, p. 14).

A second implication is that policy makers and those who hold a stake in the output and outcomes of education systems are largely ignorant about how to improve the quality of education. They need to have a far better understanding of the parts played by socioeconomic characteristics and institutional arrangements (including systems for governance, accountability and finance, teacher and school autonomy, student assessment and so on) in determining the quality of education.

Finally, an international perspective can be of great value in understanding the determinants of quality if comparable international data can be collected without sacrificing detail on student characteristics and institutional arrangements. In this regard the results of international surveys such as the IALS and PISA merit close attention.

Quality of education output and outcomes for adults

Addressing the quality of education output and outcomes for adults is more difficult than addressing it for young persons. First, 'education intervention' is difficult to define unambiguously as arrangements vary from formal classroom settings to non-formal work-related training and informal learning at work, at home, as a hobby and so on. Second, outcomes are also is difficult to define unambiguously, partly because education for adults serves multiple purposes and partly because the systems for assessing what adults have learnt are so poorly developed. Third, participation is much more *ad hoc* and less systematic. Finally, it is not clear what the findings about education quality for adults imply for action, since the responsibilities for institutional arrangements are so diffuse.

In the face of these difficulties, one way to assess the quality of education for adults is to develop core indicators of quality of outcomes without relating them to particular interventions. The OECD adopted such an approach when it compared the literacy levels of older adults with a given level of education.

Figure 2.9 shows the results for countries that participated in the IALS. It reports for each country the average literacy level (as measured by the IALS document scale) of adults aged 46–65 who completed upper-secondary education some two to four decades earlier. It estimates the additional learning that has taken place since then because it indicates the proportion of population who perform at or above the literacy level which is considered consistent with completion of upper-secondary education in earlier decades. The larger the proportion that exceed this minimum threshold, the greater the likelihood that adults have found ways of acquiring new skills and competences. There are three drawbacks to this approach. First, the literacy measure captures just a small proportion of the competences that adults acquire during their working life. Second, it fails to control for differences in literacy levels that were present when these adults left upper-secondary education (and the data in the preceding section show that differences between countries are large). Third, this measure does not allow one to identify where and how adults learn. These caveats notwithstanding, this indicator does provide a crude measure of how much the combination of formal institutional arrangements, work-related training, on-the-job learning and other factors contribute to adult learning.

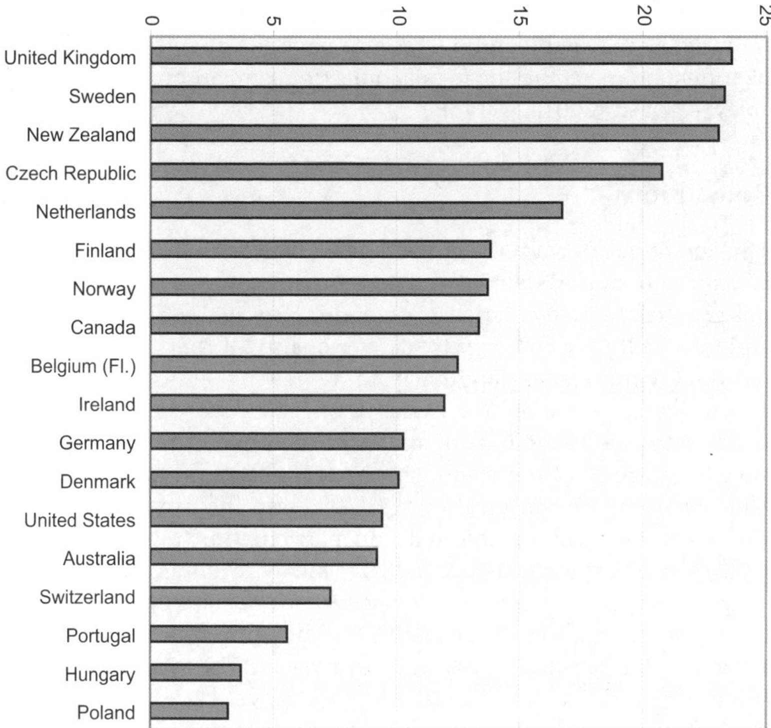

Sources: OECD and Statistics Canada; International Adult Literacy Survey.

Figure 2.9 Percentage of 46–65 year-olds with only upper secondary education and performing at literacy level 3 or above (document scale), OECD countries, (1995)

In the four countries with the highest values, adults with an upper-secondary education are roughly four times more likely to have high literacy scores than their counterparts In the three lowest ranking countries. It would appear that the nature of initial education and training systems is not associated with differences in this proxy measure of learning outside school. High- and low-ranking countries include those with strong vocational tracks and those with a more general orientation in secondary education. On the other hand differences in informal learning appear to bear some relation to opportunities for continuing education and training. The UK, Sweden and New Zealand, which have an above average performance on this indicator, have relatively high rates of participation in continuing education and training. New Zealand and the UK also have a relatively high number of annual hours of training for all adults (for comparisons of these variables see OECD 2001a, p. 146).

Conclusions

This chapter, after briefly surveying the factors that influence how education quality is defined and measured, suggested that education quality should be evaluated in terms of how inclusive systems are and how well they consistently deliver quality. It then took an international comparative approach to reviewing education quality according to these two criteria. Using national education systems/countries as the unit of analysis, The chapter presented evidence of where countries stand with regard to these additional criteria and discussed the implications. To evaluate inclusiveness it used internationally comparable data on participation rates in various sectors in which learning occurs. To evaluate levels and consistency of quality it used results from two international surveys and a more limited number of results from a third. The findings show that there are marked differences between countries, and the analysis revealed some of the factors in the structure and governance of education institutions that might contribute to the observed differences in quality. Several conclusions can be drawn:

- The circle of education stakeholders has widened as a result of social and economic developments. This has raised interest in the quality of education and led to quality being evaluated in terms of more diverse criteria.
- There has been a shift from supply-led to output/achievement as basis for assessing quality in education and training provision. This implies a shift of attention of governments from programmes and establishments to effective learning; this requires taking into account learning participation, outputs and outcomes from outside formal education institutions.
- Education systems are becoming more inclusive, partly as a result of policy and partly as a result of changes in individual behaviour. However there are considerable differences between some sectors of learning.
- There is evidence of policy intent to expand quality assessments, especially when looking at initiatives in a number of countries.

- There are substantial differences between countries with regard to the level and consistency of the quality of output and outcomes.
- In cross-country comparisons the mean quality of education systems appears to be independent of their degree of inclusiveness; moreover the mean level and consistency of the quality of outcomes appear to be independent of each other. The cross-sectional nature of the data does not allow one to evaluate the trade-off between inclusiveness and mean quality within a country, or between mean quality and consistency. But if such trade-offs exist the comparative data suggest that changes to policy and institutional arrangements might help to remedy the situations. In this regard there are good reasons for exploring how country-specific policies and institutional arrangements influence quality.

This chapter has suggested criteria by which to evaluate the quality of education systems, compared a group of countries according to those criteria and suggested features of policy and institutional arrangements within education systems that might explain the observed differences in quality. As such it has provided only a partial analysis of the causes of the observed differences in quality in that it has not considered external factors such as the impact of wage-setting practices on the wage premium for education (and thus the incentive for more individuals to participate in education). A more comprehensive analysis might obtain more realistic findings on the impact of strategies to improve quality. However the approach taken here represents a step in that direction.

Notes

1. This chapter draws heavily on OECD (2001a), ch. 2. It has benefited from the comments and suggestions provided by Andrea Montanino in the capacity of referee. The views expressed are those of the authors and do no necessarily reflect the views of the State University of New York or the OECD and its member countries.
2. The Organisation for Economic Co-operation and Development is an international organisation consisting of 30 member countries around the world. Its work includes the analysis of education and human resource policy and practice, and the collection of related statistics. This work is carried out under the aegis of the Education Committee and the Centre for Educational Research and Innovation. For further details on the Organisation, see www.oecd.org.
3. For reviews of macroeconomic and microeconomic theory and evidence see OECD (1986), ch. 2, and OECD (1996a).
4. For a review of the nature and causes of economic restructuring during this time see OECD (1994).

5. At the 1996 meeting of OECD education ministers the social partners argued strongly that steps should be taken to reduce early school leaving and increase learning opportunities for poorly qualified adults (OECD 1996c). Subsequent studies conducted for finance and economics ministries made much the same point; see OECD (2000a).
6. See OECD (1996c); European Commission (1995).
7. Evidence of this is presented in a wide range of OECD publications, including OECD (1994), (1996) and (1997). For recent data on earnings and unemployment by educational attainment level, see OECD (2000b), pp. 270, 297–8.
8. This issue was addressed at an OECD conference on 'Beyond the entrepreneurial university? Global challenges and institutional responses' in Paris on 11–13 September 2000.
9. Literacy levels were assessed in 18 countries between 1994 and 1998 by means of the International Adult Literacy Survey (IALS). Literacy was measured on the 'prose', 'quantitative' and 'document' scales. Survey participants provided information on educational attainment, other background characteristics and employment and training experience. For information on the definitions of the scales, the measurement of literacy and the results of the survey see OECD (1997a) and OECD and Statistics Canada (2000).

References

Adelman, C. (2000) *A Parallel Postsecondary Universe: The Certification System in Information Technology* (Washington, DC: Office of Educational Research and Improvement, US Department of Education).

Bradbury, B. and Jäntti, M. (1999) 'Child Poverty across Industrialized Nations', Innocenti Occasional Papers, Economic and Social Policy Series no. 71, (Florence: UNICEF International Child Development Centre).

Department of Education, Training and Youth Affairs (1998) *The Characteristics and Performance of Higher Education Institutions* (Canberra, ACT: DETYA).

Ernst & Young Center for Business Innovation and OECD (1997) *Enterprise Value in the Knowledge Economy: Measuring performance in the age of intangibles* (Cambridge, Mass.: Ernst & Young and OECD).

European Commission (1995) *White Paper on Lifelong Learning* (Brussels: European Commission).

European Commission (2000) *Key Data on Education in Europe* (Luxembourg: European Commission).

Langford, D. (1999) 'Implications of the Qualifications (Education and Training) Bill 1999', in T. Fleming, T. Collins and J. Coolahan (eds), *Higher Education: The Challenge of Lifelong Learning*, (Maynooth: Centre for Education Policy Studies, National University of Ireland).

National Center for Public Policy and Higher Education (2000) *Measuring Up 2000. The State-by-State Report Card for Higher Education* (San José, CA: NCPPHE).

Netherlands Ministry of Economic Affairs (1995) *Benchmarking the Netherlands. Test of Dutch Competitiveness* (The Hague: Ministry of Economic Affairs).

OECD (1986) *Girls and Women in Education: A cross-national study of sex inequalities in upbringing and in schools and colleges* (Paris: OECD).

OECD (1989a) *High-Quality Education and Training for All* (Paris: OECD).

OECD (1989b) *Employment Outlook* (Paris: OECD).

OECD (1994) *The OECD Jobs Study: Evidence and Explanations* (Paris: OECD).

OECD (1996a) *Measuring What People Know: Human Capital Accounting for the Knowledge Economy* (Paris: OECD).

OECD (1996b) *Technology, Productivity and Job Creation: Analytical Report* (Paris: OECD).

OECD (1996c) *Lifelong Learning for All* (Paris: OECD).

OECD (1997a) *Human Capital Investment: An International Comparison* (Paris: OECD).

OECD (1997b) 'Lifelong Learning for Employability', unpublished document (Paris: OECD).

OECD (1998a) *Technology, Productivity, and Job Creation: Best Policy Practices* (Paris: OECD).

OECD (1998b) *Redefining Tertiary Education* (Paris: OECD).

OECD (1998c) *Human Capital Investment: An International Comparison* (Paris: CERI).

OECD (1998d) *Education at a Glance: OECD Indicators* (Paris: CERI).

OECD (1999a) *Education Policy Analysis* (Paris: CERI).

OECD (1999b) *Employment Outlook* (Paris: OECD).

OECD (2000a) *Economic Outlook No. 68* (Paris: OECD).

OECD (2000b) *Education at a Glance: OECD Indicators* (Paris: CERI).

OECD (2000c) *Measuring Student Knowledge and Skills: The PISA 2000 Assessment of Reading, Mathematical and Scientific Literacy* (Paris: OECD).

OECD (2000d) *From Initial Education to Working Life: Making Transitions Work* (Paris: CERI).

OECD (2000e) *Knowledge Management in the Learning Society* (Paris: CERI).

OECD (2000f) *Employment Outlook* (Paris: OECD).

OECD (2000g) *Where are the Resources for Lifelong Learning?* (Paris: OECD).

OECD (2001a) *Education Policy Analysis* (Paris: OECD).

OECD (2001b) *Education at a Glance* (Paris: OECD).

OECD (2001c) *Starting Strong: Early Childhood Education and Care* (Paris: OECD).

OECD (2001d) *The New Economy: Beyond the Hype* (Paris: OECD).

OECD and Statistics Canada (1995) *Literacy, Economy and Society: Results of the first International Adult Literacy Survey* (Paris: OECD).

OECD and Statistics Canada (2000) *Literacy in the Information Age: Final report of the International Adult Literacy Survey* (Paris: OECD).

Quality Assurance Agency for Higher Education (2001) *The Framework for Higher Education Qualifications in England, Wales and Northern Ireland* (Gloucester: QAAHE).

Smith, J., McKnight, A. and Naylor, K. (2000) 'Graduate employment: Policy and Performance in Higher Education in the United Kingdom', *The Economic Journal* Vol. 10, pp. 382–411.

US Department of Education and OECD (1999) *How Adults Learn*, Proceedings of a conference held on 6–8 April 1998, Georgetown University Conference Centre, Washington, DC.

3
Private and Public Schools: Theoretical Considerations*

Gianni De Fraja

Introduction

There is a long-standing debate on the relative merits of state and private education. In the UK, Tony Blair is the first prime minister ever to send his children to a state school;[1] in Italy, the issue has emerged as one of the main priorities of the conservative government elected in 2001. The debate is often emotional and rarely balanced. This chapter offers a survey of an economist's view on the topic.

At a very abstract level it could be argued that what is puzzling about the coexistence of private and public education in most countries is the presence of state institutions. Education has few of the characteristics of a public good in that its consumption is clearly excludable and the marginal cost of provision is clearly different from zero.[2] Indeed state funding and provision of education are relatively recent phenomena, introduced in most countries in a systematic manner in the second half of the nineteenth and first half of the twentieth centuries. The growth of public provision has been rapid: nowadays all countries invest a very substantial proportion of their public sector budget on the provision of education, and the overwhelming majority of the world's population have received their education from a state-funded and/or state-run institution. The reasons why this should be the case are beyond the scope of this chapter (see Barr, 1998, pp. 320 ff., for a discussion of some of the arguments presented for state intervention in the education sector).

In a very broad outline that captures the organisation of the education system in many Western countries, a distinction is made between the compulsory and non-compulsory levels. At the compulsory level everybody is obliged to attend a state school, which is essentially free. Exemption is granted to children who attend a private school. The latter must normally have some form of state recognition and they usually charge a fee (which may or may not cover the full cost of attendance). For postcompulsory education, tuition at state institutions (schools and universities) is available to those who are sufficiently qualified to be admitted, and is to a greater or lesser extent subsidised by the government. Subsidies are often also available to those who opt to attend a private school or university.

The coexistence of private and state education is the focus of this chapter. We begin in the next section by asking whether this coexistence has beneficial effects. One can approach this question from a macroeconomic viewpoint by studying the effects of private schools on economic growth. As we argue, very few theoretical or empirical studies have addressed this point, and we suggest a framework for the analysis. The traditional welfarist point of view is more established, but given that the government maximises a utilitarian welfare function, should provision of education be state, private or mixed? A similar question is addressed from the political economy viewpoint: rather than by the government's preferences, the system of provision is chosen by a majority voting mechanism.

The subsequent section takes a more microeconomic approach and investigates households' choice of education acquisition and the response of providers of educational services to these choices. It begins by observing that, in order for private education to exist at all in the presence of free state education, it must be the case that private education is perceived by households to be 'better' in some sense. This idea, introduced in the previous section, is expanded to take account of the fact that schools have an objective function and will try to act to optimise it.

An important characteristic of the market for education is that price is not the main strategic variable for providers, so that the price mechanism is not the main allocative instrument in the market. In many cases institutions face substantial unsatisfied demand at the price charged for attendance, and the allocation of places to applicants is made via some administrative mechanism, the most typical of which is a quality threshold: only students whose potential (typically measured by past performance) is above a certain level may gain admission. The final section investigates the consequences of this mechanism for competition between private and state schools. Competition between educational institutions is a relatively neglected area of research in the economic theory of education, and even more so in the case of competition between state and private institutions. The last topic to be examined is the use of vouchers for education. Most of the research in this area, both theoretical and empirical, has been conducted in the US, although the topic may become politically relevant in some European countries and therefore more prominent in the European debate on education policy.

Macroeconomic effects of private education

Education and growth

This section investigates the following question: what is the effect of an increase expenditure in private education on the rate of growth of an economy? From a conceptual point of view there are two answers to this question: either private and state education have different effects (in the sense that their coefficient in a regression of the growth rate of GDP is different); or an increase in private education affects the total national expenditure on education (this happens if, for example, the government has a fixed budget for education and this budget is not reduced to correspond with an increase in private expenditure on education), and total education expenditure affects the rate of growth of an economy.

While the first of these does not appear to have been studied empirically, it is an important issue and deserves investigation. The second has been addressed both theoretically and empirically. Empirical microeconomic analyses of the effects of education on an individual's earnings consistently suggest that the private rate of return on investment in education is between 6 per cent and 10 per cent (see Card, 1998, for a recent survey and Psacharopoulos, 1994, for international comparisons). Studies that use refined techniques and account for unobservable variables such as ability in more and more ingenious ways – such as using a twins sample, where differences in incomes can be studied in relationship with differences in education while maintaining the assumption of identical abilities to remove genetic differences in ability (Ashenfelter and Kreuger, 1994; Bonjour *et al.*, 2000), or the month of birth to ascertain random differences in length of attendance at school (Angrist and Krueger, 1991) – confirm this effect of education, which tallies with our intuitive view of the world. It is therefore puzzling that what holds very consistently for individuals does not seem to hold consistently for nations. There is a very large body of literature on the relationship between investment in education and economic growth (see Krueger and Lindhal, 1999, for a survey), inspired and motivated by Lucas's (1988) theoretical model of human capital and economic growth. While vast, however, this literature is inconclusive and the link between a nation's investment in education and the rate of growth of its GDP appears weak, if not perverse (see for example Benhabib and Spiegel, 1994; Barro and Sala-I-Martin, 1995). On the other hand the level of initial education (the stock of human capital) at a given date does appear to matter for subsequent economic growth. More recently Krueger and Lindhal (1999) have shown that measurement error may be at the root of the apparent lack of a relationship between investment in human capital and GDP growth.

Although theoretical analyses of the relationship between private and state education and growth are very rare, Boldrin (1996) offers an overlapping generation model, where individuals live for three periods. In the first they may invest in human capital accumulation, which increases the productivity of the physical capital owned by elderly and middle-aged individuals: 'while the old … have little interest in future productivity, the middle age individuals have a *collective* interest in fostering society stock of human capital' (ibid., p. 2). The beneficial role of public education follows from the existence of the externality constituted by the complementarity between human and physical capital, and by the absence of perfect capital markets. This creates an interesting conflict between the generations: the elderly prefer no taxes and no education for the young (because they do not care about the future productivity of the young), while the young prefer high taxes and high education expenditure (they have no income and therefore pay no taxes). This leaves only the middle-aged with a meaningful trade-off. Not surprisingly, therefore, when voting takes place it is middle-aged voters who hold the balance of power and from whose ranks the median voter is drawn. Boldrin shows that the middle-aged may deliberately vote in favour of an increase in the taxes they pay to finance the young's education because these taxes will also be paid by the elderly: for every extra pound they pay in tax, the public funding of education is increased by more than a pound as the elderly are paying tax too.

Glomm and Ravikumar (1992) separately consider the rate of growth of the economy when education is supplied privately and that when it is provided by the government, and therefore do not study the simultaneous presence of the two modes of provision. More recently Bearse *et al.* (2001) have developed Glomm and Ravikumar's (1992) model to allow for the interaction of state and private education. They show that an increase in the share of private education may have ambiguous effects on economic growth, depending on the institutional arrangements for state provision (see below).

Welfare effects of private education

A general framework for the analysis of this issue is provided by the following model.[3] Individuals are distributed according to their ability to earn income in the future, $\theta \in [\underline{\theta}, \bar{\theta}]$ according to $F(\theta)$, with density $f(\theta) = F'(\theta)$. They have utility $u(y)$, where y is the (post-tax) income, which is a function of θ and e, y (e, θ), which satisfies y_e (e, θ), y_θ (e, θ), $y_{e\theta}$ $(e, \theta) > 0$: education increases earnings more for abler individuals. The following assumption is crucially important for many results in the area: given two equally educated individuals, a marginal increase in the education of the brighter one will increase her or his future income more than the same increase would if assigned to the less bright one.[4] This is plausible for education spending, although it would not be, for example, for health spending.

For simplicity, individuals are taxed according to lump sum taxation.[5] Individuals can purchase education privately by incurring cost p per unit. Let e_g be the education level offered by the government to every individual.[6] To maintain some generality in the range of instruments that the government can use, we also assume that a portion, $s \in [0, 1]$, of the cost of private education can be paid for by the government, for example in the form of a voucher that can be used in a private school. In order to pay for its education policy the government levies a lump-sum tax, τ. Then a household chooses to attend a private school if

$$\max_e u\left(y(e,\theta) - pe + s - \tau\right) > u\left(y\left(e_g,\theta\right) - \tau\right) \tag{3.1}$$

The LHS is the utility obtained from going private, given that by doing so an individual can choose the level of education that he or she prefers, e_p (θ). Then individuals whose ability is above θ_p (s), where θ_p (s) is the solution in θ of

$$y \ (e_p \ (\theta)) - pe_p \ (\theta) + s = y \ (e_g, \ \theta), \tag{3.2}$$

choose private education. Note of course that θ'_p $(s) < 0$.[7] The government's budget constraint is given by

$$pe_g \ F \ (\theta_p \ (s)) + s \ (1 - F \ (\theta_P \ (s))) = \tau \tag{3.3}$$

The LHS is the sum of the payment for the education of individuals who attend a state institution and the total subsidy given to those who choose private education. The government chooses e_g, s and τ, subject to Equation (3.3), to maximise its objective function, which in line with Arrow (1971) can be taken to be a utilitarian welfare function. Deriving τ from Equation (3.3) and substituting it into the objective function of the government

$$\int_{\underline{\theta}}^{\theta(s)} u\left(y\left(e_g,\theta\right) - pe_g F\left(\theta_p(s)\right) - s\left[1 - F\left(\theta_p(s)\right)\right]\right) f(\theta) \ d\theta +$$

$$\int_{\theta(s)}^{\bar{\theta}} u\left(y\left(e_p(\theta),\theta\right) - pe_g F\left(\theta(s)\right) + s - pe_g F\left(\theta_p(s)\right) + s\left[1 - F\left(\theta_p(s)\right)\right]\right) f(\theta) \ d\theta$$

The first order condition for the above with respect to the subsidy, s, is

$$\left(F\left(\theta_p(s)\right)-\left(e_g p-s\right)f\left(\theta_p(s)\right)\theta'_p(s)\right)\int_{\underline{\theta}}^{\bar{\theta}}u'(\cdot)f(\theta)\,d\theta - \int_{\underline{\theta}}^{\theta(s)}u'(\cdot)f(\theta)\,d\theta = 0 \tag{3.4}$$

Note that if $f(\underline{\theta}) > 0$,[8] when s is so low (possibly negative, so that people are penalised if they go to a private school) that $\theta_p(s) = \underline{\theta}$, that is, when nobody goes to private school, Equation 3.4 reduces to

$$-\left(e_g p-s\right)f\left(\theta_p(s)\right)\theta'_p(s)\int_{\underline{\theta}}^{\bar{\theta}}u'(\cdot)f(\theta)\,d\theta > 0 \tag{3.5}$$

That is, increasing the subsidy by a small amount so that some individuals prefer the system of private provision improves the value of the objective function. Put more simply, when the government is constrained to free provision, identical for all individuals, then optimality requires some private provision.[9]

While obtained in a specific model, this result is likely to hold in more general situations because the underlying intuition is robust. This intuition can be described as follows. If the private sector is small, then a small increase in the subsidy is cheap when measured by the social welfare function (that is, it determines a second-order increase in taxation). However an increase in the subsidy has two other (first-order) effects: (1) it induces somebody to exit the state sector, thereby reducing the amount of taxation required (and this has good redistributive consequences because those who exit the state sector are the best-off individuals), and (2) it increases the total amount of education acquired by individuals – when individuals switch from state to private they increase their education investment by a discrete amount. The total income of society increases as a consequence.[10]

To conclude this section, note that the existence of a subsidy on private education increases the total amount spent by society on education. To see this, note that $\theta'_p(s) < 0$ implies that an increase in the subsidy s, increases the number of individuals who choose private education, which is discretely higher that the publicly provided level.[11] As we shall see in the next section, this is not a general result.

Political economy models of choice between private and state schooling

A similar model is that proposed by Stiglitz in 1974 and taken up about 20 years later by Glomm and Ravikumar (1992), Epple and Romano (1996a) and others. The model is similar in that it addresses the extent of society's investment in education in the presence of a private sector.

However it differs in that it reflects the American viewpoint that the amount of state education to be provided by the government should be decided according to a democratic process: citizens vote on how much the government should spend on education (or, equivalently, on the amount of taxes to be levied to pay for education).

Stiglitz's model produces an interesting multiplicity result. He shows that *ex ante* identical communities can, as the result of the voting process, end up in very different positions: 'some communities have high quality [state] schools and a high level [of] support for public education; others, similarly situated, have low quality [state] schools and a low level of support for public education' (Stiglitz, 1974, p. 365). The reasoning is straightforward: if the quality of state education is low, then will I send my children to private school and vote for low funding for state education. Conversely if the state schools are good I will be happy to pay high taxes because I will send my children to a state school and receive immediate benefits from the funding determined by taxation. Stiglitz finds the same ambiguity with regard to the overall effect of private education on the overall amount of education acquired by the economy. As he explains, whether the total amount of education is higher or lower when the provision of private education is for bidden will in general depend on the specific functional forms used.

Epple and Romano (1996b, p. 59) study a similar set-up, and with homotetic preferences obtain the unambiguous result that overall investment in education is higher under a system where provision is mixed. However it should be noted that this result is not necessarily general. Peltzman (1983) argues that state provision of education may actually reduce the total investment in human capital: to the extent that it is difficult for households to supplement state education with private provision (because most schools are open from 9 to 3 and children cannot be in two places at the same time), individuals may settle for a low level of education, provided for free, instead of opting for private education, which they would have to pay for and would purchase in greater quantity and/or higher quality.

Stiglitz's analysis is important because it highlights a robust argument for the existence of multiple equilibria: individuals send their children to state schools when these are good but if they are not, private education will be prefered. These individuals are typically middle class (and middle income), and the tension involved is elegantly illustrated by the so-called 'end against the middle phenomenon' (Epple and Romano, 1996b; Fernandez and Rogerson, 1995). The poor prefer low-quality provision because they prefer low taxes (and the higher amount of disposable income that goes with them), while the rich prefer low-quality state provision because they send their children to private schools and therefore derive no benefit from the taxes they pay. The middle class prefer high-quality provision because they value education relatively more than they value consumption goods. When the level of education is determined by a vote, there may be an alliance between low-income and high-income voters against middle-income voters.[12] This is a symptom of the more general conflict between (traditional) left-wing and right-wing positions with regard to education. If this happens then the overall level of publicly provided education is lower than that preferred by the voter with a median income. There will, however, be more private education and the overall balance may well be ambiguous.

In concluding this section we return to the overall effects of private education on economic growth. We have already discussed the effect of private education on the overall amount of education provided, and explained that there is ambiguity with regard to the effect of private education on the overall investment in education. Moreover the effect of education on growth is also ambiguous. There is, however, a further logical link: the effect of private education on income inequality. The simple theoretical model presented above shows that if there is an increase in the subsidy on private education, financed by a reduction in the level of publicly provided education, e_g, then inequality increases as better-off individuals choose private education and the education received by the less well-off is reduced. While there is a large body of literature on the relationship between income inequality and growth, it is not appropriate to review it here except to note that its conclusions, too, are rather ambiguous, at both the theoretical and the empirical level (Atkinson, 1997; Aghion *et al.*, 1999).

Quality of private and state education

The simple models presented above made two important assumptions about for the private sector: its ability to offer any level of quality desired, in contrast to the rigidity of the state sector, which is constrained to a single level for all pupils; and that it is 'better' than state education. In the typical model illustrated above, individuals can choose either to accept the lower amount/quality of free state education, or to pay the market price and privately purchase a higher amount/quality of education.[13] In a sense this is a necessary assumption, given the price structure of the two sectors: after all, given two goods, one of which is available for free while the other must paid for, why would anyone choose the latter unless it was better in some sense? This section investigates these assumptions, beginning with an examination of the consequences of allowing schools to change their quality levels.

Free state schooling

An elegant model of the interaction between private and state education institutions is presented in Epple and Romano (1998). Households are made up of parents and children. Individuals differ in two respects: their innate ability, θ, and their parent's income, Y. These are distributed in the population according to the function $\xi (Y, \theta)$, taking values in $[\underline{\theta}, \bar{\theta}] \times [\underline{Y}, \bar{Y}]$. This formulation allows for correlation between parental income and ability.[14]

Parents are interested in their children's achievement, given simply by the result of an end of school test. To the extent that there is a positive correlation between a person's academic achievement and that person's labour market earnings, this is a reasonable objective function for parents. Achievement is given by the function $a (\theta, \theta_{av})$, where a is the achievement of a child of ability θ and θ_{av} is the average ability of the other children who attend the child's school. Both partial derivatives are positive. (See Hanushek, 1986, for a survey on the influence of a group's ability on an individual's academic achievement.) With regard to the second variable, the influence of the average ability of the student body on a child's achievement can be due to a number of factors. First, there may be a signal attached to the school: if it has a reputation for being 'good' it will attract able children and this will confirm its reputation. As a consequence employers will be more willing to offer high wages to graduates of that school. Their expectation of higher-ability graduates will on average be confirmed because of that school's better intake. Described in these terms, this is a simple case of a self-fulfilling prophecy: a certain school is better because everybody believes that it is better.

A second explanation of the positive sign of the partial derivative $\partial a/\partial\theta_{av}$ is the so-called 'peer group' effect: children learn better if they are part of a group of bright children. This is a reasonably well documented phenomenon. For example see Moreland and Levine (1992) for a survey from a psychology/education viewpoint, and Summers and Wolfe (1977) for an early economic empirical analysis. From a theoretical viewpoint, the analyses by Arnott and Rowse (1987) and de Bartolomé (1990) were among the first to take the peer group effect explicitly into account.

A third explanation relates to parental income: high-income parents are more likely to complain if the school attended by their children does not achieve the standards they expect, and are more likely to put pressure on the school and its teachers to maintain or improve its standards. If this pressure is effective, then such schools will have better results (this argument was informally proposed by a former Tory UK education minister – see Walden, 1996).

The dependence between the achievement (output) of their 'customers' and the characteristics of the 'customers' themselves render the technology of education institutions a 'customer-input technology' (Rothschild and White, 1995), that is, production costs depend on the characteristics of the customers.

The analysis of this technology is similar to the study of a 'club with non-anonymous crowding' (see Scotchmer, 1994, for a survey). Briefly, clubs provide a service with some features of a public good – the externality being determined by the fact that the utility of an individual depends on the actions of other individuals. This however, is excludable – individuals can be barred from receiving the beneficial effect of the externality. The externality, or crowding, is non-anonymous in the sense that its sign and magnitude depend on the identity of the individual bestowing it: a bright member bestows a positive externality, a less bright one a negative one. Schools can internalise this externality by pricing it. Moreover, and very importantly in the Epple and Romano (1998) model, schools can link the price they charge to individuals to their characteristics: to their ability by offering scholarship and bursaries, and to their family income by means-testing the fee they pay. Hence schools can link the price paid by individuals both to their parents' ability to pay and to the externality then bestow on the other students at the school.

Households optimise a Cobb–Douglas utility function in consumption and educational achievement, subject to a budget constraint. If p_i is the fee a household pays for admission to school i (where for state education $i = 0$ and $p_0 = 0$), they maximise:

$$(Y - p_i)\, a\, (\theta, \theta_{av}) \tag{3.6}$$

Private schools maximise profit. Their revenues come from tuition fees; their costs depend only on the number of students enrolled (and not, for example, on their ability). This dependence is non-linear so there is a cost-efficient school size. Moreover there is free entry and exit. State schools act as residual repositories, taking in all those students who do not enrol in a private school (either because they choose not to, they cannot afford to or (they are not accepted by any of them). Epple and Romano (ibid.) then proceed to solve a private school's optimisation problem, that is, the maximisation of profit, subject to the optimum behaviour of all other agents in the economy. No household whose children attend that school can obtain a higher utility by going to a different school (including a state school), and no private school can obtain a profit by entering the market.

The main theoretical result obtained by Epple and Romano is that if an equilibrium exists, then it is hierarchical. This is illustrated in Figure 3.1, which depicts the (θ, Y) Cartesian space: a point in the set $[\underline{\theta}, \bar{\theta}] \times [\underline{Y}, \bar{Y}]$ represents the characteristics of a student. The various areas are labelled according to the school to which students with certain characteristics go. The quality of the schools (measured by the average ability of the students enrolled) increases in the move from bottom-left to top-right. The state school has the lowest average ability, and therefore the lowest quality. As the figure shows, at any given income level, higher-ability students go to progressively better schools, and at any given ability level, higher-income students go to progressively better schools.

The mechanism at work here is quite subtle: schools charge a low fee to high-ability students from low-income households: this is observed in practice in the private sector in both the UK and the US in the form of

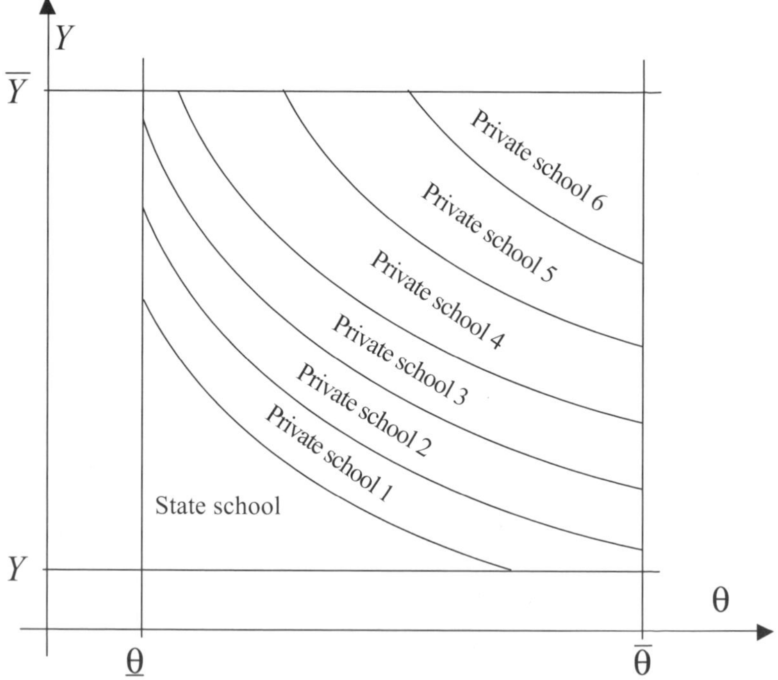

Figure 3.1 Choice of school by ability and income

scholarships or bursaries. They do so not out of any sense of philanthropy, but as a profit-maximising strategy: high-ability students bestow a positive externality on the rest of the student body (via the role of θ_{av} in function a), and therefore crucially influence their willingness to pay. In other words a profit-maximising school derives two benefits from the admission of an additional child: the direct fee paid by the child's parents, and the rise in the maximum fee that the parents of other children in the school are willing to pay; this change is positive if the additional child increases the average ability, negative if she or he lowers it. Epple *et al.* (2001, 2002) have investigated the model empirically and found some evidence that schools do behave in this fashion.

Some empirical estimates

An immediate consequence of the model is that private schools offer better quality than state schools: no private school can charge a positive price – and therefore continue to exist – unless its offerings are of better quality than those which state schools provide for free. In practice, whether private schools are better than state schools is an empirical point. Surprisingly, relatively few tests have been conducted to determine the validity of this. In a study that focused on the effects of school quality, measured mainly by the number of pupils per teacher and the nature of the selection mechanism, Dearden *et al.* (2000) drew on NCDS data (a survey that followed the progress of all UK children born in a certain week in March 1958) and found that 'the impact on educational qualifications of attending a state selective school (grammar) or a private school is large and significant even after controlling for tests at 11 which are the primary selection mechanisms into these schools' (ibid., p. 21). In an international comparison of Belgium, France, New Zealand, Ontario and the US, Toma (1996) also found that private schooling had effect on attainment. On the other hand Feinstein and Symons (1999, p. 310) found that 'Contrary to received wisdom in the UK, attendance at private school is nowhere significant.' More recently Naylor *et al.* (2002), found that UK university graduates who had previously attended a private school on average obtained better results at university than graduates who had attended a state school (3.4 per cent for females and 3.1 per cent for males), but their subsequent earnings were not significantly different. However in a similar study of Italian students, Bertola and Checchi (2002) found the opposite: attendance at a private school prior to university lowered a student's performance at university.

In their influential study Coleman *et al.* (1981) found that US students in private schools were higher achievers. This study was subsequently repeated by other researches (Evans and Schwab, 1995; Sander, 1997;

Neal, 1997) and the results were qualified. One constant, however, was the finding that Catholic schools performed better than state schools: 'Catholic schools would, in some subjects, offer six years of achievement for four years of attendance' (Neal, 1998, p. 82). However, this finding should be treated with caution because in general parents who send their children to religious schools (which in the US usually means Christian) are likely to have instilled moral values and a work ethic in their children, and this might well result in better behaviour, and hence better achievement at school. Moreover there are likely to be large differences between countries, especially between the US and Western European countries. For example in a UK study Marks *et al.* (2001), found that while attendance at religious schools in the state sector could be associated with small improvements in average attainment there was considerable variation among schools: some were very good but others were very poor.

Most comparative studies of the performance of private and public institutions relate to primary and secondary schooling. One exception is Goudriaan and Degroot (1993), who studied the relative performance of state and private universities. They were unable to find significant difference between the two types of institution with regard to cost efficiency.

Fee-charging state schools

There is of course no reason why state-provided education should be free, and indeed many state-owned universities do charge for tuition. By the same token there is no reason why state provision should be uniform, that is, why all state schools should be identical. To the extent that the quality of a state school depends on the ability and social background of its pupils, this assumption is unlikely to correspond to reality even in countries such as Italy, where a degree or diploma obtained from one state institution is legally treated as being equal in value to the same degree or diploma obtained from any other state institution.[15] Conceptually this has important consequences: unless there are additional constraints on the state sector, then anything the private sector can do the state sector can do just as well. If such constraints do exist, then they should be justified and modelled explicitly, rather than implicitly assuming their consequences. Examples of constraints could be the need for state schools to respond to (direct or indirect) electoral pressure to conform to certain principles,[16] constraints that affect the cost of providing the service, such as a strong union presence, self-imposed requirements with regard to the hiring and firing of teachers, and excessive bureaucracy and paperwork.

It will be instructive to consider one model in which private and state institutions are subject to the same constraints. In particular the state is not required to offer identical provisions to all its pupils or to educate its pupils free of charge. One of the questions that can be addressed by this model is whether the uniform and free provision assumed by other models is optimal.

The model, based on De Fraja (2002), is relevant for the current analysis because the private sector acts as a constraint on the behaviour of the state sector, and therefore it limits the range of policies that the government can implement using state education institutions. As before, households differ in income, $Y \in [\underline{Y}, \bar{Y}]$, and in the ability of their children, $\theta \in [\underline{\theta}, \bar{\theta}]$. A household's utility depends on current consumption and future income, subject to budgetary constraints on current consumption expenditure, c, and expenditure on education. Education can be either purchased privately at cost k per unit, or obtained from the state in amount e, which is paid for by an up-front fee, f, and a postponed payment, m.[17] Moreover households can transfer income from parent to child, but not *vice versa*: this is due to the presence of capital market imperfections that prevent parents from borrowing to finance the household's current consumption using a child's future income as collateral. Thus if a child attends a private school the parents choose the amount of education and a monetary transfer to the child to solve

$$U_{pr} (Y, \theta) = \max_{e,t} [u (Y - t - ke) + y (e, \theta, E) + t] \qquad (3.7)$$

where $y (e, \theta, E)$ captures the functional relationship between the parents' income, y, their ability, θ, and the education they have received, e, with the additional variable measuring the total amount of education in the economy, E. Again y satisfies y_e, $y_\theta > 0$ and $y_E > 0$, implying that E is a positive externality. The model makes the crucially important assumption that $y_{e\theta} > 0$, as discussed in the second section and note 4. If parents send a child to a state school they obtain utility

$$U_{pub} (Y, \theta) = u (Y - f (Y, \theta)) + y (e (Y, \theta), \theta, E) - m (Y, \theta) \qquad (3.8)$$

Note that the state is not constrained to uniform provision, and so the household's characteristics, income and ability can affect both the education received, $e (Y, \theta)$, and the payment required, $f (Y, \theta)$.[18] The government maximises a utilitarian welfare function given by the sum of utilities in society, subject to a budget constraint: it cannot spend on current education more than it can collect from parents, either as fees or as loans, plus transfers from the general budget. The government also faces an incentive compatibility constraint: since a person's ability is private information, as recognised in a tradition dating back to Mirrlees (1971), the government must provide incentives for each household to choose the 'appropriate' education level. Finally, the government must ensure that households have at least as much utility as they would receive if they could choose their preferred form of education, $U_{pub}(Y, \theta) \geq U_{pr}(Y, \theta)$. The solution to the government's problem is shown in Figure 3.2, which illustrates the education received by an individual as a function of his or her ability, θ, and parental income, Y. The thin lines are the education levels acquired in the private market in the absence of any public intervention and at various income levels: this is given by the condition that marginal cost equals marginal benefit, $k = y_e(e, \theta, E)$, for those households which can afford this amount – the highest of the thin lines is the locus of points, such that $k = y_e(e, \theta, E)$ holds. If a household does not have enough income to pay for this amount, then the amount of education acquired is reduced. The other thin lines depict the education received at various income levels, with lower-income households receiving less education.

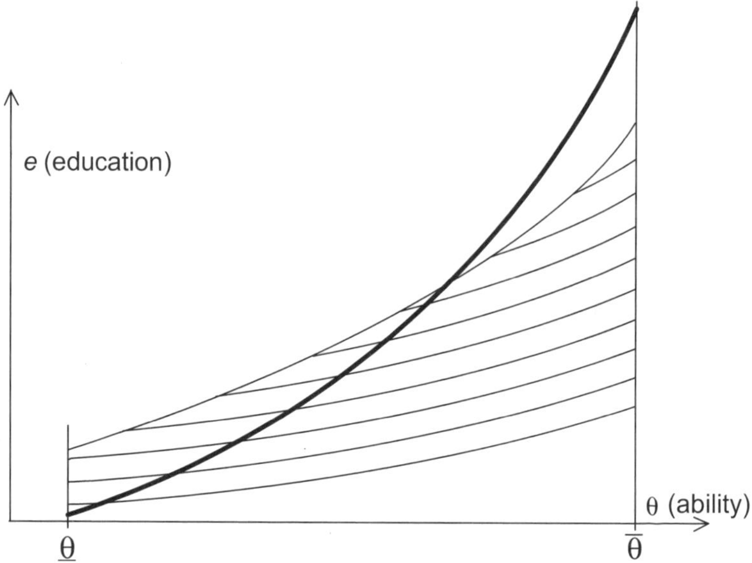

Figure 3.2 Education and ability when private education is possible

When the government intervenes it internalises externality. *E*, as well as taking into account the shadow cost of public funds. If there were no private provision it would choose to give each person the education level denoted by the thick line. This curve represents a trade-off between internalisation of the externality (which tends to increase the level of education each receives) and the need to provide incentives to self-select (which lowers the curve, except for those with the highest ability – the standard 'efficiency at the top'). The latter effect is weaker for high-ability individuals: they receive more education than they would purchase privately. Given that private education is allowed, the government is unable to impose, the level of education it would prefer on households where the child has low ability, but must let them acquire the education they would choose privately (the thick line is below the relevant thin line). This is how the presence of a private sector acts as a constraint. Note also the unexpected implication that the introduction of a private education loan market, which would allow households to borrow to finance education, would reduce welfare. This is because it would enable less well-off households to choose too high a level of education.[19] One interpretation of this model is that the outcome produced by a model such as Epple and Romano's (1998), in which better-off students go to private schools, only applies (when the government implements a welfare-maximising policy) to low-ability students.

The model illustrated above reflects a utilitarian, rather European viewpoint. In Bearse *et al.* (2001) the point of view is more American. They study the effect of the possibility of private schooling on individual behaviour. In their model households make a number of choices. First they choose where to live; then they vote on the level of income taxation their district should levy in order to pay for free state education; and finally they choose whether to send their children to state or private schools. In each stage households predict and take into account the choices, that will be made in the subsequent stages. The focus of Bearse *et al.*'s study is the difference between a decentralised and a centralised mechanism for the provision of state education, and they show how the possibility of private education profoundly affects the relative merits of the two mechanisms for the determination of public expenditure on education. This topic is important in view of the fact that the US Supreme Court requires all states to provide education to all individuals 'on equal terms'.[20]

To understand their argument, note first of all that in the absence of private education households will be stratified according to income in the standard Tiebout fashion: high (low) income households choose high (low) taxes and high (low) public education. When provision is centralised (in the simple terms of the model, when there is only one district), the level of education provision is the average of the education levels of the various decentralised districts, and therefore centralisation makes the provision of education more uniform (and income distribution less unequal). This ceases to be the case when private education is available: in the case of a single district, better-off households will send their children to private schools (because state provision is lower) and consequently will vote for low taxes. This may well lower the amount of education received by children from poor households with regard to a decentralised mechanism.

Competition

Competition between private and state institutions

So far in the analysis schools have been given a fairly passive role. Their quality is either given or is simply determined by the quality of their intake. For example in Epple and Romano's (1998) model, schools can only do something about their quality by changing their tuition fee, which is directly related to the average ability of its pupils. This is clearly unrealistic and is related to another important feature of the market for education that is not adequately captured by the models described above, which assume that individuals are able to purchase the services of any institution as long as they are willing to pay the relevant price. This is patently not the case in the education market: in many countries admission to an institution is determined by a type of administrative rationing, typically based on an assessment of the applicant's ability (see Clotfelter, 1999). This is true of universities (state and private) in most countries, and often of secondary (or even primary) schools, both private and state. This has important implications for competition between institutions, and in particular – given the topic of this chapter – between private and state institutions.

The model by Oliveira (2001) provides a simple illustration of this point. Students differ in ability, $\theta \in [0, 1]$ (an innocuous normalisation). There are two institutions (universities) competing in the market: one state, one private. The latter maximises profit and chooses the fee charged for tuition (for simplicity this is the same for all students, irrespective of their ability, although this assumption could be relaxed). The former, as before, has an objective function that is given by the sum of the utility of all individuals in the economy, and it provides its services free of charge.

The difference between this model and these discussed above is that universities are not passive but impose admission criteria: only students whose ability is above a certain threshold will be admitted.

Students derive utility from the receipt of education: this is given by the expected increase in their lifetime earnings, less the tuition fee they have to pay, if any. There is a peer group effect: academic attainment, and therefore lifetime earnings, depend positively on the average ability of the students who attend the institution. A student's utility function is given by

$$w(\theta, \theta_{av}) = \theta + a\theta_{av} - p = \theta + a\frac{\int_0^1 \theta f(\theta)\, d\theta}{\int_0^1 f(\theta)\, d\theta} - p \qquad a \in (0, 1) \tag{3.9}$$

where p is the tuition fee paid for attendance. The parameter a measures the strength of the peer group effect. The function w is a simplifying assumption that does not carry important consequences: what Equation 3.9 captures is the plausible fact that, by setting a stricter admission standard, a university improves the labour market earnings of its students. The earning of a student who does not attend university are given by $w_0(\theta)$.

The solution of the game between the institutions is based on the assumption that because the private institution is a profit maximiser it will charge the highest fee the market is willing to bear, given the admission standard it chooses. Let x_{pr} and x_{pub} be the admission standard set by the private and the state university, respectively. Let $\theta^H(x_{pr}, x_{pub})$ and $\theta^L(x_{pr}, x_{pub})$ be the ability of the least able student who can gain admission to the university with the higher or lower admission standard, respectively. Likewise let $\theta^H_{av}(x_{pr}, x_{pub})$ and $\theta^L_{av}(x_{pr}, x_{pub})$ be the average ability of students who accept a place at the university with the higher or lower admission standard respectively. The fee charged by a private university is given by

$$p(\cdot) = \begin{cases} w\left[\theta^H(\cdot), \theta^H_{av}(\cdot)\right] - w\left[\theta^H(\cdot), \theta^L_{av}(\cdot)\right] & \text{if } \theta_{pr} > \theta_{pub} \\ w\left[\theta^L(\cdot), \theta^L_{av}(\cdot)\right] - w_0\left[\theta^L(\cdot)\right] & \text{If } \theta_{pr} \leq \theta_{pub} \end{cases} \tag{3.10}$$

where, to lighten the notation, $(\cdot)$ stands for (x_{pr}, x_{pub}). According to the first line, the fee charged by a high-quality private university is such that the least able student who can gain admission – that is, the student whose ability is $\theta^H(\cdot)$ – is indifferent between attending the private university (where her or his postgraduate salary, net of the fee, will be $w[\theta^H(\cdot), \theta^H_{av}(\cdot)] - p$) or going to the state university, where her or his postgraduate salary will be $w[\theta^H(\cdot), \theta^L_{av}(\cdot)]$. The second line is the equivalent statement for a state university with a higher admission threshold. The alternative for the weakest student who will be accepted is not to attend university at all, which will give him or her a salary of w_0 [$\theta^L(\cdot)$]. From Equation 3.10 the payoff for the two institutions is given by

$$\begin{array}{ll} p\left(\cdot\right)\int_{\theta^H(\theta)}^{1} f\left(\theta\right) d\theta - c\left(\int_{\theta^H(\cdot)}^{1} f\left(\theta\right) d\theta\right) & \text{if } \theta_{pr} > \theta_{pub} \\[2em] p\left(\cdot\right)\int_{\theta^L(\cdot)}^{\theta^H(\cdot)} f\left(\theta\right) d\theta - c\left(\int_{\theta^L(\cdot)}^{\theta^H(\cdot)} f\left(\theta\right) d\theta\right) & \text{if } \theta_{pr} \le {}_{pub} \end{array} \tag{3.11}$$

for the private institution and

$$\begin{array}{ll} \int_{\theta^H(\cdot)}^{1}\left[w\left(\theta, \theta_{av}^H(\cdot)\right) - p\right] f\left(\theta\right) d\theta + \int_{\theta^L(\cdot)}^{\theta^H(\cdot)} w\left(\theta, \theta_{av}^L(\cdot)\right) f\left(\theta\right) d\theta & \\[1em] + \int_{0}^{\theta^L(\cdot)} w_0(\theta) f\left(\theta\right) d\theta & \text{if } \theta_{pr} > \theta_{pub} \\[2em] \int_{\theta^H(\cdot)}^{1} w\left(\theta, \theta_{av}^H(\cdot)\right) f\left(\theta\right) d\theta + \int_{\theta^L(\cdot)}^{\theta^H(\cdot)}\left(w\left(\theta, \theta_{av}^H(\cdot)\right) - p\right) f\left(\theta\right) d\theta & \\[1em] + \int_{0}^{\theta^L(\cdot)} w_0(\theta) f\left(\theta\right) & \text{if } \theta_{pr} \le \theta_{pub} \end{array} \tag{3.12}$$

for the state university.

Oliveira shows that two equilibrium configurations can result, depending on the value of the parameters.

$$x_{pr} > x_{pub} \tag{3.13}$$

$$x_{pr} < x_{pub} \tag{3.14}$$

These are illustrated in Figure 3.3. In area A there is only one (pure strategy) Nash equilibrium, which satisfies (3.13): the private institution has stricter standards than the state one. In area B there are two (pure strategy) Nash equilibria, one of which satisfies (3.13) and the other satisfies (3.14). Note that, given the functional forms assumed, whenever a configuration that satisfies (3.14) is an equilibrium, so is a configuration that satisfies (3.13). This is probably due to the specific functional forms and it is unlikely to be generalisable.

Configurations that satisfy (3.13) correspond to the assumption made in most models that private institutions have high-ability students and charge accordingly. State institutions, given the location of private ones, prefer to set a low admission threshold in so that more students can obtain an education. However, note that, unlike in the model described above, they do not admit all students because this would have a negative effect on the achievement of the students admitted.

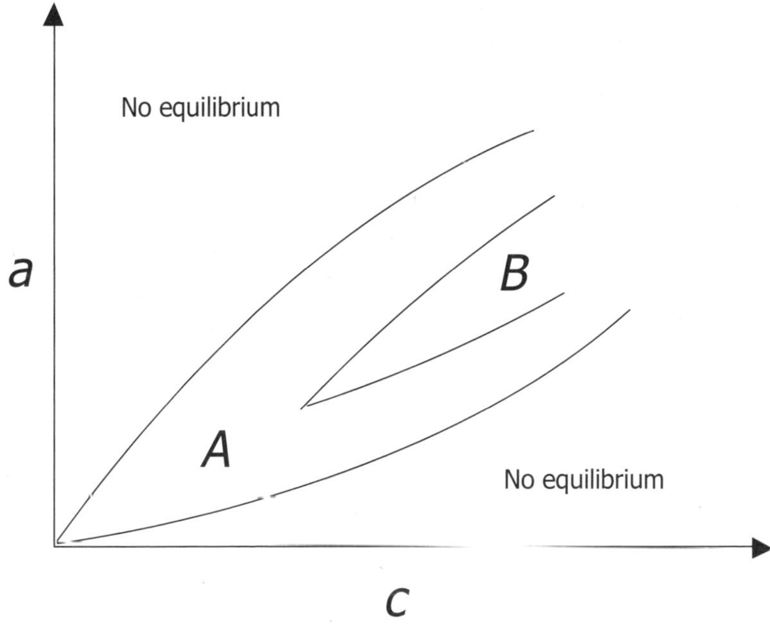

Figure 3.3 Equilibria in the game between private and public schools

Equilibria that satisfy (3.14) are more intriguing. Here the state institution has a high admission standard and captures the brightest students. How can this be an equilibrium? Consider the decision of the private institution, which takes as given the location of the state institution. It can either settle for low-ability students: this will result in low fees but many students, in light of the fact that the state institution has a strict admission standard and therefore few students are admitted. Or it can leapfrog the state institution and set an even higher admission standard. However, given the high standard of the state institution it cannot charge too high an admission fee; moreover the pool of high-ability students that can be captured is quite small. For some parameters the private institution does prefer the former strategy and so (3.14) is an equilibrium.

Although Oliveira's (2001), analysis is simple the results are likely to be quite robust, and it illustrates the importance of rigorously capturing the interaction between private and state schools. In her analysis full account is taken of the fact that institutions ration their allocation of places according to criteria other than price. In this case the standard conclusions can be reversed. Not also that the equilibria are asymmetric – other models of competition where educational institutions set admission standards also display asymmetric equilibria (for example Effinger and Polborn, 1999; De Fraja and Iossa, 2002).

Empirical evidence

Evidence of the effects of competition between private and state institutions is scarce. An interesting study is that by Allen and Shen (1999), who consider a private religious University and calculate the cross-price elasticity of its demand for admission with the tuition fee charged by three other relevant institutions: a state university located in the same town, a state university (research oriented)[21] located in the same state and a private secular university located in a neighbouring state. Allen and Shen's main finding (which reflects the results obtained from earlier studies, such as that by McPherson, 1978) is that state universities do not affect the admission policy of private universities. This is attributed to the large difference between the fees charged by two types of institution. Substitutability between institutions is much stronger between private universities. While these studies are interesting they suffer from the limitation of considering just one institution, and therefore they are unable to distinguish a general causal relationship between fees and admission and the possibility that local effects may overwhelm the price effects. The topic is clearly an important one, and in view of the importance that competition between schools and universities is likely to play in the future, more research is clearly needed.

Among the other authors who have studied the interaction between private and state schools, Brasington (2000, p. 583) has studied quality and found that quality in public schools 'is responsive to private-school competition but not to competition from other public schools'. Similar results have been obtained by Couch *et al.* (1993), but Newmark (1995) and Simon and Lovrich (1996), among others, have disputed these results. See also Dee (1998).

Vouchers

A complaint often made by those who favour private schooling is that competition from the state sector is unfair. After all, if private car manufacturers were to face competition from a state manufacturer that gave away free cars, with production being paid for out of general taxation, there would ear-splitting howls of protest. Indeed there have been proposals to abolish all state intervention in the provision of education. One should not be surprised to learn that such proposals have come mainly from right-wing US academics (Lott, 1987; McGee, 1996). One way of addressing this perceived unfairness, without going to the extreme of abolishing state intervention, is to issue vouchers. In its basic form a voucher is a lump sum given to the parents of school-age children to put towards the cost of education at a private institution. The debate on vouchers is hottest in the US, because in Europe many schools that would be considered private in the US typically receive public funding in some form or other.[22] In 1993 Californian voters rejected the proposed introduction of a state/wide voucher system. However there are many places that have adopted such a system, usually on a more limited scale. For example the city of Milwaukee in Wisconsin introduced a voucher system in 1989. Vouchers to the value of about $4000 (in 1996 prices) were assigned to children from low-income households; these could be spent at one of about 20 approved schools. The results have been ambiguous. According to Rouse, the finding of possible or insignificant effects of vouchers on to maths and/or reading performance depends on how family background and student's ability are controlled for in econometric regressions (Rouse 1998b, p. 62).

Epple and Romano (1998) have used the model described above to analyse the effect of vouchers on various parameters of education. They calibrated the parameters of the model roughly to fit the US economy, and studied how the diagram in Figure 3.1 varied as the value of the voucher varied. Their analysis shows that the adoption of vouchers causes the state education sectors to shrink: it attracts fewer students, and these tend to come from the poorest households and have the lowest levels of ability. Their analysis has produced a number of other important findings. For example even when there are aggregate gains from the introduction of a voucher system, these gains are not equally distributed: 'there is a majority with relatively small losses and a minority with relatively large gains' (ibid., p. 50). Another interesting finding is that to a certain point the tax rate necessary to finance a voucher system decreases as the value of vouchers increases. This is due to the fact that while the vouchers must be paid for by taxation, they induce a reduction in the size of the publicly funded state school sector. This reduction has a built-in multiplier: parents who choose state schools in the absence of vouchers opt for private schools when vouchers are introduced. This is essentially the same mechanism as that illustrated in the second section. But because these marginal parents are the parents of high-ability children, their 'defection' to the private sector reduces the average ability of pupils in state schools, which induces more parents to opt for private provision under the voucher system. Eventually, for a voucher sufficiently high, most individuals will be in the private sector and so a further increase in the voucher increases the tax rate necessary to finance it.

Important lessons can be learnt from the Czech and Hungarian experiences. After the fall of the Berlin wall the rigid state school system was replaced in these two countries by a system in which private and state schools coexisted. This was achieved by allowing free entry to private entrepreneurs who were willing to offer school services. Filer and Münich (2000) have empirically investigated whether private schools chose to locate where the quality of state schools was weakest. Related to this was the question of whether state schools responded to the new competition by improving their quality. These were clearly important questions, and Filer and Münich found a qualified 'yes' to both. They measured quality by the probability of a secondary school graduate being admitted to university, and estimated the following simple linear model:

$$S_{j,}d = \beta D_{j,d} + \epsilon_{j,}d$$

where S is the supply of certain education places and D is a vector of the determinants of local demand for education.

Filer and Münich found that both types of school increased their provision of subjects in high demand, such as business and financial subjects. However private schools were responsive to the wages offered in these sectors while state schools were not. While their analysis reflects the special features of the education system in these countries in the 1990s, a time of exceptional circumstances in a region with low intracountry mobility, there are clearly lesson to be learnt with regard to the response of various agents in the education sector to changed incentives.

Privately run state schools

This type of institution is likely to become more widespread in most countries if the US experience in education and the European experience in other areas of public provision are anything to go by. Essentially the government allows a private agent to run a public activity. This idea is not new: tax collection in ancient Rome was franchised to private entrepreneurs, and this practice survived until relatively recently in Italy and other countries. Today many prisons are run by private companies, who receive a payment based on certain parameters and achievements; the construction of public roads is usually undertaken by private contractors; and nursery facilities are often provided by private nurseries when state or local council provision is insufficient.

An important example in the education sector is the US Edison company. This commercial organisation already has contracts to run more than 100 schools in 21 states, and in 20 years time it hopes to control 10 per cent of the country's state schools.[23] Among the relatively few analyses of the types of problem faced by privately run, state-financed schools are those by Hart *et al.* (1997) and Besley and Ghatak (2001). However these studies do not deal directly with the interaction between private and state schools, and therefore will not be discussed here. Further theoretical research into this topic is needed.

Conclusion

This chapter has investigated some of the conceptual problems posed by the existence of private schools. The theoretical literature on the topic is underdeveloped and there is no established analysis. Hence any survey of the literature is bound to fall short of exhaustive coverage of the topics and problems involved. This chapter has therefore been limited to particular ideas that both illustrate the importance of the research area and give a feel for areas of inquiry to be pursued in the future. There is little doubt that this area of research will prove to have important practical applications. The present model of monolithic and uniform state provision with a separate and small private sector – which is perhaps an extreme characterisation anyway – is likely to be replaced by a variety of modes of education provision, with the distinction between private and state becoming ever more blurred. Theoretical instruments will be needed to analyse this, and in my opinion these instruments will be based on the types of model and idea presented in this chapter.

Notes

* This chapter was first presented at the conference on 'Education, Training and Labour Market Outcomes in Europe, held in Milan on 16–17 November 2001. I wish to thank the discussant, Andrea Ichino, the other participants at the conference for helpful comments on an earlier draft.

1. A point-of terminology here: in the UK the term public school refers to a private (or independent school). This confusing terminology dates back to the time when children were educated by private tutors. When (private) schools came into being they were called public schools because they were open to the public, unlike the lessons given by private tutors.

   While the term state schools avoids the possibility of confusion, this can also be a misnomer as very often schools funded from the public budget are run and/or financed by local or regional institutions. This chapter will use the term private schools to denote fee-paying institutions, and state schools to denote institutions run by a public body (local or central government).

2. Other justifications offered for public intervention are the presence of externalities and capital market imperfections. However externalities are likely to be restricted to the primary education sector and, according to a rare attempt to quantify them, are limited in extent (Wyckoff, 1984, p. 349). Moreover, while it is true that capital markets for the financing of education are severely impaired, this logically justifies state intervention in the capital markets, not necessarily the state provision of education.

3. This is loosely inspired by Marchand and Schroyen (2001), who show that when high-income individuals dislike queuing for health care, a large public sector may be beneficial.

4. While this appears to be intuitively plausible, or at least for education above the compulsory level, and it tallies, for example, with the practice followed by government agencies, foundations and similar institutions to award scholarships on the basis of ability, empirical work should attempt to confirm it by ascertaining the effects of ability at different schooling levels. The typical estimate of the Mincerian equation of the returns from education posits a linear relationship between additional earnings and additional amount of education, and is therefore unable to shed light on this particular point. To the extent that e is higher for academic than for vocational qualifications, the results by Dearden *et al.* (2002), who show that academic qualifications have higher returns than vocational ones, lend support to the assumption that $y_{e\theta} > 0$.

5. This rules out taxing ability: it could be due to incentive problems, according to the standard Mirrlees (1971) argument, or to the (related) fact that taxes are levied on current rather than future income.

6. It is clearly unrealistic to assume that all individuals receive the same level of education from the government. However it is a standard assumption in many models. The consequence of relaxing it is illustrated below.

7. To see this, totally differentiate (2) to get

$$\frac{d\theta}{ds} = \frac{-1}{y_\theta\big(e_p(\theta), \theta\big) - y_\theta\big(e_g, \theta\big)} < 0$$

in view of the fact that $e_p(\theta) > e_g$ and $y_{e\theta}(e, \theta) > 0$.

8. The argument for $f(\theta) = 0$ is slightly less immediate, but identical in essence.

9. Related models are those by Grout (1983) and Ireland (1990). The former uses a model where optimal (redistributive) taxation and state provision of education make the market for private education redundant only if the government has perfect information on individuals' abilities. With asymmetric information there is a role to play for private education. The latter studies the role of vouchers, and identifies conditions such that a reduction in state spending constitute a Pareto improvement, making every member of

society better off. The mechanism that causes this to happen is as follows in a reduction in tax, accompanied by an increase in vouchers, causes more individuals to use the private sector and thus allows an increase in per capita expenditure on education in the state sector.

10. Incidentally this simple model illustrates the result obtained by Marchand and Schroyen (2001), that if a state sector is optimal then it must be 'large' it s is large enough to make the state sector shrink to 0. To see this, note that when $\theta_p(s)$ tends to θ, then (3.4) tends again to (3.5), implying that a small increase in the state sector decreases welfare.

11. Note that the amount of education acquired does not depend on the level of the subsidy. This is a consequence of the lump-sum nature of the subsidy: if the subsidy were proportional to the cost incurred, then the amount of private education would rise with the subsidy.

12. Whether such an alliance occurs depends in general on the shape of the utility functions, and more specifically on the 'relative magnitudes of the price and income elasticities of the (implicit) demand for' education (Epple and Romano, 1996a, p. 71; see also Kenny, 1978).

13. In Epple and Romano (1996a) households top-up the education they receive for free from the state by purchasing an additional amount from the private sector. Clearly the principle is unaltered.

14. This is a delicate point and is worth a footnote, even if it is orthogonal to the present topic. The correlation between fathers' and sons' income can be as high as 0.4 (see Solon, 1992, and Zimmerman, 1992, for the US and Dearden *et al.*, 1997, for the UK). Schematically, there is a right-wing explanation of why there should be a positive correlation between these measures: bright people have high earnings, and in view of the fact that intelligence is hereditary, on average their children will be of higher ability and hence earn higher incomes. There is also a left-wing explanation: intelligence is only one of the factors that affect earnings and family connections are also important: to the extent that wealthy, well-connected parents are more likely to find good jobs for their children, the latter will enjoy a higher income.

15. In other countries, such as the UK, this type of legal equality has never been on the statute books. Traditionally the civil service and other prestigious public sector institutions have recruited from only a handful of select universities, at and the secondary state school level there have always been variations in provision (see Lawton, 1992, for information on the history of education policies in the UK).

16. This is a self-imposed constraint and it is often the case that a state school can remain independent of current political opinion and elected politicians' preferences. The Oxbridge colleges are examples of institutions with such independence. Other institutions, such as the judicial system in most developed countries, some nationalised enterprises and organisations such as the BBC also hold themselves aloof from political pressure.

17. This corresponds to student loans, whereby students borrow from government agencies to finance their attendance at university. See Barr (1993) for a discussion, and Chapman (1997) for an evaluation of the Australian experience.

18. Also note that household transfers are channelled through the state sector: thus both f and m include the transfer, t.
19. This is a typical application of the second-best principle: with symmetric information, the optimal policy amounts to relaxing the household budget constraint and subsidising everyone's education. This, however, is worse than no intervention when the constraint constituted by the asymmetry of information is taken into account.
20. Brown vs Board of Education of Topeka, 347 US 483 (1954).
21. And doctorate granting: in the US there is a substantial difference between the overall culture of institutions that grant doctorates and the culture of those which do not.
22. Until recently all private schools in the UK had 'assisted places' – essentially scholarship paid for by public funds. The Labour government elected in 1997 abolished the assisted places scheme, but ituition fees at private schools remained VAT exempt. This has reduced the cost to parents, so in effect is a form of voucher. In many countries in continental Europe a substantial proportion of education is privately provided but government funded (see Toma, 1996).
23. A variation on this theme is the contract school – see Hill *et al.* (1997). Here a private company is awarded the franchise to run a school or set of schools. Elsew here I have reviewed the drawbacks of this form of organisation (De Fraja, 1997).

References

Aghion, Philippe, Caroli, Eve and Garcia-Penalosa, Cecilia (1999) 'Inequality and economic growth: The perspective of the new growth theories', *Journal of Economic Literature*, vol. 37, pp. 1615–60.

Allen, Robert F. and Shen, Jianshou (1999) 'Some new evidence of the character of competition among higher education institutions', *Economics of Education Review*, vol. 18, pp. 465–70.

Angrist, Joshua D. and Krueger, Alan B. (1991) 'Does compulsory school attendance affect schooling and earnings?', *Quarterly Journal of Economics*, vol. 106, pp. 979–1014.

Arnott, Richard and Rowse, John (1987) 'Peer group effects and educational attainment', *Journal of Public Economics*, vol. 32, pp. 287–305.

Arrow, Kenneth J. (1971) 'A utilitarian approach to the concept of equality in public expenditures', *Quarterly Journal of Economics*, vol. 38, pp. 175–208.

Ashenfelter, Orley and Krueger, Alan B. (1994) 'Estimates of the economic return to schooling from a new sample of twins', *American Economic Review*, vol. 84, pp. 1157–73.

Atkinson, Anthony B. (1997) 'Bringing income distribution in from the cold', *Economic Journal*, vol. 107, pp. 297–321.

Barr, Nicholas A. (1997) 'Student loans: Towards a new public/private mix', *Public Money and Management*, vol. 17.

Barr, Nicholas A. (1998) *The Economics of the Welfare State*, 3rd edn (Oxford: Oxford University Press).

Barro, Robert J. and Sala-I-Martin, Xavier (1995) *Economic Growth* (New York: McGraw-Hill).

Bearse, Peter, Glomm, Gerhard and Ravikumar, B. (2001) 'Education finance in a dynamic Tiebout economy', unpublished.

Benhabib, Jess and Spiegel, Mark (1994) 'The role of human capital in Economic development: evidence from aggregate cross-country data', *Journal of Monetary Economics*, vol. 34, pp. 143–74.

Bertola, Giuseppe and Checchi, Daniele (2002) 'Sorting and private education in Italy', in the present volume.

Besley, Timothy and Ghatak, Maitreesh 'Government versus private ownership of public goods' (London: Centre of Economic Policy Research).

Boldrin, Michele (1996) 'Public education and long-run capital accumulation', Universidad Carlos III De Madrid unpublished.

Bonjour, Dorothe, Cherkas, Lyn, Haskel, Jonathan, Hawkes, Denise and Spector, Tim (2000) *Estimating Returns to Education Using a New Sample of UK Twins* (London: Queen Mary and Westfield College).

Brasington, D. W. (2000) 'Demand and supply of public school quality in metropolitan areas: The role of private schools', *Journal of Regional Science*, vol. 40, pp. 583–605.

Card, David (1998) 'The causal effect of schooling on earning', in Orley Ashenfelter and David Card (eds), *Handbook of Labour Economics* (Amsterdam: North-Holland), pp. 909–47.

Chapman, Bruce (1997) 'Conceptual Issues and the Australian Experience with Income Contingent Charges for Higher Education', *The Economic Journal*, vol. 107, pp. 738–51.

Clotfelter, Charles T. (1999) 'The Familiar but Curious Economics of Higher Education: Introduction to a Symposium,' *Journal of Economic Perspectives*, vol. 13/1: pp. 3–12.

Coleman, James, Kilgmore, Sally and Hoffer, Thomas (1981) *Public and Private High Schools* (Washington, DC: National Center for Eduicational Statistics).

Couch, J. F., Shughart, W. F. and Williams, A. L. (1993) 'Private School Enrollment and Public School Performance', *Public Choice*, vol. 76, pp. 301–12.

Dearden, Lorraine, Ferri, Javier and Meghir, Costas (2000) *The Effect of School Quality on Educational Attainment and Wages* (London: Institute for Fiscal Studies).

Dearden, Lorraine, Machin, Steven and Reed, Howard (1997) 'Intergenerational mobility in Britain', *Economic Journal*, vol. 107, pp. 47–66.

Dearden, Lorraine, McIntosh, Steven, Myck, Michal and Vignoles, Anna (2002) 'The Returns to Academic and Vocational Qualifications in Britain', *Bulletin of Economic Research*.

de Bartolome, Charles (1990) 'Equilibrium and inefficiency in a community model with peer group effects', *Journal of Political Economy*, vol. 98, pp. 110–33.

Dee, T. S. (1998) 'Competition and the quality of public schools', *Economics of Education Review*, vol. 17, pp. 419–27.

De Fraja, Gianni (1997) 'Review of Paul T. Hill, Lawrence C. Pierce, James W. Guthrie: *Reinventing Public Education. How Contracting Can Transform America's Schools*, The University of Chicago Press, Chicago and London, 1997', *Journal of Economics*, vol. 66, pp. 214–17.

De Fraja, Gianni (2002) 'The Design of Optimal Education Policies', *Review of Economic Studies*, vol. 69(2), pp. 437–466.

De Fraja, Gianni and Delbono, Flavio (1989) 'Alternative strategies of a public enterprise in oligopoly', *Oxford Economic Papers*, vol. 41, pp. 302–11.

De Fraja, Gianni and Iossa, Elisabetta (2002) 'Competition among Institutions and the Emergence of the Elite University', *Bulletin of Economic Research*, vol. 54(3) pp. 275–93.

Effinger, M. and Polborn, M. K. (1999) 'A Model of Vertically Differentiated Education', *Journal of Economics*, vol. 69, pp. 53–69.

Epple, Dennis, Figlio, David and Romano, Richard E. (2000) 'Competition Between Private and Public Schools: Testing Stratification and Pricing Predictions', NBER Working paper (Cambridge, Mass.: NBER).

Epple, Dennis and Romano Richard E. (1996a) 'Public Provision of Private Goods', *Journal of Political Economy*, vol. 104, pp. 57–84.

Epple, Dennis and Romano, Richard E. (1996b) 'Ends against the middle: Determining public service provision when there are private alternatives', *Journal of Public Economics*, vol. 62, pp. 297–325.

Epple, Dennis and Romano, Richard E. (1998) 'Competition between provate and public schools, vouchers and peer group effects', *American Economic Review*, vol. 62, pp. 33–62.

Epple, Dennis, Romano, Richard E. and Sieg, H. (2001) 'Peer Effects, Financial Aid and Selection of Students to Colleges and Universities: An Empirical Analysis', *Journal of Applied Econometrics*.

Evans, William and Schwab, Robert (1995) 'Finishing high school and starting college: Do catholic schools make a difference?', *Quarterly Journal of Economics*, vol. 110, pp. 947–74.

Feinstein, L. and Symons, J. (1999) 'Attainment in Secondary School', *Oxford Economic Papers*, vol. 51, pp. 300–21.

Fernandez, Raquel and Rogerson, Richard (1995) 'On the Political Economy of Education Subsidies', *Review of Economic Studies*, vol. 62, pp. 249–62.

Filer, Randall K. and Münich, Daniel (2000) *Responses of Private and Public Schools to Voucher Funding: The Czech and Hungarian Experience* (Prague: CERGI-EI).

Glomm, G. and Ravikumar, B. (1992) 'Public versus Private Investment in Human Capital Endogenous Growth and Income Inequality', *Journal of Political Economy*, vol. 100, pp. 818–34.

Goudriaan, R. and Degroot, H. (1993) 'State Regulation and University Behavior', *Journal of Economic Behavior and Organization*, vol. 20, pp. 309–18.

Grout, Paul A. (1983) 'Imperfect information, markets and public provision of education', *Journal of Public Economics*, vol. 22, pp. 113–21.

Hanushek, Eric A. (1986) 'The economics of schooling: Production and efficiency in public schools', *Journal of Economic Literature*, vol. 23, pp. 1141–77.

Hart, Oliver, Shleifer, Andrei and Vishny, R. W. (1997) 'The proper scope of government: Theory and an application to prisons', *Quarterly Journal of Economics*, vol. 112, pp. 1127–61.

Hill, Paul T., Pierce, Lawrence C. and Guthrie, James W. (1997) *Reinventing Public Education. How Contracting Can Transform America's Schools* (Chicago, Ill.: University of Chicago Press).

Ireland, Norman (1990) 'The mix of social and private provision of goods and services', *Journal of Public Economics*, vol. 43, pp. 201–19.

Kenny, Lawrence W. (1978) 'The collective allocation of commodities in a democratic society: A generalization', *Public Choice*, vol. 33, pp. 117–20.

Krueger, Alan B. and Lindah, Mikael (1999) 'Education for growth', *Swedish Economic Policy Review*, vol. 6, pp. 291–339.

Lawton, Denis (1992) *Education and Politics in the 1990s: Conflict or Consensus?* (London: Falmer).

Lott, John R. (1987) 'Why is Education Publicly Provided. A Critical Survey', *Cato Journal*, vol. 7(2), pp. 475–501.

Lucas, Robert J. (1988) 'On the mechanics of economic development', *Journal of Monetary Economics*, vol. 22(1), pp. 3–42.

Marchand, Maurice and Schroyen, Fred (2001) *Markets for Public and Private Health Care: Redistribution Arguments for a Mixed System* (Louvain, Belgium; Core).

Marks, John, Burn, John, Pilkington, Peter and Thompson, Penny (2001) *Faith in Education* (London: Institute for the Study of Civil Society).

McGee, Robert W. (1996) *A Solution to the Education Crisis* (Dumont, NJ: Dumont Institute for Public Policy Research).

McPherson, Michael (1978) 'The demand for Higher Education', in D. W. Brennan and C. E. Flinn Jr (eds), *Public Policy and Private Higher Education*, (Washington, DC: The Brookings Institution).

Mirrlees, James A. (1971) 'An exploration in the theory of optimum income taxation', *Review of Economic Studies*, vol. 38, pp. 175–208.

Moreland, Richard L. and Levine, John M. (1992) 'The composition of small groups', in E. J. Lawler, B. Markovsky, C. Ridgeway and H. Walker (eds), *Advances in Group Processes*, vol. 9 (Greenwich, CT: JAI Press), pp. 237–80.

Naylor, Robin, Smith, Jeremy and McKnight, Abigail (2002) 'Why is there a graduate earnings premium for students from Independent schools?', *Bulletin of Economic Research*, vol. 54(4), pp. 315–39.

Neal, Derek (1997) 'The effect of Catholic secondary schooling on educational achievement', *Journal of Labor Economics*, vol. 15, pp. 98–123.

Neal, Derek (1998) 'The effect of Catholic secondary schooling on educational achievement. What have we learned about the benefits of private schooling', *Economic Policy Review*, (Federal Reserve Bank of New York), vol. 4, pp. 79–86.

Newmark, C. M. (1995) 'Another look at whether private schools influence public-school quality – comment', *Public Choice*, vol. 82, pp. 365–73.

Oliveira, Tania (2001) 'How public and private universities compete for students', University of York PhD dissertation, Economics Department.

Peltzman, Sam (1993) 'The political economy of the decline of American public education', *Journal of Law and Economics*, vol. 36 pp. 331–70.

Psacharopoulos, George (1994) 'Returns to investment in education: A global update', *World Development*, vol. 22, pp. 1325–43.

Rothschild, Michael and White, Lawrence J. (1993) 'The university in the marketplace: Some insights and some puzzles', in Charles T. Clotfelter and Michael Rothschild (eds), *Studies of Supplies and Demand in Higher Education* (Chicago, Ill.: University of Chicago Press).

Rothschild, Michael and White, Lawrence J. (1995) 'The Analytics of Pricing in Higher Education and Other Services in Which Customers are Inputs', *Journal of Political Economy*, vol. 103(3), pp. 573–86.

Rouse, Cecilia E. (1998) 'Private school vouchers and student achievement: An evaluation of the Milwaukee parental choice program', *Quarterly Journal of Economics*, vol. 113, pp. 553–602.

Rouse, Cecilia E. (1998b) 'Schools and student achievement: More evidence from the Milwaukee parental choice program', *Economic Policy Review* Federal Reserve Bank of New York, vol. 4, pp. 61–76.

Sander, William (1997) 'Catholic high schools and rural academic achievement', *American Journal of Agricultural Economics*, vol. 79, pp. 1–12.

Scotchmer, Suzanne (1994) 'Public goods and the invisible hand', in John Quigley and E Smolensky (eds), *Modern Public Finance* (Cambridge, Mass: Harvard University Press), pp. 98–119.

Simon, C. A. and Lovrich, N. P. (1996) 'Private school enrollment and public school performance: Assessing the effects of competition upon public school student achievement in Washington state', *Policy Study Journal*, vol. 24, pp. 666–75.

Solon, Gary (1992) 'Intergenerational income mobility in the US', *American Economic Review*, vol. 82, pp. 393–409.

Stiglitz, Joseph E. (1974) 'The demand for education in public and private school systems', *Journal of Public Economics*, vol. 3, pp. 349–85.

Summers, Anita A. and Wolfe, Barbara L. (1977) 'Do schools make a difference?', *American Economic Review*, vol. 67, pp. 639–52.

Toma, Eugenia Froedge (1996) 'Public funding and private schooling across countries', *Journal of Law and Economics*, vol. 39, pp. 121–48.

Walden, George (1996) *We Should know Better* (London: Fourth Estate).

Wyckoff, James H. 'The nonexcludable publicness of primary and secondary public education', *Journal of Public Economics*, vol. 24, pp. 331–51.

Zimmerman, David J. (1992) 'Regression toward mediocrity in economic stature', *American Economic Review*, vol. 82, pp. 409–29.

4
Sorting and Private Education in Italy

*Giuseppe Bertola and Daniele Checchi**

Introduction

The economics and politics of private education are complicated and controversial. Recent efficiency-oriented reforms of public transportation, urban sanitation, health care and even prison administration have involved the replacement of public provision of goods and services with private provision at subsidised rates. The question of whether governments should issue tax-financed vouchers to private non-profit suppliers of education is particularly topical in Italy, where the constitution stipulates that state and private schools have equal rights but the latter should not be state-funded. Regional governments, however, have begun to issue means-tested vouchers to offset either state or private schooling costs. Moreover the education minister in the Berlusconi government, Letizia Moratti, was among the signatories of the 1999 *'Scuola Libera'* manifesto, which advocated the radical privatisation of schooling provision in Italy.[1]

Interest in the motivation and effects of education policy has also been boosted in Italy by reforms of the primary, secondary and university-level curricula. These reforms are now being implemented after an extremely long gestation period. Gambetta (1987, ch. 2) provides a very useful description of the Italian education system in the early 1980s and analyses the effects of previous reforms. That description and analysis remain interesting today because even though reforms were being discussed at the time, the system remained virtually unchanged until the late 1990s. The policy debate was then (and still is) centred on whether the Italian secondary school system should conform to the Anglo-American comprehensive model, or remain similar to those of continental Europe countries where the vocational and generalist tracks are separated early in students' school careers. Advocates of reform claimed that comprehensive schooling would prevent the segregation of low- and middle-class children; opponents emphasised the advantages of school selectivity for elite formation.

A reform legislated by the left-wing majority of the late 1990s moved the Italian education system towards the former model, and was quite clearly designed to eliminate elitist stratification.[2] The right-wing government elected in 2001 campaigned against the reform, pledging to stop its implementation and preserve the elitist high-schools (*licei*, which the government wanted to keep distinct from vocational schools and lengthen attendance by one year). The plans of the current Italian government include a school voucher programme to increase equality of opportunity and allow talented children from poor families to obtain a high-quality education in the private sector.

Issues to do with school stratification and freedom of choice in education are also quite important in other countries, including the US, where the Bush administration planned to introduce tax-financed subsidies for private religious schools. In many of those countries, and especially in the US, a substantial number of academic researchers, have tried to assess the efficiency and distributional implications of maintaining the *status quo* in education provision, and of possible reforms. In Italy, however, much of the policy debate has been largely ideological, and scarcity of data has so far prevented serious evaluation of the matter.

This chapter first reviews scientific perspectives on education systems and then offers a statistical analysis of university records, focusing on the implications of the current mixed system of private and public, vocational and generalist education in Italy. Theoretical arguments and empirical evidence suggest that deregulation of education provision (with or without state funding) might not be as beneficial as it would be in a simpler environment. In Italy, where vocational and generalist tracks coexist, private schools appear to cater to segments of the population that are not only wealthier but may also be less likely to perform well in school. This is not being taken into account in the debate on state versus private provision, and therefore a potentially undesirable side effect of increased reliance on private schooling is being ignored.

Economics and education

In education, demand and supply are quite distant from the competitive paradigm of textbook economic models. The economic benefits of education accure much later than the time its costs are paid. Moreover they are random and hardly verifiable since they depend on school leavers' behaviour in the labour market as well as on the quality of education (which is difficult to evaluate). Such problems generally prevent markets from ensuring that private costs and benefits are fully accounted for by appropriate intertemporal, state-contingent contracts. Moreover some of the benefits of education are public in nature, that is, they accure to society as a whole rather than to specific individuals.

Checchi (1999) discusses the interactions between state and private education, and their implications for economic efficiency and resource distribution. Briefly, education plays three related but conceptually distinct socioeconomic roles. First, the school system provides young individuals with the communication and behavioural skills they will need to interact with other members of society. In primary school, children learn not only how to read and write, but also to respect each other and obey rules. Such skills are essential for the smooth functioning of any organised social system.

The second role is to supply the labour market with suitably trained factors of production. Schools instil in new generations advanced productive skills (human capital) in the form of an ability to formulate, analyse and solve problems, and/or technical know-how. The former skills are general and can be learned by exercising and refining one's ability to reason at an abstract level; the latter skills can be learned more mechanically for specific applications. Schools also select (screen) individuals and sort them according to their ability to perform different tasks. The curriculum followed by a student has value in the labour market if it enhances general and/or specific skills and talents. Hence not only society but also individual students benefit (in the form of higher wages and/or better employment opportunities) from school curricula that transmit (and certify) skills that increase workers' productivity. The private value of education is obviously higher when high-quality curricula are scarce in the labour market, and more generally in the socioeconomic system.

In order to interpret many features of school systems in market economies it is important to consider their third role, that of shaping the social structure: Schools select and sort the members of successive generations according to their socioeconomic duties in society, and the structure of a schooling system can prevent or foster intergenerational mobility across the social strata.

What bearing does the coexistence of state and private education have on these roles, and on other institutional features of socioeconomic systems? Clearly it is easier for (primary) schools to foster social cohesion if their students are representative of a cross-section of society and they are managed by civil servants. As far as the first role of schools is concerned, their output is a public good, valued by society as a whole rather than by each individual in isolation. Hence it is easy to see why Article 34 of Italy's constitution prescribes free (state-financed), comprehensive and mandatory education for at least eight years. Just as clearly, however, the other two purposes of school systems (which offer private benefits to individual students) may not be served as well as the first one by a comprehensive state school system.

State schools can be more or less selective at different stages of the student's career, and the simultaneous presence of private schools has important implications for the scope and character of education. To see why, it is useful to suppose that the cost of private education is born directly by families, and to recognise that financial market imperfections generally constrain poor families' educational investment. Hence the student base of private schools predominantly consists of children from relatively rich families, which also offer a better cultural background when educational achievement and financial resources are correlated. In terms of the first role of schools, this implies that the children of better-off families will learn to interact only with each other, and not with their poorer contemporaries, who remain segregated in cheaper state schools.

As regards the economic role of schools – the transmission of knowledge and selection of skills – private schools have important efficiency advantages. Because parents have to pay for the services their children receive they are more likely to monitor the quality of the education provided. Hence competition among private schools and with state schools can increase the efficiency of the education supply. The quality of education, however, is not as easy to determine as that of groceries. Education inputs (such as the number and qualifications of teachers and the size and quality of classrooms) are to some extent observable and measurable, but education output depends on the quality of the students attracted. In principle the quality of education should be evaluated on the basis of students' labour market experience in the decades after graduation. In practice the perceived quality of education is strongly influenced by a school's reputation, which changes very slowly and effectively prevents new entrants from contesting the incumbent's market position; and by a variety of spurious indicators, such as the pleasantness of the premises. The position of private schools is much clearer in respect of the third role of education: social stratification. To the extent that financial resources and social connections limit access to private education, private schools effectively exclude members of other social strata. Suppliers of private education compete with each other and with state schools along this dimension, positioning along an ideal line of more or less exclusiveness (in terms of focusing wealth, social prestige and selectiveness of access).

The supply of private schooling in Italy and elsewhere

The education sector produces a less than purely private good, and since the impact of education on life outcomes takes years if not decades to become apparent, the private aspects of the quality of output are relatively hard to assess for final users. Moreover, the choices made by parents may or may not be aimed at maximising the payoffs to their children in later life. All this may explain why (as with justice administration, medical services and pharmaceutical production) education is heavily regulated and/or publicly provided. This section discusses some aspects of competition in the market (also see De Fraja, 2004, and the references therein), and argues that the sector's supply interacts in complex ways with self-sorting of students on the demand side providing a multiplicity of equilibria in the education market.

Education has many dimensions, and different market failures have different relevance to different types of education. Public-good factors are most relevant for primary education, whose main purpose is to instil basic social skills. At higher levels of education, schooling offers private benefits in the form of specialised skills and certification, and sometimes also in the form of exclusive status. On the basis of these considerations we shall document the characteristics of private education in Italy and other countries, particularly the US, as it represents an interesting opposite case and is a source of extensively researched data.

Data on the incidence of private education at different levels of schooling and for different population groups are of interest in this respect. Among the 2 693 328 Italians enrolled in secondary schools during the 1994–95 school year, only 6.5 per cent were enrolled in private schools. This percentage varied across secondary school types, ranging from 1.2 per cent for vocational schools to 9.8 per cent for *liceo* high schools. Figure 4.1 shows the historical evolution of private education's share of the Italian student population from 1945 to 1995. While the share of private primary education hovered slightly below 8 per cent during this period, private lower-secondary and

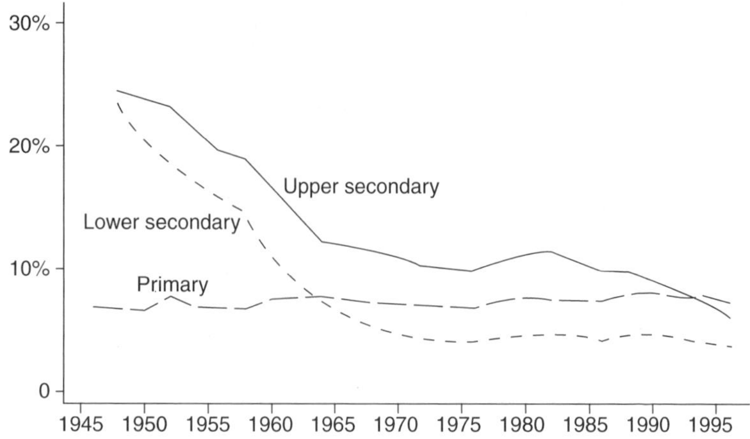

Figure 4.1 Evolution of the share private education in Italy, 1945–95

upper-secondary schools' shares declined over time. However, in absolute numbers, enrolment in private schools remained quite stable at all educational levels. Private schools were popular among the upper and middle classes and enrolment was almost unaffected by the unification of lower-secondary schools in 1962. Meanwhile enrolment in lower-secondary state schools, including training schools (*avviamento professionale*), rose from 572 306 in 1950–1 to 2 795 522 in 1978–79, when the baby-boomers completed their compulsory schooling. A similar trend was followed (with a lag) by upper-secondary state schools: enrolment was slightly below 100 000 at the beginning of the 1950s but had soared to 2 599 452 by 1990–91.

For economic as well as politico-ideological reasons, the existence of church schools is an important aspect of the topici-question. Roughly 1000 of the 1800 or so private schools in Italy are Catholic. This has important implications in that a religious orientation may affect both the demand for educational services and the conditions under which they are supplied. As outlined above, schools not only supply skills and certificates that are privately valuable (because they improve individuals' labour market opportunities), but also instil successive generations with socially valued ethical and social characteristics. Clearly the second of these is particularly important in the case of Catholic and other church schools. A religious orientation certainly affects families' decision to purchase private education when state education is available. The religious character of many educational establishments also has important implications for the quality of education they supply. For example their religious orientation may enable them to obtain high-quality factors of production at relatively low prices, such as the labour of teachers who are not motivated by wages alone, or better facilities financed by bequests. Historically, religious orders have competed very successfully in the various school sectors. Some, such as the Jesuits, have specialised in offering extremely high quality (and not inexpensive) education to the elite. Others, such as the Scolopians, were specifically founded (much earlier than state elementary schools) to cater to the primary schooling needs of the poor, and more recently the Salesians have focused on preparing urban working-class youths for the labour market.[3] Thus religiously oriented education interacts in interesting ways with the comprehensive versus vocational and private versus public classification of schools in general.

Catholic and other religious organisations are active in supplying and funding education not only in Italy, but also in the US and many other countries. At the aggregate level, private education accounts for about 8 per cent of the school population in Italy and about 10 per cent in the US, but the characteristics of the two countries are very different at more disaggregated levels. In the 1980s the extensive 'High School and Beyond' survey enabled American economic and social researchers to study the relationship between family background, school curricula and subsequent labour market success. A controversial but robust finding was that Catholic on average students from schools tended to enjoy slightly more favourable further education and labour market outcomes, and that this was not strictly related to family background.[4] It is important to note that in the US Catholic schools are not only attended by Catholic students. Many of the Catholic schools were built in the relatively poor urban neighbourhoods in which Irish and Italian Catholic immigrants settled before moving to the suburbs, when they were replaced by other poor minorities, not all of them Catholic. So the schools are now attended by students from heterogeneous backgrounds, although enrolment in a Catholic school is still more likely for the children of Catholic families. This has made it possible for researchers to disentangle the effects of schooling from those of background, under the working assumption that a Catholic background makes Catholic schooling more likely but does not otherwise influence a student's performance in higher education and the labour market.

In the US, state education is locally funded, hence its quality is far from uniform and it is not surprising to find that private schools offer better education. It is harder, however, to understand why attendance at Catholic schools should not only benefit students in general (in terms of better opportunities for and better performance in higher education, and better labour market outcomes), but also be especially beneficial for students from disadvantaged backgrounds. It has been suggested that a student culture based on self-discipline, on the notion that 'No one fails who works hard', and on the feeling of belonging to a voluntary community may be an important asset for primary and secondary Catholic educational establishments. There is also some evidence that the teachers employed by Catholic schools are better monitored and more highly motivated than their colleagues who work – for significantly higher wages – in state schools (for a recent review of the literature see Bryk *et al.*, 1993; Lazear, 1999).

Information on teacher motivation and effectiveness is not available for Italy, but it may be of interest to look at comparative pay. According to the most recent figures, teachers who work in state secondary schools earn a gross salary of 1 750 000 lire per month (approximately 900 €) at the start of their teaching career.[5] At the end of their career, with 35 years of seniority, they earn 3 084 000 lire (approximately 1593 €). In private church schools the equivalent monthly salaries are 1 792 000 lire (approximately 925 €) and 2 328 000 lire (approximately 1202 €) respectively,[6] and in private secular schools they are 1 516 000 lire (approximately 783 €) and 2 086 000 lire (approximately 1077 €) respectively.[7] Hence private and state school teachers are similarly paid at the beginning of their career, but private school teachers' salaries rise considerably less thereafter. One possible explanation of this is that work in private schools is considered to be a starting point, to be replaced sooner or later by a job in the state education system.

An empirical exercise

In the light of US evidence and current policy debates, it is quite interesting to consider whether and how similar phenomena may be relevant in Italy, where Catholics are not a minority and Catholic schools need not cater to the needs of particularly poor segments of the population, as is the case in the US. Unfortunately in Italy relevant statistical information is scarce, and no survey comparable to the American 'High School and Beyond' has been conducted. Hence our analysis is restricted to individual data on the university-level performance of pupils from state and private high schools. Our data set, covering the 1999–2000 academic year, is drawn from the administrative files of the University of Milan, the state university in a city where private universities also exist. The files contain information on all enrolled students' backgrounds (the type of secondary school they attended will be of particular interest to our analysis) and their academic performance, which we shall use as a proxy for (relative) economic success in the labour market.

Descriptive statistics

Our data set cannot be taken as representative of all Italian or even Milanese secondary school students. First, while Milanese students' distribution across school types is similar to the national average (Table 4.1), a larger proportion attend private educational establishments, especially in the case of high schools (Table 4.2). This probably reflects the fact that family incomes are higher in Milan than in Italy as a whole, but it may also relate to supply factors. Second, the sample only contains high school students who went on to tertiary education. Not surprisingly, by far the largest fraction of the sample attended *licei* high schools and relatively few came from technical or vocational schools – students from the latter are more likely to enter the labour market straight from school (Table 4.3). The incidence of private *licei* is the same in the sample as in the population, while private technical and vocational schools are overrepresented. Third, the sample was drawn only from the state university, and not from the three private universities in Milan. Table 4.4 shows the distribution of our sample of students by state/private education. These statistics do not coincide with those for the entire population in Table 4.2, but this could reflect the self-sorting of students into different higher-education establishments.

Making generalisations from such a selected sample is clearly very difficult. In order to control for different distortions leading to our data set, we would need information on the probability of transition by individuals from various types of high school into our state university,

Table 4.1 Distribution of students by type of secondary school, 1994–95 (per cent)

	City of Milan	*Lombardy*	*Italy*
Vocational schools	17.8	18.8	19.0
Technical schools	44.2	44.4	41.6
High schools (*licei*)	29.9	26.9	28.2
Other schools	8.1	9.9	11.2
Total	100.0	100.0	100.0

Table 4.2 Distribution of students by state and private secondary schools, 1994–95 (per cent)

	Province of Milan		Italy	
	State schools	*Local and private schools*	*State schools*	*Local and private schools*
Vocational schools	96.0	4.0	98.0	2.0
Technical schools	90.1	9.9	94.0	6.0
High schools (*licei*)	75.9	24.1	89.7	11.3
Other schools	80.4	19.6	87.0	13.0

Table 4.3 Students enrolled at the University of Milan: distribution of students by type of secondary school attended, 1999–2000 (per cent)

	City of Milan	*Lombardy*	*Italy*
Vocational schools	6.9	6.8	6.6
Technical schools	24.0	25.2	25.2
High schools (*licei*)	63.9	62.0	62.1
Other schools	5.2	6.0	6.1
Total	100.0	100.0	100.0

rather than into the labour market or other (private) universities. Since a sample of high-school students with suitable covariates was not available to us, our results may be distorted by selection bias. The various sources of such bias, however, to some extent cancel each other out. If for example students from richer families tended to be underrepresented in both state secondary schools and universities, we would expect the private education fraction to be smaller in Table 4.4 than in Table 4.2.[8] Overall, in our sample students from university-oriented secondary schools are overrepresented whereas the opposite situation applies to students from high-income families within the population of university students. With regard to attendance at private secondary schools these two situations should partially offset, because the former induces overrepresentation of private schools, while the latter works in the opposite direction.

Comparing Tables 4.2 and 4.4, we can see that private school attendance appears to be associated with a higher probability of university entry. If we take the share of private schools in each type of secondary school (the second column of Table 4.2) and multiply this vector of

Table 4.4 Students enrolled at the University of Milan: distribution of students
by state/private education, 1999–2000 (per cent)

	Province of Milan		*Italy*	
	State schools	*Local and private schools*	*State schools*	*Local and private schools*
Vocational schools	86.6	13.4	84.9	15.0
Technical schools	85.1	14.9	86.5	13.5
High schools (*licei*)	74.4	25.6	77.4	22.6
Other schools	79.6	20.4	79.9	20.1
Total	78.1	21.9	80.4	19.6

number by the secondary school origin of the students (the first
column of Table 4.3), we find that if public/private school origin were
irrelevant to further education, 19.1 per cent of the students in our
sample should have originated from private schools. Since the proportion observed in our sample was slightly higher at 21.9 per cent, the
likelihood of university entry is confirmed as being higher for students
from private schools.

We shall now look at the main differences between students from
state secondary schools and students from private schools. From
Table 4.5 we can see that the private school students in our sample
tended to be less academically gifted. Not surprisingly, students from
private schools belong to richer families. The average difference is
5 million lire – nearly 2600 € – in yearly net income and 39 million –
nearly 20 000 € – in self-reported wealth.[9] The university career of students from private secondary schools proceeded at as lower pace (as
measured by the average number of exams passed per year of enrolment) and yielded lower average grades.[10] Since students can choose
how much time to devote to preparing for each exam, slower students
should, *ceteris paribus*, obtain higher marks. Hence a summary indicator of a student's performance versus was computed as the ratio of the
cumulative sum of marks and the number of enrolment years, or the
product of the average mark and the exams-per-year measure of speed
(Table 4.5). In terms of this indicator, the performance of the private
school students in our sample was unambiguously worse than that of
their state school contemporaries because they were slower and
obtained lower marks.

We shall now relate university performance to the type of secondary
school attended and the student's background, which also bears on

Table 4.5 Statistical profile of students enrolled at the University of Milan by state/private education, 1999–2000

	State secondary schools (n = 51 341)		Private secondary schools (n = 12 636)			
	Mean	*St. dev.*	*Mean*	*St. dev.*	*Minimum*	*Maximum*
Sex (1 = woman)	0.56	0.50	0.56	0.50	0	1
Age	24.88	5.51	25.36	5.37	18	79
Number of members of the family	3.55	1.03	3.42	1.05	1	11
Final mark at secondary school	45.81	7.01	44.66	6.88	36	60
Normalised final mark at secondary school	0.035	0.99	−0.144	0.97	−2.013	3.579
Family income (lira)	58 223 530	37 542 330	63 240 460	47 373 250	0	1 611 686 000
Equivalised family income (lira)*	31 623 020	18 601 920	35 663 020	23 617 640	0	657 968 100
Family wealth indicator (lira)	65 365 470	193 683 500	104 482 700	411 776 300	0	36 227 815 000
Number of passed exams	14.06	9.01	14.18	9.15	0.5	80.5
Number of exams passed per year (speed)	2.88	1.84	2.66	1.78	0.04	31
Average mark in exams	25.21	2.43	24.67	2.47	18	31
Performance (average mark × speed)	73.91	49.80	66.98	47.16	1	799.80

*Equivalence scale is the square root of the number of family members.

secondary-school choice and is difficult to characterise precisely. The data set includes indicators of family income but does not contain information on the cultural background of the students, such as their parents' educational achievements. We do have information on the marks students obtained at the end of their secondary schooling. Exams and marks are hardly comparable across school types, but the Board of Public Education administers uniform, nationwide examinations for each type of school. Hence by normalising the grades each of the 80 secondary school diplomas (and converting the 60–100 scale adopted in 1998 to the earlier 36–60 scale, and adding one point to account for *cum laude* scores) we can obtain an indicator of each individual's academic prowess at the end of secondary school. On this basis, Table 4.5 shows that the average final mark of private school students was lower than that of state school students by more than one point in 1999–2000. This conveys some, albeit imperfect, information about variations between individuals that can be attributed to family background, rather than innate characteristics, that is, 'everything that contributes to the child's income potential, is in the child at the time he takes his education decision, and cannot be purchased on the market' (Rubinstein and Tsiddon, 1998, p. 19).

For the sake of brevity we shall refer to such characteristics as 'talent'. In their empirical analysis Rubinstein and Tsiddon (ibid.) use the parents' educational level as a proxy for this notion. Here we measure talent by secondary school exit marks, normalised within each type of secondary school (vocational or generalist).[11] We acknowledge, however, that the use of this term is potentially misleading in the context of our analysis, because measured performance at the end of secondary school is affected both by the individual's ability (or talent) and by the school's contribution to his or her development. To the extent that observable indicators of talent are correlated over time for a given individual, good performance at the time of secondary school graduation is an indicator that students were viewed as talented at the end of lower secondary school.[12] The information conveyed by the final secondary school mark about an individual's ability to perform well at university, of course, may well depend on whether she or he followed a vocational or generalist track, and the division of students into tracks might further distort the relationship between the observable talent proxy and their family background characteristics. The limitations of our data make it impossible to address these concerns rigorously, but we shall bear them in mind when discussing the empirical results.

As shown in Table 4.6, attendance at private school appears to be correlated with the subsequent choice of faculty. In our sample the share of students from private church schools was highest in the faculties of law, medicine and pharmaceutics, all of which were likely to professional, better-paid jobs.[13] This raw correlation could be spurious, however, in that the decision to attend a private high school generally depends on characteristics that also affect faculty choice. Table 4.7 reports a multinomial logit estimate of the determinants of faculty choice. The model fits the data rather poorly but suggests that attendance at a private secondary school is not particularly relevant to faculty choice, which is much more strongly related to attendance at a specific type of secondary school (for example a *liceo* high school in the case of law).[14]

Self-sorting and secondary schools

Before proceeding to evaluate empirically the relationship between university performance and secondary school types, we need to discuss the self-sorting of students. As mentioned earlier, one salient feature of the Italian education system is its stratification into a generalist training track (in high schools: *licei*) and a vocational training track (in technical and professional schools: *istituti tecnici* or *istituti professionali*). Thus while in countries such as the US students are sorted in terms of state and private schools (or in some cases private Catholic and state schools), in the Italian case the sorting is the generalist versus vocational. Outcomes can be tabulated in six categories: state high schools, private church high schools, private secular high schools, state vocational schools, private church vocational schools and private secular vocational schools (Table 4.8).

Private secondary schools are not all alike.[15] We can see from Table 4.8 that the sample of students from private church schools came from wealthy families and were richer than the students from secular private schools. Moreover, without taking income and other available information into account the performance of the former was superior to that of the latter, but comparable to that of students from state schools. From this table it is impossible to ascertain whether students from private church schools outperformed students from state schools, but some idea can be obtained by comparing our evidence with theoretical expectations. Human capital theory predicts that if talent is observable, and subject to resource constraints, parents will invest more in more talented children.[16] So more financial resources will be spent on the education of children who are very talented and/or (in

Table 4.6 Students enrolled at the University of Milan: choice of faculty by type of secondary school, 1999–2000 (per cent)

	State high school	Church high school	Private high school	State vocational school	Church vocational school	Private vocational school
Agricultural sciences	48.35	4.74	2.49	39.21	1.81	1.53
Pharmaceutics	58.09	9.45	3.72	22.74	1.90	1.05
Law	44.40	9.40	5.80	31.65	3.06	2.81
Literature and philosophy	53.52	6.24	5.93	27.37	2.84	1.08
Medicine	49.69	9.11	3.28	25.43	2.46	4.25
Veterinary science	52.17	6.67	4.39	30.14	2.07	1.33
Sciences (maths, chemistry, physics)	49.95	5.71	2.69	36.69	1.61	1.25
Physical education	34.53	4.89	3.91	50.49	3.26	1.63
Political sciences	37.52	5.88	6.38	40.85	2.96	3.19
Total	*48.27*	*7.12*	*4.76*	*32.17*	*2.51*	*2.10*

Table 4.7 Students enrolled at the University of Milan: choice of faculty – multinominal logistic regression, robust standard errors, 1999–2000

	Agricultural science	Pharmaceutics	Law	Literature and philosophy	Medicine	Veterinary science	Science (maths, chemistry)	Political science
Age	0.529**	0.586**	0.633**	0.635**	0.620**	0.559**	0.602**	0.651**
Sex	0.457**	1.326**	0.862**	1.068**	0.869**	1.057**	0.230*	0.520**
Log (family income)	–0.044	–0.084**	–0.073*	–0.055	–0.064*	–0.064**	–0.038	–0.053
High school (*liceo classico*)	–13.738**	–14.055**	–12.814**	–13.126**	–14.594**	–14.122**	–13.975**	–13.646**
High school (*liceo scientifico*)	–14.462**	–15.144**	–15.200**	–15.690**	–16.254**	–15.283**	–14.847**	–15.297**
Technical school	–15.026**	–16.709**	–15.399**	–16.464**	–17.930**	–16.122**	–15.524**	–15.362**
Teaching school (*magistrale*)	–16.559**	–17.216**	–16.489**	–16.168**	–17.575**	–17.405**	–16.775**	–16.430**
Vocational school	–14.787**	–15.728**	–16.000**	–16.251**	–15.985**	–16.180**	–15.835**	–15.733**
High school (*liceo artistico*)	–15.937**	–16.988**	–16.523**	–15.296**	–17.805**	–16.182**	–16.160**	–16.566**
High school (*liceo linguistico*)	–15.911**	–16.531**	–15.571**	–14.945**	–17.616**	–16.355**	–15.958**	–14.862**
European secondary school	3.736	3.281**	2.552**	2.950**	2.880**	3.359**	3.099**	2.425**
State secondary school	0.672	0.505	0.321	0.770	0.266	0.262	0.634	0.233
Local authority secondary school	–0.170	–1.099	–0.209	0.455	–0.119	–0.641	–0.357	–0.292
Private Catholic secondary school	0.449	0.762	0.694	0.572	0.637	0.312	0.495	0.276

Other private church secondary schools	19.557**	18.674**	19.312**	19.990**	19.287**	18.256	19.059**	19.644**
Secular private secondary school	0.168	0.291	0.642	0.648	0.554	0.196	0.049	0.395
Constant	5.370**	5.122**	4.976**	4.805**	5.998**	5.587	5.534**	4.372**
No. in samples:	61 314							
Log likelihood:	−111 475.95							
Pseudo R^2:	0.0591							

Notes: * Significant at the 95 per cent level. ** Significant at the 99 per cent level. The physical education faculty (*Scienze Motorie.*) formerly ISEF is the comparison group.

Table 4.8 Statistical profile (means) of students enrolled at the University of Milan, by type of secondary school, 1999–2000

	State high school	Church high school	Private Secular high school	State vocational school	Church vocational school	Private secular vocational school
Sex (1 = woman)	0.60	0.56	0.57	0.51	0.69	0.28
Age	24.26	24.28	25.41	25.96	25.70	27.38
Final mark at secondary school	45.54	45.12	43.47	46.28	46.44	44.16
Final normalised mark at secondary school	0.06	−0.02	−0.29	0.05	0.02	−0.16
Family income (lira)	63 392 570	70 925 540	62 242 520	52 395 630	60 214 410	58 200 570
Equivalised family income (lira)*	34 232 620	39 887 010	35 536 680	28 732 100	33 836 000	32 651 280
Family wealth of (lira)*	75 185 830	129 288 000	92 460 630	53 489 290	125 192 100	86 477 140
Number of passed exams	14.62	14.71	13.90	13.26	13.90	12.85
Number of exams passed per year (speed)	3.03	2.96	2.42	2.62	2.62	2.38
Average mark in exams	25.59	24.99	24.41	24.64	24.66	23.81
Performance (average mark × speed)	78.86	75.37	60.26	65.58	65.76	57.94
No. in sample	29 857	4354	2804	18938	1476	1160

* Equivalence scale equal to the square root of the number of family members.

the presence of financial market imperfections) whose families are relatively rich. If private education improves education outcomes and the effect is more pronounced for highly talented students, then heterogeneous families will sort themselves along a downward-sloping line in [talent, income] space (see figure 3.1 and 3.2 in previous chapter).

Our data set does not contain information on the (perceived) talent of students at the age of 14, when the state/private choice was made. As argued above, however, the normalised final mark at secondary school provides a clue to individual talent at the time of secondary school choice. Figure 4.2 shows the distribution of students at the six types of secondary school according to this proxy for talent, and to current income as a proxy for the family's financial circumstances at the time of secondary school choice. The circles are positioned according to the average talent and income of the students at each of the secondary schools in our sample, and the (size of the circles is proportional to the number of sampled students from those schools.[17] The horizontal and vertical lines indicate the median talent and equivalised income in the full sample. Interestingly, highly talented students were abundant in private church schools but relatively rare in other private schools. The theory outlined above predicts that private school students should cluster in the top-left (highly-talented offspring of poor families) and bottom-right (low-talented offspring of rich families) quadrants of each graph. Many of the private secular schools in our study, however, appear to have catered to students whose financial and talent resources lie in the bottom right quadrant of the graphs. If university-level performance is the objective of secondary-school attendance, the families' decision to send their children to such schools cannot be interpreted as a decision to purchase high-quality education in the sense used in human capital theory.

Before discussing other possible determinants of schooling choice in the next section, we shall analyse the relationship about which our data set is most informative, namely that between private schooling (and other observable characteristics of students) and academic performance at university.

Tables 4.9–4.11 show the results of descriptive regressions on the complete data set. As already mentioned, the variable 'talent' is only loosely related to individual characteristics before secondary school. To the extent that different schools provide different educational experiences, final secondary school marks are in principle jointly determined with the choice of attending different secondary schools (on the basis of unobservable individual characteristics). For this

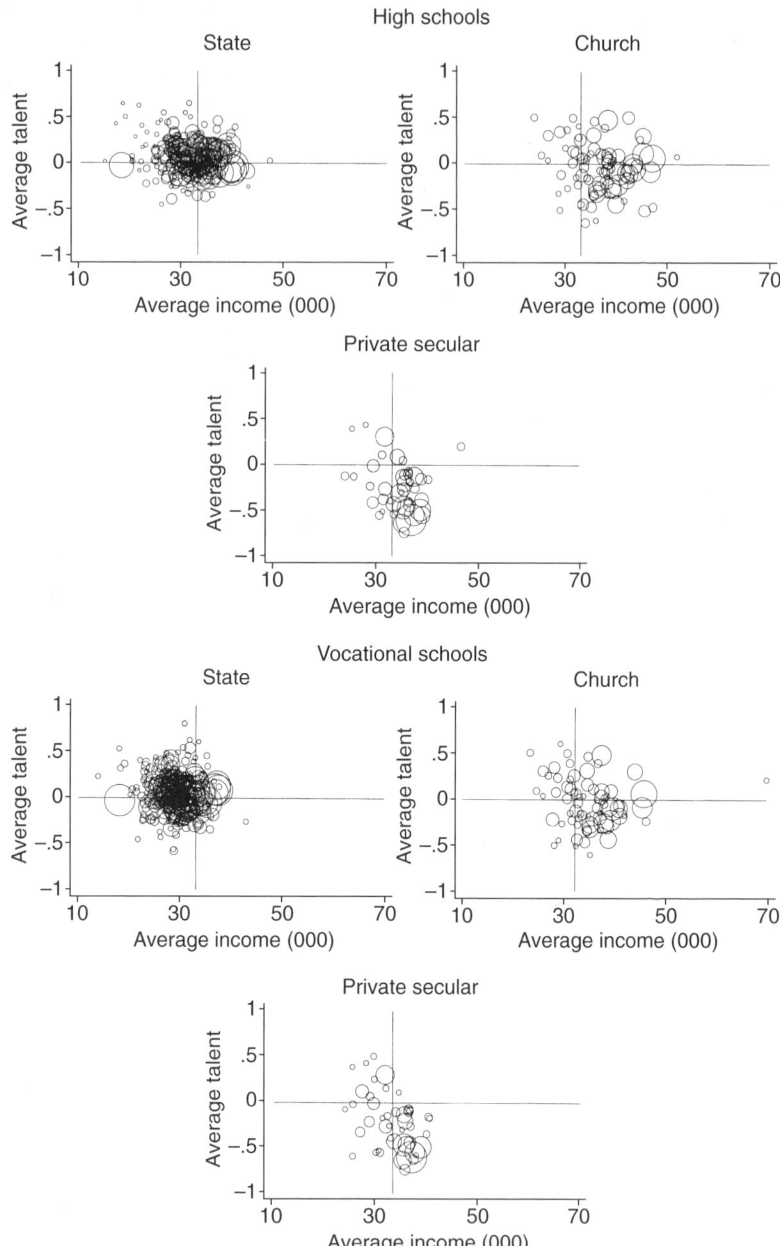

Figure 4.2 Distribution of talent and resource proxies by type of secondary school

Table 4.9 Students enrolled at the University of Milan: determinants of student performance, excluding secondary school mark, 1999–2000 (robust standard errors. t-statistics in parentheses)

	(1) *Average mark*	(2) *Speed*	(3) *Student productivity*	(4) *Average mark*	(5) *Speed*	(6) *Student productivity*
Sex (1 = woman)	0.149	0.20	5.490	0.605	0.241	6.520
	(7.84)	(15.10)	(15.41)	(11.62)	(17.85)	(18.04)
Log equivalised	0.037	0.032	0.937	0.177	0.046	1.267
family income	(5.24)	(4.80)	(5.22)	(8.47)	(7.05)	(7.33)
Public high school	1.278	0.262	10.242	3.619	0.490	15.657
	(20.76)	(4.53)	(6.63)	(17.93)	(9.01)	(10.91)
Church high school	0.785	0.121	5.148	2.793	0.319	9.850
	(11.19)	(1.94)	(3.09)	(12.79)	(5.38)	(6.28)
Private secular high	0.102	−0.146	−3.255	1.478	−0.019	−0.196
school	(1.36)	(−2.31)	(−1.94)	(6.14)	(−0.31)	(−0.12)
State vocational	0.520	−0.025	0.697	1.754	0.097	3.525
school	(8.35)	(−0.44)	(0.45)	(8.52)	(1.77)	(2.45)
Church vocational	0.357	−0.098	−1.686	1.587	0.010	0.862
school	(4.36)	(−1.39)	(−0.91)	(5.89)	(0.15)	(0.48)
Private secular	−0.187	−0.385	−10.122	−0.188	−0.377	−9.939
vocational school	(−2.04)	(−4.92)	(−4.98)	(−0.62)	(−5.09)	(−5.20)
No. in sample	56 282	56 282	56 282	59 665	59 665	59 665
R^2	0.231	0.33	0.328	0.066	0.307	0.308

Note: Additional controls: intercept, age, living area, faculty, whether attending a three-year course and whether graduating that year.

Table 4.10 Students enrolled at the University of Milan: determinants of student performance, including secondary school mark, 1999–2000 (robust standard errors, t-statistics in parentheses)

	(1)	(2)	(3) Student productivity	(4)	(5)	(6) Student productivity
	Average mark	*Speed*	*productivity*	*Average mark*	*Speed*	*productivity*
Sex (1 = woman)	−0.023	0.146	3.60	0.310	0.175	4.312
	(−1.33)	(11.17)	(10.36)	(6.12)	(13.15)	(12.29)
Log equivalised	0.024	0.028	0.799	0.154	0.040	1.092
family income	(3.71)	(4.28)	(4.57)	(7.54)	(6.37)	(6.51)
Secondary school mark	0.917	0.287	10.087	1.508	0.339	11.267
(normalised mark)	(106.38)	(42.78)	(55.58)	(59.97)	(49.76)	(61.51)
State high school	1.194	0.236	9.317	3.476	0.457	14.591
	(19.66)	(4.08)	(6.04)	(17.27)	(8.42)	(10.17)
Church high school	0.761	0.114	4.878	2.755	0.311	9.563
	(11.25)	(1.83)	(2.95)	(12.71)	(5.27)	(6.15)
Private secular high school	0.255	−0.098	−1.579	1.755	0.043	1.873
	(3.50)	(−1.56)	(−0.95)	(7.37)	(0.72)	(1.19)
state vocational school	0.339	−0.082	−1.297	1.487	0.037	1.533
	(5.51)	(−1.41)	(−0.84)	(7.24)	(0.67)	(1.06)
Church vocational school	0.229	−0.138	−3.096	1.422	−0.027	−0.372
	(2.87)	(−1.97)	(−1.68)	(5.35)	(−0.40)	(−0.21)
Private secular vocational	−0.223	−0.396	−10.512	−0.185	−0.377	−9.922
school	(−2.54)	(−5.10)	(−5.22)	(−0.62)	(−5.13)	(−5.26)
No. in sample	56 282	56 282	56 282	59 665	59 665	59 665
R^2	0.362	0.353	0.367	0.120	0.336	0.354

Note: Additional controls: intercept, age, living area, faculty, whether attending a three-year course and whether graduating that year.

reason, we report regressions of academic performance first on a set of explanatory variables excluding normalised high-school marks (or talent), then on sets that include 'talent' and that interact it with the type of secondary school. (Namely we take the product of talent by each dummy variable indicating the type of secondary school attended in order to see whether it plays a differential role according to the type of secondary school attended.)

The first three columns of Table 4.9 omit students who had passed no exams; the other three columns consider all those in the sample for whom information was available.[18] The students from richer families performed better in terms of both average marks and speed of progress. Attendance at a state *liceo* high school was invariably associated with the highest performance for all three indicators. Students from church *licei* high schools and secular private high schools displayed the next-best performances, and the ranking of those who had attended state, church, and secular private schools was similar in the case of vocational schools. If we compare vocational and generalist schools we can see that a vocational background appeared to slow down a student's university career.

The regressions reported in Table 4.10 controlled for normalised final secondary school marks, or talent. They provide identical ranking of different secondary school tracks. Not surprisingly, normalised secondary school marks (talent) seem to be a good predict or of academic performance at university.[19] Of course this does not necessarily offer additional information on the determinants of the choice of private schooling, since those grades depend not only on talent as perceived at the time of secondary school enrolment, but also on further development of students' skills during their time at high school. In other words private schooling and talent are potentially endogenous variables. However private schooling appears to be associated with poorer university performance regardless of whether or not the talent proxy is controlled for, and this casts considerable doubt on the notion that private schools are unequivocally better.

The development of academic skills during secondary school may differ according to educational track, so the regression reported in Table 4.11, the coefficient of the final secondary school mark was allowed to differ across school types. The interaction coefficients in lower half of the table indicate that the impact of the final mark on university performance tends to be larger for *licei* high schools than for vocational schools, and larger for state than for private schools (separate regressions by type of school, which are not reported in the table,

Table 4.11 Students enrolled at the University of Milan: determinants of student performance, including secondary school mark interacted with school type 1999–2000 (robust standard errors, t-statistics in parentheses)

	(1) *Average mark*	(2) *Speed*	(3) *Student productivity*	(4) *Average mark*	(5) *Speed*	(6) *Student productivity*
Sex (1 = woman)	−0.024	0.145	3.563	0.311	0.174	4.281
	(−1.41)	(11.11)	(10.27)	(6.14)	(13.10)	(12.22)
Log equivalised	0.023	0.027	0.772	0.154	0.040	1.068
family income	(3.53)	(4.17)	(4.43)	(7.52)	(6.27)	(6.39)
Secondary school mark	0.544	0.092	3.801	1.034	0.134	4.577
(normalised mark)	(8.09)	(1.37)	(2.09)	(4.77)	(2.09)	(2.65)
State high school	1.215	0.247	9.636	3.526	0.475	15.132
	(20.02)	(4.18)	(6.11)	(17.59)	(8.50)	(10.23)
Church high school	0.790	0.128	5.355	2.802	0.332	10.261
	(11.69)	(2.03)	(3.17)	(13.01)	(5.49)	(6.42)
Private secular high	0.281	−0.062	−0.739	1.901	0.095	3.108
school	(3.83)	(−0.96)	(−0.43)	(8.15)	(1.52)	(1.88)
State vocational school	0.371	−0.065	−0.730	1.535	0.057	2.188
	(6.04)	(−1.09)	(−0.46)	(7.51)	(1.02)	(1.47)
Church vocational school	0.264	−0.120	−2.520	1.470	−0.008	0.245
	(3.32)	(−1.69)	(−1.34)	(5.54)	(−0.11)	(0.14)
Private secular vocational	−0.207	−0.393	−10.558	−0.077	−0.363	−9.749
school	(−2.37)	(−4.93)	(−5.09)	(−0.26)	(−4.78)	(−4.96)
Secondary school mark	0.458	0.243	8.134	0.430	0.247	8.459
State high school	(6.74)	(3.59)	(4.44)	(1.97)	(3.82)	(4.85)
Secondary school mark	0.531	0.264	8.502	0.498	0.263	8.656
church high school	(7.19)	(3.68)	(4.38)	(2.15)	(3.81)	(4.66)
Secondary school mark	0.377	0.282	7.890	0.799	0.315	8.815
private high school	(4.65)	(3.84)	(3.98)	(3.14)	(4.42)	(4.61)

Secondary school mark state vocational school	0.256 (3.73)	0.122 (1.80)	3.691 (2.01)	0.502 (2.26)	0.143 (2.19)	4.304 (2.46)
Secondary school mark church vocational school	0.157 (1.83)	0.097 (1.23)	3.012 (1.43)	0.592 (2.11)	0.137 (1.78)	4.105 (2.02)
Secondary school mark private vocational school	0.303 (3.23)	0.125 (1.41)	3.267 (1.39)	0.766 (2.46)	0.178 (2.09)	4.588 (2.06)
No. in sample	56 282	56 282	56 282	59 665	59 665	59 665
R^2	0.364	0.354	0.369	0.12	0.338	0.356

Note: Additional controls: intercept, age, living area, faculty, whether attending a three-year course and whether graduating that year.

deliver a similar message). To the extent that both secondary and university performance and school choice are jointly determined by unobservable family characteristics, these coefficients (like those in Tables 4.9 and 4.10) cannot be free of selection bias. The finding, however, is quite intriguing, and could be rationalised by a structural model whereby private schools offer smaller payoffs to relatively less talented students and attract a relatively large share of such students from the population.

The same pattern of productivity rankings is confirmed on a faculty-by-faculty basis in Table 4.12, and in similar regressions where coefficients were allowed to vary by type of secondary school. In such smaller samples, however, the coefficients were not always statistically significant (especially in the case of the medical school, where the results were possibly influenced by the fact that some medical schools were associated with private church hospitals).[20]

Because the students were self-sorted into different secondary schools, these statistical results merely show correlations and cannot be interpreted in causal terms. For example the coefficient associated with attendance at a state *liceo* high school does not imply that a randomly selected student would have improved his or her average mark by 1.194 points if he or she had been forced to attend that type of secondary school (column 1 of Table 4.10). The coefficient measures the average effect for an average member of the group that had attended a state *liceo*, but its estimated value could be entirely attributable to unobservable characteristics of that group. In order to control for self-sorting, we would have to exploit variations in the data with respect to factors that are relevant to the choice of secondary school but irrelevant to performance at university.[21]

Since our data set included some information on family wealth, we experimented with that variable as an instrument for the choice of private schooling. For simplicity we applied standard IV estimation techniques to the (discrete) choice under study. An appropriate instrument would have to be relevant to the choice of attending different schools, which would arguably be the case if the cost of private education were more or less burdensome for families with different current resources and imperfect access to financial markets. To validate exclusion from the outcome equation, the instrument would have to have no relation to university performance after controlling for other observable characteristics of the student's background.[22] Lacking a better instrument, we had to assume that the financial wealth indicator's variance component that was orthogonal to family income and other observable covariates was not structurally related to university

Table 4.12 Students enrolled at the University of Milan: determinants of student productivity by faculty, 1999–2000 (robust standard errors, t-statistics in parentheses)

	Agricultural science	Pharmaceutics	Law	Lit. and Philosophy	Medicine	Veterinary science	Sciences	Political sciences
Sex (1 = woman)	−0.214	−0.521	−1.702	1.453	27.853	−2.722	5.884	3.028
	(−0.14)	(−0.42)	(−2.51)	(2.22)	(14.48)	(−1.56)	(8.46)	(3.69)
Log equivalised	1.297	1.640	1.147	0.508	1.106	1.698	1.238	0.784
family income	(2.16)	(4.25)	(3.88)	(1.63)	(1.38)	(2.34)	(3.76)	(1.85)
Secondary school mark	15.701	16.871	11.864	10.767	4.526	10.653	11.493	9.108
(normalised mark)	(19.57)	(26.16)	(30.34)	(34.87)	(4.94)	(11.47)	(32.17)	(17.65)
State high school	24.089	14.879	18.413	10.451	13.387	3.048	4.185	19.860
	(3.87)	(3.95)	(7.55)	(4.45)	(2.75)	(0.53)	(0.82)	(8.76)
Church high school	15.116	6.324	17.901	4.894	2.841	−7.003	0.767	13.559
	(2.17)	(1.53)	(6.84)	(1.87)	(0.52)	(−1.11)	(0.14)	(4.50)
Private secular high	−1.862	1.552	5.341	0.302	5.338	−12.349	−9.619	3.958
school	(−0.25)	(0.35)	(1.98)	(0.12)	(0.74)	(−1.83)	(−1.76)	(1.49)
State vocational	4.571	2.662	3.072	−6.409	29.940	−8.412	−4.541	5.128
school	(0.73)	(0.69)	(1.26)	(−2.72)	(5.84)	(−1.46)	(−0.88)	(2.33)
Church vocational	−8.739	−6.533	2.223	−2.685	24.248	−15.624	−14.881	2.132
school	(−1.07)	(−1.17)	(0.75)	(−0.92)	(2.91)	(−1.92)	(−2.66)	(0.76)
Private secular	6.550	−12.307	−1.90	−12.661	−5.604	−25.543	−13.830	−2.385
vocational school	(0.81)	(−1.86)	(−0.65)	(−3.48)	(−0.86)	(−3.10)	(−2.30)	(−0.79)
No. in sample	2804	3301	11 630	13 895	5945	2293	11 236	8359
R^2	0.217	0.304	0.228	0.174	0.291	0.176	0.229	0.166

Note: Additional controls: intercept, age, living area and whether graduating that year.

performance, and allowed it to affect the choice between private and state school.

To focus on binary choices we considered in turn three alternatives: state versus private schools, state versus church schools and state versus church *liceo* high schools. Table 4.13 summarises the students' performance in terms of the overall productivity measure (average marks multiplied by speed), and reports the coefficients for these three binomial alternatives, estimated by ordinary least squares and with family wealth as an instrument. The regression was not conditioned on 'talent', but a similar message was conveyed by an IV estimation (not reported) of the other specifications considered in Table 4.10, while the average least square effect was negative, the marginal effect of attending a private (or a church) school was positive. This may indicate that those students who attended expensive private schools because of their families' relatively greater wealth did benefit from attending private schools, and even more so when they were less talented.[23] Conversely the effect of private schooling on university performance was negative when the student's talent, as measured by the normalised final secondary school mark, was used as an instrument for private-school

Table 4.13 Students enrolled at the University of Milan since 1994: determinants of student productivity, 1999–2000 (robust standard errors, t-statistics in parentheses)

Model:	(1)	(2)	(3)	(4)	(5)	(6)
Sex (1 = woman)	5.442	8.505	5.729	6.601	6.159	6.428
	(14.82)	(14.92)	(15.60)	(15.01)	(17.17)	(14.87)
Log equivalised	0.974	1.084	0.988	0.931	1.096	1.010
family income	(5.44)	(5.34)	(5.50)	(4.59)	(6.03)	(4.77)
Private school	−7.240	62.217	–	–	–	–
	−14.75)	(7.06)				
Church private school	–	–	−3.211	83.365		
			(−5.32)	(7.02)		
Church high school	–	–	–	–	−0.375	109.682
					(−0.54)	(8.01)
No. in sample	56 282	56 282	56 282	56 282	56 282	56 282
R^2	0.328	0.094	0.326	0.085	0.318	0.019

Notes: (1) student productivity; (2) student productivity – wealth used as instrument for estimation of the effect of private school; (3) student productivity; (4) student productivity – wealth used as instrument for estimation of the effect of church school (5) student productivity; (6) student productivity – wealth used as instrument for the estimation of the effect of church high school. Additional controls: intercept, age, living area, type of secondary school (first four columns only), faculty, whether attending a three-year course and whether graduating that year.

choice. The evidence is admittedly far from robust, since both family wealth and talent were measured after secondary-school choice in our data set, and the proxy for talent was in principle jointly determined with the chosen type of secondary school. However it is *prima facie* consistent with the idea of a remedial role for private schools a stratified, multitrack education system. On average it seems that private schooling improved the performance of the students from rich families, but their value added of private schools seems to lie in their remedial work with less able students rather than providing across-the-board, high-quality education.

The results in the last two columns of Table 4.13, which examine the determinants of enrolment in a church *liceo* high school, can be interpreted differently. In this case the students were doubly selected (according both to the funding and to orientation of their secondary school) and it appears that their university performance benefited strongly from their attendance at this type of school. As long as the families' choice of secondary school was constrained by financial considerations, the IV results can be given a causal interpretation – that private/church schooling is beneficial for rich and less talented students.

The empirical perspective of our IV exercise offers useful insights into the possible implications of state funding of privately supplied education. Like the component of wealth that is orthogonal to other observable family characteristics (and by assumption to the component of university performance outcomes that is unexplained by such characteristics), vouchers would increase the propensity to choose private schools. Even private schooling is especially beneficial for less talented students from rich families, a school voucher programme would make no difference to their financially unconstrained choice. Of course such a programme might enable less talented students from poor families to take advantage of private schools' remedial capacity. The social implications of this, however, are not as clear as those of programmes that enable relatively talented but financially constrained students to obtain a better education, whether in state or private establishments. It is also quite likely that the industrial organisation of the private education sector would not remain unchanged in the new circumstances.

In summary, there is a positive correlation between average student performance and the type of secondary school attended, ranked in the following order: state high schools, private church high schools, private secular high schools, state vocational schools, private church vocational schools and private secular vocational schools. Allowing for the self-sorting of students into different types of secondary school, there is evidence that private (or church) schools offer a remedial service to students from wealthier families.[24]

Discussion

What is purchased by families who pay for private schooling? According to the results presented above, the answer cannot simply be better quality education. Attendance at a private school does not guarantee access to desirable university faculties, and its effects on students' performance are positive only in the case of less talented children from wealthy families. Moreover the average performance of students from private schools is lower, and this could have negative implications in terms of stigma. Our findings are consistent with the hypothesis that the pay-off from private education is not uniformly higher than that from state education. Rather, the education technology of Italian private schools appears superior to that of state schools when applied to low-talent students, not when applied to high-talent students. Allowing for such heterogeneity of schooling technologies, rather than focusing on a single index of 'quality' (as in models surveyed in the previous chapter by De Fraja) can explain why private and state educational institutions coexist, and why the latter tend to be attended by relatively talented and poor students. Outline some possible reasons why families send their children to private secondary schools when this will not result in a better performance at university (and presumably in the labour market). It should be noted, however, that the available data are not very informative on all relevant factors. For example private schools may be attractive to families, especially those in which both parents work, because they offer convenience in terms of proximity, extended care facilities, infrequent teacher strikes and less disruption by student protests, but the lack of suitable family background information in our data makes it impossible to test this hypothesis against other plausible alternatives, such as the idea for example that the parents choose private schooling under the expection of a differential benefit for talented children.

The finding that university performance is not necessarily improved by private schooling need not imply that the money spent on fees is wasted. Since private school students are somewhat more likely to enrol in higher education (see Tables 4.2 and 4.4 above), families may trade off this greater likelihood against a less than optimum academic performance. A somewhat different explanation, and one backed up by our data, is that tuition fees prevent the children of poorer families from attending private schools (in the absence of targeted school vouchers) which may be desirable from some better-off families' point of view.[25] An empirical counterpart to the economic return on investment in social exclusion is the peer effect: having 'better' schoolmates could improve a child's performance and/or provide access to social networks that could later prove helpful in the labour market. We tried to assess the strength of these effects by averaging the final marks at secondary school according to a single school and year of exit (deducting the individual contribution to the average).[26] Similarly we tested for a 'neighbourhood effect' (i.e. the characteristics of the social environment) by controlling for average family income at secondary school level.[27] Table 4.14 shows regression estimates of university performance according to these and other family background indicators (to avoid selection bias from drop-out attrition the sample includes only recently enrolled students). The estimates indicate that a peer effect only becomes apparent when it is allowed to differ across different school types. When we interacted the type of school with our measure of the peer effect, we found that the students from non-vocational private high schools seemed to benefit from the average talent of their schoolmates. Conversely it seems that the performance of students from state high schools was negatively affected by the same variable. In the case of vocational schools, however, students at both types of school appear to have benefited from the peer effect. The existence of a peer effect does not contradict the general finding that on (average) the students from state high schools performed better than the others. In fact if we sum the coefficients of the corresponding dummies we can see that the state high school effect dominated all the other effects.

The results show with a strong neighbourhood effect on the outcomes of further education, in that university performance increased with average family income for all school types (only students from church schools exhibit coefficients on interacted variables that are statistically significant).[28] But the results offer very limited support to the idea that the peer effect should be more pronounced in more homogeneous environments (Coleman *et al.*, 1982), and the overall evidence is quite mixed.

Our estimates and inferences are hampered by our lack of information on outcomes other than performance at university. In Italy, university exam results do not appear to have a significant effect on subsequent labour market outcomes (Boero *et al.*, 2004), which are more influenced by pre-university qualifications and family background. If

Table 4.14 Determinants of student performance: students enrolled at the University of Milan since 1994 and coming from schools from which at least 10 of the students originated, 1999–2000 (robust standard errors, t-statistics in parentheses)

Model: Dependent variable:	1 Average mark	2 Average mark	3 Speed	4 Speed	5 Productivity	6 Productivity
Sex (1 = woman)	−0.046	−0.053	0.234	0.228	5.725	5.546
	(−1.77)	(−2.05)	(11.66)	(11.32)	(10.61)	(10.25)
Log equivalised	0.006	0.008	0.035	0.035	0.881	0.901
family income	(0.52)	(0.72)	(3.11)	(3.16)	(2.99)	(3.06)
Log family wealth	0.014	0.015	0.010	0.011	0.321	0.330
	(5.45)	(5.69)	(4.87)	(5.02)	(5.68)	(5.85)
Secondary school mark	1.032	1.031	0.381	0.381	13.280	13.279
(normalised mark)	(80.21)	(80.11)	(37.40)	(37.45)	(47.75)	(47.79)
State high school	1.179	0.841	0.251	−0.338	10.20	−4.119
	(8.59)	(1.01)	(2.18)	(−0.52)	(3.40)	(−0.24)
Church high school	0.798	−0.850	0.113	0.693	5.237	14.888
	(5.46)	(−0.63)	(0.92)	(0.58)	(1.64)	(0.47)
Private secular high school	0.135	−7.780	−0.218	−4.072	−4.650	−122.486
	(0.89)	(−3.31)	(−1.80)	(−2.86)	(−1.48)	(−3.33)
state vocational school	0.40	−3.134	−0.137	−4.188	−2.491	−112.071
	(2.88)	(−2.18)	(−1.17)	(−3.90)	(−0.82)	(−3.86)
Church vocational school	0.066	−6.586	−0.092	−7.348	−1.799	−211.210
	(0.34)	(−1.67)	(−0.61)	(−2.33)	(−0.45)	(−2.51)
Private vocational school	−0.776	−13.771	−0.839	−1.020	−22.951	−72.590
	(−3.45)	(−2.03)	(−4.80)	(−0.20)	(−5.11)	(−0.59)
Peer effect × mark at	−0.004	—	0.007	—	0.143	—
secondary school	(−0.68)		(1.31)		(1.06)	
Peer effect × state high school	—	−0.042	—	−0.014	—	−0.487
		(−4.79)		(−2.10)		(−2.70)

Peer effect × church high school	—	0.032	—	–0.020	—	–0.375
		(1.67)		(–1.24)		(–0.90)
Peer effect × private high school	—	0.087	—	0.058	—	1.663
		(3.41)		(3.24)		(3.58)
Peer effect × state vocational school	—	0.024	—	0.035	—	0.930
		(1.94)		(3.52)		(3.56)
Peer effect × church vocational school	—	0.137	—	0.129	—	3.858
		(3.09)		(3.27)		(3.59)
Peer effect × private vocational school	—	0.002	—	–0.068	—	–1.831
		(0.03)		(–1.38)		(–1.51)
Neighbourhood effect × family equivalised income	0.248	—	0.112	—	3.506	—
	(5.00)		(2.91)		(3.42)	
Neighbourhood effect × state high school	—	0.236	—	0.131	—	3.901
		(3.30)		(2.38)		(2.63)
Neighbourhood effect × church high school	—	0.034	–	0.043	–	1.052
		(0.33)		(0.49)		(0.44)
Neighbourhood effect × private high school	—	0.431	—	0.145	—	4.843
		(2.50)		(1.43)		(1.88)
Neighbourhood effect × state vocational school		0.255		0.252		6.877
		(1.95)		(2.77)		(2.77)
Neighbourhood effect × church vocational school	—	0.048	—	0.139	—	3.426
		(0.18)		(0.57)		(0.53)
Neighbourhood effect × private vocational school	—	1.306	—	0.327	—	13.343
		(2.72)		(0.86)		(1.41)
No. in sample	26 110	26 110	26 110	26 110	26 110	26 110
R^2	0.384	0.386	0.34	0.341	0.369	0.371

Notes Model 1: average mark – peer effect; model 2: average mark – peer effect interacted with type of secondary school; model 3: exams per year – peer effect; model 4: exams per year – peer effect interacted with type of secondary school; model 5: student productivity – peer effect; model 6: student productivity – peer effect interacted with type of secondary school. Additional controls: intercept, age, living area, faculty of attendance, whether attending a three-year course and whether graduating that year.

private secondary education provides access to socioeconomic networks (rather than influencing university-level education outcomes), it might conceivably constitute a valuable asset. However a preliminary analysis of survey data collected from a sample of recent graduates from the same university indicates that private schooling does no more than good university results to improve labour market outcomes.

Concluding remarks

Our empirical findings offer interesting insights into the nature of self-sorting mechanisms when, as is currently the case in Italy, students with varying degrees of talent and from diverse family backgrounds can choose from a wide range of generalist/vocational, public/private and secular church schooling options. In our study, on average the students from state schools achieved the best academic performance. However private schooling (both church and secular) improved the performance of a subgroup of students whose choice of private school was correlated with family wealth. There was evidence of peer effects of varying intensity and sign across school types. In both vocational and generalist schools the students' performance also appears to have been influenced by a neighbourhood effect, or at least in the case of secular schools.

How do the findings bear on the general issues discussed in the theoretical sections of this chapter? In general the self-sorting (or segregation) of students can be problematic in two respects: imperfect socialisation due to lack of exposure to the full range of social diversity, and inefficient allocation of students of different abilities in the presence of peer effects. The former involves an unavoidable trade-off between individuals' freedom to choose (and to self-sort) and social obligations. The latter is irrelevant when student interactions do not create externalities, but becomes more and more problematic the stronger the peer pressure grows. In addition the efficiency consequences are strongly interwined with the type of sorting device used.[29]

The Italian education system allows students to sort themselves according to talent and to family income. The 'best' students (in terms of personal ability and family background) self-sort into *liceo* high schools. Of these, students from wealthier families also appear to self-sort into private and church schools. Such sorting can have negative implications in the presence of peer and neighbourhood effects, which amplify differences between the academic performance of students.

The previous government's proposed secondary school reforms were aimed at removing one of the divides by standardising school curricula up to the age of 16, abolishing the formal distinction between high schools and vocational schools, and easing mobility between the educational tracks. However the current government wants to preserve the distinction between high schools and vocational schools, and to subsidise private school attendance. This would add to the self-sorting opportunities in an education system that already features extensive choice.

Of course maintaining the differentiation of school curricula and introducing school vouchers could increase efficiency by encouraging competition between state and private schools.[30] In order to enhance competition, however, it would be necessary to remove the market imperfections reviewed in the second section of this chapter, for example by officially rating schools and teachers on the basis of objective performance criteria, an issue that has not arisen in the Italian policy debate. Distributing school vouchers unconditionally would do little to reduce financial inequality among families. It would simply increase the demand for private education by making it affordable for somewhat poorer (but still relatively rich) families, and might merely intensify competition within the private education sector. Our findings indicate that private schools do not offer uniformly better education, rather the returns on talent appear to be higher in the state sector, especially in *licei* high schools. While further work is undoubtedly needed to improve the statistical measurement of the relevant effects and to analyse the nature of competition among schools, it is difficult to argue that stronger competition from private schools would necessarily improve efficiency. In order to be competitive, private schools would have to attract good students (who are both customers and inputs of the educational process) and good experienced teachers. At the moment the latter tend to work in the state sector (especially in *licei* high schools) because, as noted earlier, wages are higher there than in the private sector. To increase teachers' salaries, private schools would have to increase their tuition fees (or become better at attracting donations), thus discouraging parents from enrolling their children.

In the light of the above, it will not be as easy as many think to improve the Italian education system via increased competition by the private sector. The reform process will presumably reinforce the stratified nature of the system. To improve efficiency in such a setting, it will be necessary to focus resources on primary schools to compensate for differences in family backgrounds and to base entrance to all secondary and tertiary institutions on merit (with exam-based admission) rather than family wealth. In this regard school vouchers would play a significant role if they were suitably targeted at poor families and made conditional on adequate student performance. Otherwise they would create an additional demand for private schooling without improving human capital formation.

Notes

* We would like to thank Christopher Flinn (the discussant) and other participants at the conference on 'Education, Training and Labour Market Outcomes in Europe' (Milan, 16–17 November 2001) for their helpful comment.

1. See *Liberal*, 18 November 1999, or http://www.agesc.it/Liberal.htm. The manifesto insisted that the state should (1) finance, not provide education, (2) support a variety of educational options, (3) ensure equal dignity among all schools, (4) deprive all degrees of legal validity, (5) set an annual per-pupil educational expenditure, (6) pay the latter to families, and (7) set the value of vouchers below the cost of state education, but by no more than 10 per cent, in order to support universal service.

2. *Legge quadro* no. 30 of 10 February 2000 combined *scuola media* (the lower secondary school, whose curriculum was unified in the late 1960s reform – see Gambetta, 1987) and elementary schools into a single primary school curriculum; abolished its final examination (*esame di licenza media*); increased the lowest learning age to 16 (from 15), with two additional years of compulsory on-the-job training for school leavers (*obbligo formativo*); shortened the total duration of primary and secondary school by one year (from 13 to 12 years); reformed the secondary school curriculum, as composed by an initial biennium, common to all tracks to be followed by additional three years which are track-specific. The law also prescribed that all secondary schools curriculum regardless of their vocational orientation, must be named '*liceo*' (high school), like the non-vocational schools of the existing system.

3. Interestingly these and other religious orders have retargeted their educational products, responding in economically sensible ways to the competition by state schools and to the changing character of their customer base.

4. See for example Coleman *et al.*, Kilgore (1982); Evans and Schwab (1995); Neal (1997); Altonji *et al.* (2000).

5. Individual teachers are also paid an additional amount based on cumulated past inflation (*indennità integrativa speciale*). These figures are drawn from the national contract for public school professors.

6. Figures drawn from the national contract between workers' unions and the association of religious schools (AGIDAE). There is also a provision for additional 'merit' pay (*Superminimi*) of 99 000 (50 €) 675 000 lire (355 €), determined on an individual basis.

7. Figures drawn from the national contract between workers' unions and the associations of private secular schools (ANINSEI and ASSOSCUOLA).

8. We can approximately assess the potential impact of this selection bias by looking at average family incomes. Using the 1998 Bank of Italy survey on household incomes, we find that the median family, net income was 70 385 200 (37099 €) lire in the city of Milan (14 observations from families with at least one student member who had graduated from secondary school) and 57 158 490 (30083 €) lire in the as a whole country (784 observations from similar families). In our student sample the median family's net income was 54 227 500 (28540 €) lire in the province of Milan (36 416 observations) and 52 751 000 lire (27763 €) for the as a whole population (61 343 observations). Thus we undersampled the richest families whose offspring attended college.

9. Self-reported wealth is the value of real estate declared for fiscal purposes. It excludes the value of the family residence, if owned (100 million lire are deducted from the value of other real estate if the residence is rented), and all financial wealth. Thus it is a downward-biased measure of the family's resources, and even more so for richer families since financial assets tend increase more than proportionately with total wealth (see Cannari-D'Alessio in Rossi, 1994).

10. We excluded from the computation students that had not yet passed an exam (3959 students, or two thirds of those who began in 1999).

11. The two proxies are both imperfect, and are obviously related. In a different data set (a representative sample of 6377 Italian students surveyed in 1993 at the completion of secondary school – see Gasperoni, 1996), the partial correlations of marks (measured in 60ths) and parents' education are:

$$\text{Mark} = 40.6 + 0.56 \times \text{father's education} + 0.95 \times \text{mother's education};$$

$$\quad\quad\quad (120.3)\quad (4.9)\quad\quad\quad\quad\quad\quad\quad\quad\quad (8.2)$$

$$R^2 = 0.04; \text{RMSE} = 7.01$$

12. In the alternative sample of 6377 Italian students surveyed in 1993 at the completion of secondary school, the average final mark (measured in 60ths) varied according to the students' evaluation at the end of lower secondary school, as follows: 40.9 for 'adequate', 42.8 for 'good', 45.8 for 'distinctive' and 50.3 for 'optimum'.

13. Checchi (2000, table 2), estimates the return of different university subjects using the 1995 Bank of Italy survey on household incomes. Controlling for sector and job position, he reports that the highest return is associated with a degree in law (the estimated coefficient is 0.54), followed by a degree in medicine (0.48), economics (0.37) and engineering (0.30).

14. In this case, partitioning schools according to type and sector (see below) yields at most marginally significant results, probably because the type of secondary is excessively aggregated:

15. The administrative file identifies only private/non-private secondary schools. Using name and address of secondary schools generically coded as private, we were able to classify 643 out of 678 private institutions: thus only 113 students were left unclassified with respect to the type of secondary school attended. We thank Chiara Colleoni for research assistance.

16. See for example Owen and Weil (1997) and DeFraja (2004).

17. To avoid excessive clutter, schools with fewer than 10 students in the university enrolment sample have been omitted. Family income is converted

    into per capita income taking into account the sufficient marginal cost of each child. We use a commonly used equivalance scale consisting of the square root of the number of family members.

18. We set to zero the average mark of students who had not yet taken an exam. Hence the independent variable is distinctly not normal, with a discrete probability mass of zero and a continuous distribution of 18–31.

19. This predictive ability is even probably greater when we consider the fact that the sample was self-selected, given the high drop-out rates in the initial years of attendance. Checchi (2000) estimated a probit model of drop-out during the academic career and found that the final secondary school mark was negatively related to the probability of drop-out.

20. We omitted the *Scienze motorie* faculty (which trains physical education teachers and began operating in 1998), because only 307 were enrolled in it.

21. The US empirical work briefly reviewed above, for example, measured the effect of Catholic schools (which cater to both Catholics and non-Catholics in the US) according to the assumption that the family's religious orientation was relevant to the choice of a Catholic school, but did not otherwise affect labour market outcomes. Altonji *et al.* (2000) exploited a large set of additional information to model the choice of a private Catholic school. This strategy would not be practical for Italy, where the population is almost completely Catholic.

22. When included on the right-hand side of regression, such as those reported in Tables 4.9–4.11, financial wealth is significantly correlated with university performance outcomes. Of course in an OLS regression the coefficient of wealth may pick up the indirect role of that variable in determining secondary school choice and, through that channel, university performance. It may also be the case that correlation between financial wealth and the family's earned income (human wealth) is generated by an unobservable ability of the parents: if talent has some persistence across generations, children's talent and financial wealth are correlated. 'Wealth', as measured in our data set (see note 9) has a low correlation with income as many families report zero. In a just-identified structural system, of course, the identifying assumption cannot be tested.

23. For example a maximum likelihood probit regression for attending a private school reads as follows (SE in parenthesis):

$$\text{prob(private school} = 1) = -1.09 + 0.018 \times \log(\text{wealth}) - 0.095 \times \text{talent};$$
$$ (0.009) \quad (0.001) (0.006)$$
$$\text{pseudo } R^2 = 0.001; n = 61\ 343$$

24. Students from private schools and from lower-income families were over-represented in our sample. It is unlikely, however, that this substantially affected our results: since family income (or wealth) and private school attendance are positively correlated, the two selection-induced biases have opposite signs.

25. See De Fraja (2002) for models of school competition where admission criteria play a role along with tuition fees. From the social point of view, as remarked earlier and discussed formally by Bénabou (1996) and others, segregation across social census lines may have a detrimental effect on an education system's efficiency. Gradstein and Justman (2001) discuss the

implications of education funding schemes in the presence of cultural differences, as may result from mass immigration.
26. Even though we are not sure that students with the same peer effect actually attended the same classes, we are at least sure that they attended the same school during the same years. We stress that our peer effect measure is very imperfect since we could not control for the self-sorting of students. Only with the random allocation of students to schools could a more precise measure of the peer effect be obtained. See Hoxby (2000) for a discussion of this issue.
27. Family wealth produced similar results. Including both variables reduced their individual significance, due to collinearity. The results were very similar when the schools attended by only a few students in the sample were omitted, and robust to a variety of slightly different specifications.
28. When we combined the average peer effect with its dispersion (measured by standard deviation) the results were similar: the inverse of the coefficient of variation was positively significant with regard to income but not to talent.
29. Fernandez and Gali (1999) show that sorting can occur either through the market mechanism (families compete for the best schools allowing schools to choose potential customers using school fees) or through meritocratic screening (only the best students are admitted). In a world of imperfect financial markets, the latter alternative is Pareto superior to the former.
30. For New Zealand's experience of school competition see in Fiske and Ladd (2000).

References

Altonji, J., Elder, T. and Taber, C. (2000) 'Selection on observed and unobserved variables: assessing the effectiveness of Catholic schools', NBER Working Paper no. 7831 (Cambridge, Mass.: NBER).

Bénabou, R. (1996) 'Heterogeneity, stratification, and growth: Macroeconomic implications of community structure and public finance', *American Economic Review*, vol. 89, pp. 584–609.

Boero, G., McKnight, A., Naylor, R. and Smith, J. (2004) 'Graduates and Graduate Labour Markets in the UK and Italy', in the present volume.

Bryk, Anthony S., Lee, Valerie E. and Holland, Peter B. (1993) *Catholic Schools and the Common Good* (Cambridge, Mass.: Harvard University Press).

Checchi, D. (1999) *Istruzione e mercato – Per una analisi economica della formazione scolastica* (Bologna: Il Mulino).

Checchi, D. (2000) 'University education in Italy', *International Journal of Manpower*, vol. 21, nos. 3–4, pp. 160–205.

Coleman, J. S., Hoffer, T. and Kilgore, S. (1982) *High School Achievement: Public, Catholic, and Private Schools Compared* (New York: Basic Books).

De Fraja, G. (2004) 'Private and Public Schools' in the present volume.

Evans, William N., and Schwab, Robert M. (1995) 'Finishing high school and starting college: Do catholic schools make a difference?', *Quarterly Journal of Economics*, vol. 110, no. 4, pp. 941–74.

Fernandez, R. and Gali, J. (1999) 'To each according to ...? Markets, tournaments and the matching problem with borrowing constraints', *Review of Economic Studies*, vol. 66, pp. 799–824.

Fiske, E. and Ladd, H. (2000) *When Schools Compete – A Cautionary Tale* (Washington, DC: Brookings Institution).

Gambetta, Diego (1987) *Were They Pushed or Did They Jump? Individual Decision Mechanisms in Education* (Cambridge: Cambridge University Press).

Gasperoni, G. (1996) *Diplomati e istruiti* (Bologna: Il Mulino).

Gradstein, M., and Justman, M. (2001) 'Public Education and the Melting Pot,' CEPR Discussion Paper no. 2924 (London: CEPR).

Hoxby, C. (2000) 'Peer effects in the classroom: learning from gender and race variation', NBER Working Paper no. 7867 (Cambridge, Mass.: NBER).

Lazear, E. (1999) 'Educational production', NBER Working Paper no. 7349 (Cambridge, Mass: NBER).

Neal, Derek (1997) 'The effects of Catholic secondary schooling on educational achievement', *Journal of Labor Economics*, vol. 15 no. 1, pp. 98–123

Owen, A. and Weil, D. (1997) 'Intergenerational earnings, inequality and growth', *Journal of Monetary Economics*, vol. 41, no. 1, 71–104.

Rossi, N. (ed.) (1994) *La transizione equa* (Bologna: Il Mulino).

Rubinstein, S., and Tsiddon, D. (1998) 'Coping with technological progress: The role of ability in making inequality so persistent', Tel Aviv University working paper 27–98 (December).

5
The Impact of Research Assessment and Teaching-Quality Exercises on the UK University System

Peter J. Sloane

Introduction

Historically, decisions relating to resource allocation in British universities were largely left to the universities themselves,[1] but in the 1980s the Conservative government attempted to introduce accountability and performance measurement into the public sector and this also applied to the universities. This involved not only selectivity in the distribution of resources but also rationalisation and, where appropriate, the closure of small departments, firmer financial control and attempts to improve the standard of teaching (Cave and Weale, 1992). Two reasons for this intervention were suggested in a 1991 white paper, *Higher Education: A New Framework*, namely the considerable growth in student numbers and the development of competition among institutions as a result of changes to the funding mechanism.

Increased attention was paid to the two major activities of universities – teaching and research. Fundamental questions were whether funding and incentives should be based on the supposition that all universities were essentially equal, with profiles reflecting similar mixes of research and teaching, or whether universities should specialise in diverse ways. One possible model was the so-called R-T-X model proposed by the Advisory Board for the Research Councils in a 1987 HMSO report, *A Strategy for the Science Base*. This three-way classification model would have divided universities into those with research strengths in most or all departments ('R'), those funded only to undertake teaching ('T') and those with recognised research strengths in only a few departments ('X'). This raised questions about the fundamental nature of universities and the relationship between teaching and research.[2]

What is the objective function of universities?

In attempting to apply the theory of the firm to universities, Hare and Wyatt (1992) suggest that whilst all but one British university is the public sector, universities possess a degree of independence that is not shared by other public bodies because of the protection provided by their royal charters.

There appears to be general agreement that since there is no residual claimant for any profit stream that might arise, universities should be regarded as not-for-profit organisations, one variant of which is the labour-managed firm. In this model the maximisation of income per worker replaces the profit maximisation assumption. In universities, however, salaries are fixed nationally and since profit sharing is absent the degree to which academics can maximise economic rents is limited. There remains, however, a principal–agent problem insofar as asymmetric information prevents the principal (either the government or the various funding councils) from ensuring that the agent (the academic staff) acts in its interests. There is a further principal–agent problem in relation to academic staff (as the principal) and students (as the agent). The product in higher education is not only informational in character but also its value as information is not precisely known until it has been acquired. Nerlove (1972) points out that one of the most important non-market responses to such uncertainty is licensing. In the higher education sphere this takes the form of accreditation, which Nerlove sees as a type of basic quality control that is designed to compensate for the lack of a market mechanism for allocating the risk and uncertainty that arises from the purchase of an informational commodity. This is buttressed by restrictions on the entry of new institutions of higher education. James and Neuberger (1981) argue that all universities are effectively captured by their academic staff and that the latter run the universities in their own interests. Shirking behaviour has traditionally been regarded as a significant issue, but James and Neuberger place more emphasis on allocation inefficiency. The assumption is that academics have a preference ordering that tends to favour research over teaching, and that there is a preference for graduate or advanced undergraduate courses over introductory courses. There is also a strong preference for teaching high-quality rather than weaker students. Implicit in this analysis is the likelihood that costs will exceed the minimum levels achievable under profit maximisation. Constraints on the freedom to pursue these goals include the nature of the production function for teaching and research, the institutional budget constraint and the demand function for student places.

Much has been made in the literature of the fact that teaching and research are joint products. More specifically, basic research and postgraduate training are regarded as perfect complements whilst applied research is of a somewhat different character as it can be accomplished in the absence of students (see Nerlove, 1972). To some extent undergraduate teaching and research are joint products as they are frequently conducted in the same institutions by the same individuals. The reason for complementarity or economies of scope is the joint use of common facilities such as buildings, libraries and computers, so that fewer scarce resources are needed to provide services jointly than to provide them separately.

Because of these shared inputs the production possibility curve for a university will be as shown in Figure 5.1. If all university resources are devoted to teaching, value added is given by OX, which measures the difference between the social productivity of students before entering

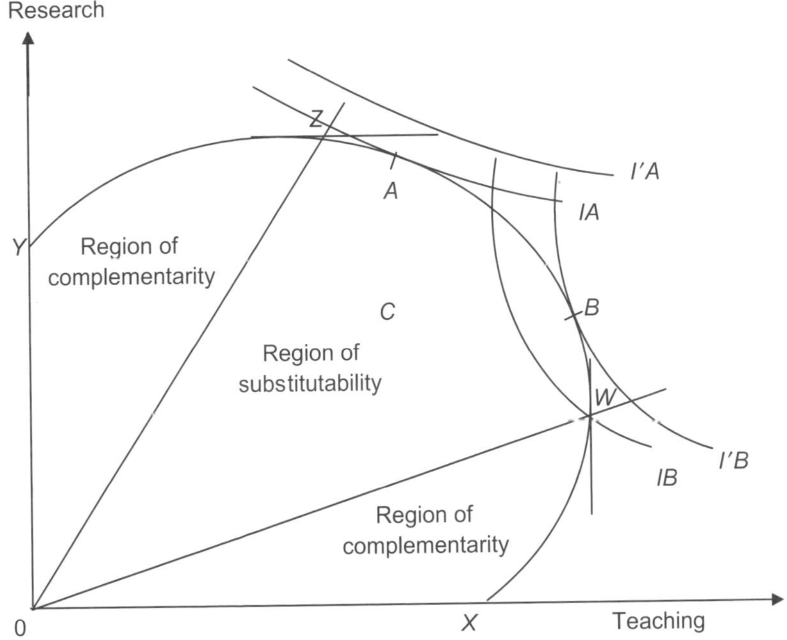

Figure 5.1 Production possibility curve and resource allocation

university and their productivity after leaving it. If in contrast all resources are devoted to research, with the results being provided free of charge to the community, the value of output is O*Y*. The curve *YZWX* shows the maximum production possibilities for the university.

The ranges *YZ* and *XW* are positively sloped and no efficiently run organisation would operate in these segments as it would be possible, by reallocation, to increase one type of output without any loss of the other. Depending on taste, universities would end up in the range *ZW*, in which teaching and research are substitutes. University A, which has a relative preference for research, would operate at *A* and university B, which has a relative preference for teaching, would end up at *B*.

The implication of economies of scope is that it would be ineffic-ient to have teaching-only universities or research-only universities. Further-more efficiency only requires one to operate on the produc-tion possibility frontier in the region of substitutability. This suggests that teaching and research assessment should be undertaken jointly. Further efficiency requires that universities should not operate within the production possibility curve at outputs such as *C*. This suggests that teaching and research assessment should attempt to ascertain whether resources are being used efficiently.

Recently there have been some attempts to apply data envelopment analysis (DEA) to evaluate the technical efficiency of individual univer-sity departments. This allows one to assign in a non-arbitrary fashion input and output weights, which perform the same function as market prices. However this cannot address the question of allocative efficiency. In one such study of UK departments of economics for the period 1984–88 (see Cave and Weale, 1991), considerable variation in technical efficiency was found. The departments at Birkbeck College and York University were found to be technically efficient with scores of 1, while the scores of the remaining 34 ranged from 0.24 (Strathclyde) to 0.88 (Aberdeen).

A number of studies have examined whether economies of scale exist in universities, but relatively few have attempted to estimate economies of scope. Two exceptions were those conducted in the United States by Cohn *et al.* (1989) and de Groot *et al.* (1991). Both sets of authors recognised that there were problems with defining outputs. Cohn *et al.* estimated multiple output cost functions for 1887 institutes of higher education in 1981–82. They included three 'outputs' (under-graduate student enrolment, graduate enrolment and size of research grants). They found that, except for output levels below 150 per cent of output means in (public sector institutions, economies of scope occurred at all output levels in both public and private sector institutions. Thus when all outputs were at 300 per cent of their respective means, the costs of production for single output institutions were 8.4 per cent higher than those in multiple-output public sector institutions and 33.2 per cent higher than in private sector ones. De Groot *et al.* extended the above analysis by focusing on 147 doctorate-granting universities in 1982–83 using translog variable cost functions. They too used student enrolment as an output measure, but also tested for degrees awarded and peer ratings of graduate programmes, together with a direct measure of research output: number of publications. They found evidence of economies of scope between undergraduate and graduate instruction at the sample mean, which they explained by the cost savings obtained by employing graduate students as teaching assistants at relatively low salaries. However they were unable to detect any economies of scope between graduate teaching and research. Clearly we require more studies of this phenomenon before we can be certain of its significance.

The UK research assessment exercise

The objective of the research assessments in conducted in the UK is clearly indicated by the fact that they were initially referred to as research selectivity exercises. That is, there was concern that research resources were being spread too thinly and a greater return might be obtained by concentrating resources among more research-active departments in each discipline across universities.

A process of expansion and refinement took place during the five exercises conducted so far (in 1986, 1989, 1992, 1996 and 2001). In 1986 and 1989 only universities were included in the exercise, but in 1992 polytechnics, Scottish central institutions and colleges of higher education were invited to participate. Some of these were later designated as universities. Because non-university institutions were less active in research it was recognised that requiring them to consider all staff would mean that in most cases they would receive no funding. Hence from 1992 they could choose whom to consider as research-active while excluded staff could be disregarded. However the reduction in volume would come at a cost, since only those considered as research active would be allocated research funding in line with their average rating. This meant that an element of gaming was introduced into the exercise, since the monetary value attached to any rating was not revealed until after documentation had been presented. Talib

(1999) suggests that the two key decisions were the quantity versus quality trade-off decision and the decision as to which unit of assessment to submit. For example just as many economists were submitted to the Management and Business Studies Panel as to the Economics and Econometrics Panel. In part this may have reflected the location of some economists in business schools, but it may also have reflected a belief that the Management and Business Studies Panel would be more lenient or less demanding in terms of the requirement to publish in leading international journals.

To some extent the 1986 exercise should be regarded as a trial run. Universities were requested to complete a four-part questionnaire covering various aspects of income and expenditure, planning, priorities and output. This information was used by the subcommittees of the University Grants Committee (UGC) to establish ratings on a four-point scale after consultation with the research councils. Possible ratings were below average, average, above average and starred, and were therefore relative rather than absolute scores. These ratings were then used for selective allocation of part of the research resources (see Adams *et al.*, 2000). The exercise was criticised on a number of grounds. According to Johnes (1988) the criteria for assessment were unclear, the process did not allow for a proper assessment of interdisciplinary research, there was a bias in favour of large departments, different assessment standards were applied to different disciplines, it was retrospective (taking no account of future potential) and there was no appeals mechanism. To varying degrees these criticisms also applied to later exercises.

In the 1989 research assessment exercise information was requested on the total number of studies published over the period 1984–88 in each unit of assessment, bibliographic details of up to two nominated published works for each member of staff over this period, together with up to two other items of output, the number and value of research grants and contracts, and the number of research studentships. A five-point rating scale was introduced, ranging from research quality that equated to attainable levels of national excellence in none, or virtually none, of the subareas of activity (1) to research quality that equated to attainable levels of international excellence in some subareas of activity, and attainable levels of national excellence in virtually all others (5). These ratings largely survived in later exercises, though with some redefinitions and the addition of a 5* category. A rating of 1 meant zero funding in 1989, as did a rating of 2 in 1996, and it was suggested that a rating of 3 should be treated likewise in 2001, or at least in Scotland.

The 1992 exercise covered the period from 1 January 1989 to 30 June 1992. The main difference with the 1992 exercise was increased participation, with only one former polytechnic declining to participate. There were no fewer than 2700 submissions, requiring the work of 45 000 research staff to be assessed. In some cases panels read widely and in other cases selectively from the submitted research output. To allow for the non-submission of staff, each quality rating was given a letter qualifier to indicate the percentage of total eligible staff submitted. The enlarged participation rate also had an impact on funding allocations per unit of assessment. This was further affected by the fact that the University Funding Committee had been replaced by separate funding bodies for England, Scotland, Wales and Northern Ireland, and these had chosen to allocate funds for given ratings in distinctive ways (see McNay, 1997).

The 1996 exercise broadly followed the same approach as in 1992, but research staff were invited to detail up to four published works, as opposed to two in 1992. However the requirement to list the total number of publications for each unit of assessment was dropped in order to emphasise that the exercise was concerned with the quality of output rather than the quantity. The assessment panels produced statements of their individual criteria for assessment and some details of their working methods, which were published in time to inform decisions. On this occasion there were 2898 submissions from 92 participating institutions with 55 893 active researchers. This represented an increase of 6 per cent in the number of submissions and 11 per cent in the number of researchers submitted.

In 1996 the rating was amended by the addition of a 5* category, denoting research quality that equated to attainable levels of international excellence in a majority of subareas of activity and attainable levels of national excellence in all others. Moreover rating of the 3 was split into 3(a) and 3(b), so there were now seven points on the scale. The assessment period for publications and research income ran from 1 January 1992 to 31 March 1996 (4.25 years) and therefore overlapped the 1992 exercise.

The fifth exercise covered the period 1 January 1996 to 31 December 2000, and again there were modifications to the rating scale and the inclusion of a new category, A*, for staff who had left one UK institution for another during the period 1 April 2000 to 31 March 2001. This was designed to reduce the transfer market in academic staff that research assessment encouraged. Such staff could specify two works published (as opposed to four for A category staff) while at the institution they had left and at the one they had joined, but only in the latter case would they add to the quantity for research income allocation purposes. Another change was the introduction of international advisory panels for each unit of assessment.

An important element of the exercises was peer review by a group of nominated experts who agreed on the ranking of units of assessment in each discipline based on their own subjective opinions. This had the advantage of allowing all aspects of research performance to be taken into account, but was subject to potentially biased judgements based on the panel members' particular disciplinary expertise and personal contacts (Johnes, 1992). Whilst early in the process the possibility of using citation counts was considered, this was never applied. There were a number of difficulties with this approach, including the fact that reference was made only to the first-named author, not all journals were included in citation counts and the citations did not necessarily measure the quality of the output (see Johnes, 1988). As far as journals were concerned, it was recognised that some were more prestigious than others. The assessment panels, however, avoided an explicit ranking of journals, leaving such judgements to the individual panel members. As far as economics was concerned, an analysis covering the period 1984–1988 by Johnes (1990) revealed that the 10 journals in which UK economists published most often – accounting for 18 per cent of the total – included only four core journals (*Economic Journal, Oxford Economic Papers, Oxford Bulletin of Economics and Statistics* and *European Economic Review*).

There have been a number of attempts to explain the differences between the ratings obtained in the research assessment exercises. Johnes and Taylor (1992) and Johnes *et al.* (1993) attempted to explain the variation in rankings in the 1989 exercise using a cumulative logit model and a proportional hazards model for each cost centre. A high proportion of the variation in research ratings across universities could be explained by a handful of variables. The most significant finding was that the size of the unit of assessment (UoA) was strongly (positively) correlated with the research rating in 12 of the 18 UoAs analysed. This might have reflected the importance of critical mass, economies of scale, visibility or the ability to attract research funding. Thus the potential existence of two-way causation did not necessarily mean that panels were biased in favour of large departments. A further finding was that the probability of a UoA obtaining a high research rating was substantially higher if it was located in a university with a high overall rating. This might have represented increased competitiveness in research-intensive institutions or a halo effect. The influence of research expenditure per member of staff was found to be patchy. There was, however, a certain type of institution effect, with former colleges of advanced technology (such as Aston, Bradford, Loughborough and Surrey) tending to have lower research ratings. The same was true of institutions in Scotland, Wales and Northern Ireland.

Taylor (1995) conducted a similar analysis of the 1992 exercise. The general form of the regression model applied to each unit of assessment was:

$$RR_j = b_0 + \sum_i b_i X_{ij} + u_j \tag{5.1}$$

where RR_j was the research rating awarded to institution j (within a unit of assessment). A set of 19 explanatory variables (x_0) was constructed from the research assessment database in order to identify which research inputs and outputs were significantly related to research-active staff to and standardise for variations in the size of UoAs. As in the earlier studies, five or six explanatory variables explained 75 per cent of the variation in research ratings. For economics and econometrics the following result was obtained using an OLS regression, which produced similar results to ordered probit – a more appropriate estimation method given the nature of the dependent variable:

$$RR = 0.74 + \underset{(5.11)}{0.111} \text{ Staff} - \underset{(-3.60)}{1.08} \text{ Staff Squared} + \underset{(5.10)}{0.31} \text{RJA}$$
$$+ \underset{(2.02)}{0.013} \text{RCGrants (£1000)}$$
$$R^2 = 0.66$$

Thus three variables – number of staff, number of refereed journal articles (RJA) and amount of research council grants (RCGrants) – explained two-thirds of the variation in research ratings in economics. Even though the exercise was supposed to be about quality, these were all quantitative measures.

In a subsequent analysis of economics and econometrics departments, Taylor and Izadi (1998) founded that the research rating was maximised when the number of research-active staff was 45–50, but very few British economics departments were of that size. They also found that the average grade score had risen over time, and relative to other UoAs. Thus in the 1989 exercise the mean rating for economics departments was 2.7 compared with 3.1 for all UoAs. In 1992 the mean rating for economics departments was 3.76 compared with 3.44 for all subjects and in 1996 there was a further rise to 4.27. Whether this represented a general improvement in performance or a tendency for the economics panel to become more lenient is a moot point. It should, however, be noted that there was some truncation of the sample, with 50 submissions in 1996 compared with 60 in 1992, and weaker UOAs had migrated elsewhere.

Nonetheless there was a general belief that research performance had improved as a consequence of the assessment exercises. Adams *et al.* (2000) found that the effectiveness and productivity of the UK research base had significantly increased, especially in larger universities with medical schools. Bibliometric impact measures suggested that the timing of change was closely associated with the exercise cycles. Williams (1991) noted that among the effects of the exercises were the early retirement of less productive senior staff and the recruitment of research professors, the closure or merger of low-rated departments, better planning and monitoring of research, and the creation of funds to pump-prime research initiatives.

A more recent study of the publications listed on a sample of UK academic economists' *vitae* (Moore *et al.*, 2001) confirmed that the 1992 exercise had a positive impact on performance for those in stronger departments and led to an improvement in output in lesser journals for those in weaker departments. The 1996 exercise strongly reinforced these patterns. The increased productivity resulting from these two assessment exercises had more to do with an improvement in the performance of existing staff than with the entry of new, higher-quality staff into the system.

Teaching-quality assessment

Responsibility for assuring the quality of teaching, learning and assessment and the maintenance of academic standards rested ultimately with the universities themselves. However an element of external scrutiny was established to provide some measure of accountability for the public funding of higher education. External evaluation of the provision of degree education at the subject level became the statutory responsibility of the Funding Councils in 1992. Further external audits were carried out by the Higher Education Quality Council (HEQC) until 1997 and by a newly established Quality Assurance Agency for Higher Education (QAA) from August 1997. The HEQC was 'owned' by the universities while the QAA was set up as a replacement for the HEQC in response to the Dearing Report.

External audits covered the individual institutions as a whole and involved the submission of documents prepared by the institution in respect of its quality assurance procedures, scrutiny of these documents by a team of academics trained by the agency, a visit by an audit team to the university to hold meetings with groups of staff and students, and the production of an academic quality audit report, which was made available to the public. Traditionally universities had maintained their standards through a system of external examiners, consisting of senior academics from other universities. The HEQC was more concerned with strengthening the mechanisms by which standards were determined than with defining academic standards *per se*.

As for teaching-quality assessment of individual subjects, each of the three funding councils – the Higher Education Funding Council for England (HEFCE), the Scottish Higher Education Funding Council (SHEFC) and the Higher Education Funding Council for Wales (HEFCW) – developed their own particular methods of assessment. However there were certain common elements, including scrutiny at the subject level, the use of subject assessors who were drawn from academia and industry and were specialists in their fields, the scrutiny of an institution's submission by a visiting team of assessors (undertaking three- to five-day visits to meet with staff and students and observe teaching), and the publication of a report that contained an overall judgement of the quality of teaching in the subject area.

In 1992–93 teaching-quality assessment began in Scotland. This involved a three-point scale in which teaching was judged to be excellent, satisfactory or unsatisfactory. Between 1993–94 and 1997–98 an additional category of highly satisfactory was added. In England and Wales only the three-point scale was used. Subsequently the HEFCE and HEFCW adopted a graded quality-profile system supported by a 24-point grading system divided into six aspects of assessment, each with a four-point scale. This scheme was also applied in Scotland from 1997–98 onwards. Any institution judged to be unsatisfactory was in danger of losing its funding for teaching in that area if the problems identified were not rectified within a specified time. In general the rewards for good performance were limited to reputation, with the ratings being used as a partial basis for the construction of university league tables by various national newspapers. In Scotland, however, an award of excellent led to a 5 per cent increase in funded students in the relevant areas. Similar arrangements were introduced in Wales.

There was a considerable overlap in the type of information requested by academic quality auditors and teaching-quality assessors, and concern was expressed by the Committee of Vice Chancellors and Principals about the overlap between the two systems. One of the roles of the newly formed QAA was to develop a single, UK-wide system of quality assurance, embracing both audit and assessment. The QAA proposed that teaching-quality assessment and the academic quality audit should be replaced by an integrated process of subject review and institutional review. In support of this the QAA published a plethora of documents on programme specifications, subject benchmark statements, codes of practice and a handbook for academic reviews.

The QAA established 42 benchmarking panels (comprising subject specialists drawn from the academic community) for each subject group. These panels developed benchmark statements to indicate the standards (expressed in terms of knowledge, understanding and skills) that all honours graduates in the subject would be expected to attain. It was argued that such benchmarking would inform the public about the nature of higher education awards, inform prospective students, employers and others about the range of provisions, provide institutions with a framework for developing and specifying the intended learning outcomes of programmes, and help QAA reviewers to make judgements about the appropriateness of standards. One issue was whether the standard should be set at the level of the typical (modal) student, the threshold for obtaining an honours degree (third class) or the two-two/two-one borderline needed for progression to professional status. The danger with this approach was that it could tend to stifle diversity and impose a national curriculum. Some benchmarking panels attempted to avoid this. For example the economics panel stated that the content of curricula could be adapted to meet the nature and objectives of the degree programme and that this was a matter for each institution to decide. Meanwhile there was increasing criticism by universities, and notably the Russell Group of research-active universities, about the excessive bureaucracy of the new system, although the QAA promised a light touch in the case of mature institutions.

The system was introduced in Scotland in 2000–1 and was due to be introduced in the rest of the UK the following year. Following lobbying the secretary of state for education and employment announced in March 2001 that the burden of the system would be greatly reduced. However the Russell Group continued to oppose its introduction, suggesting that inspection of even 10 per cent of teaching in subject level reviews was excessive, and insisting that there should be immediate cessation of subject reviews in Scotland. It was noted that research by PA Consulting for the HEFCE had found that universities spent about £250 million per annum (4 per cent of their public income) on meeting accountability requirements.

The major criticism that could be made of teaching-quality assessment, as practised in the UK, was that it focused unduly on process rather than value added. Performance indicators were used only to a limited extent. Value added, according to Arestis and Young (1994), was not used as a measure of quality because it would not be entirely consistent with fitness for purpose. Self-assessment was deemed important and assessors looked for evidence of systematic, self-critical approaches by departments. Thus quality was defined as fitness for purpose, which permitted institutions to define their own goals and presented the danger of institutions setting unambitious targets. As noted in a Royal Economic Society newsletter, (Harrison and Lockwood 2001) a system that ranked departments according to their ability to achieve their own specified objectives but then defended publication of such scores on the ground that this would enable consumers to make their own comparisons was a nonsense. According to Harrison and Lockwood, one study of 665 QAA reports from the 1998–2000 inspection rounds found that there was a tendency for grade inflation, which in part was associated with the ability of institutions to define their aims and objectives in such a way as to maximise their grades. Very few degree programmes were in fact found to be unsatisfactory. Cave (1994), for example, notes that by autumn 1994 only a handful of courses in England had been declared unsatisfactory, and most of these had gone to appeal. In Scotland only two unsatisfactory departments were identified in over 100 inspections of 11 disciplines. There were also wide variations across disciplines in the percentage of departments found to be excellent, ranging from 28 per cent in law to 19 per cent in history and 12 per cent in mechanical engineering. Over time excellent ratings tended to rise across the system. Harrison and Lockwood (2001) argue that the QAA had an incentive to overregulate – with excessive performance criteria, benchmarking and so on – in order to extract the rents to be had from the funding councils, thereby imposing a large deadweight loss on society through the increased cost of higher education.

What has been the impact of external assessment?

As discussed earlier, it has been suggested that universities have promoted and valued research at the expense of the quality of teaching. Indeed the Dearing Report commented that 'one current barrier is that staff perceive national and institutional policies as actively encouraging and recognising excellence in research, and not in teaching' (National Committee into Higher Education, p. 115). Little has been done to test this assertion, but McNabb *et al.* (2002) have cast some light on it. Controlling for a number of variables, they have attempted to ascertain the extent to which teaching and research quality affect degree performance. They included one direct measure of teaching quality, namely the percentage of departments in each institution graded as excellent in teaching-quality assessments, and three indirect measures: total university expenditure per student, library expenditure per student and the staff–student ratio. Research intensity was measured by the percentage of a university's total income that came from research grants and contracts.

Educational attainment was measured by class of degree according to a five-point point scale that ranged from O (fails and drop-outs) to 5 ± (first-class honours). Given the ordered nature of the degree-class variable, estimation was by ordered probit. It was assumed that there was comparability in standards across the system (limited to pre- 1992 universities), (enforced by the system of external examiners. Table 5.1 shows the results for the institutional variables, which are the primary interest here, and separately by gender, given that the probability of obtaining a good degree varied by gender. It was found that higher research income and teaching quality had a strong positive impact on female student achievement. This was consistent with the joint-product nature of research and teaching, and also raised some doubt about the claim that the research assessment exercises had caused staff to neglect their teaching duties in favour of pursuing their research interests, as implied in the Dearing Report. A strong research record also enhanced male degree attainment, though in this case teaching quality did not appear to have any significant effect.[3]

Related issues are whether rewards to academics are in fact biased in favour of research or whether good researchers are also good teachers. The latter has been tested by Euwals and Ward (2000), who ran a probit regression of teaching skill against individual, job and research productivity characteristics for a sample of academics in five Scottish universities. They found no significant relationship between research

Table 5.1 The impact of institutional variables on degree performance in England and Wales, 1993

Variable	Ordered probit analysis			
	Female students		Male students	
	Coefficient	t-ratio	Coefficient	t-ratio
Percentage of income from research contracts/grants	0.017	8.61	0.013	7.83
Percentage of departments graded excellent in teaching-quality assessments	0.007	2.77	0.0005	1.39
Number of students	0.000001	0.35	−0.000001	−0.61
Staff–student ratio	3.247	3.96	1.705	2.43
Expenditure per student	−0.033	−9.22	−0.020	−7.85
Library spending per student	0.027	0.60	0.266	6.96
No. in sample	33,666		40,849	
Log-likelihood	−43065.55			−59221.80

Note: Other controls include entry qualifications, school type, age, marital status, whether born in the UK, subject of degree and parental occupation.
Source: Adapted from McNabb *et al.* (2000).

productivity variables and the probability of being a skilled teacher (defined in terms of student evaluation). However they did find a positive correlation between number of books published, number of refereed papers published, number of grants awarded and high teaching ability at the non-professional level. A simulation exercise revealed a career-progression reward for good teaching skills that equalled the reward for 12–15 refereed papers.

Overall, therefore, there is no evidence to support the conjecture that academics have ignored their teaching duties in favour of research activities.

Conclusions

That research and teaching-quality assessment have had an impact on UK universities is not in doubt. However, whether this intervention has been generally beneficial is much more questionable. The institutions themselves seem much readier to accept research assessment than teaching-quality assessment. Outsiders have argued that this may reflect the fact that academics have tended to neglect teaching in favour of research. However there is no evidence of this. Indeed teaching and research quality tend to be positively related. The main complaint against external assessment is that it is excessively costly and bureaucratic.

It is also questionable whether it is appropriate to separate teaching from research assessment. To the extent that economies of scope are present it may be equally efficient to combine teaching and research in different proportions, provided both are undertaken together. Further more the question of efficient use of resources has been almost completely neglected in the assessment exercises. Thus in research assessment, institutions can choose which staff to include as research-active and this will not count against them other than in terms of the volume of financial rewards obtained. In teaching assessment the institutions themselves can decide the goals against which they are to be assessed. The question of what degree of selectivity is optimal has been almost wholly neglected. If economies of scope apply, removing research funding from certain institutions may not be appropriate. Moreover, whether certain institutions should be closed or merged when there are economies of scale has not been addressed.

The incentive structures differ between teaching and research. Though it is true that institutions obtain more income from teaching than from research, research assessment can change financial allocations at the margin much more than is the case for teaching assessment. Further more research assessment has encouraged a transfer market for academics, thereby inflating wage costs. Finally, the objectives of external regulation have not always been clearly thought through. In the case of teaching-quality assessment, allowing institutions to define their own objectives means that no objective comparisons can be made across institutions, thereby frustrating the objective of informed consumer choice. All of this has led to calls for reform, but it is far from clear what would be the most appropriate regulatory regime for the UK university system.

Notes

1. Polytechnics, which increasingly offered degree-level courses, had their degrees validated by the Council for National Academic Awards and this required approval by visiting teams of academics drawn largely from universities. The universities themselves relied on self-regulation, with comparability being assured by external examiners chosen by the universities. Universities were empowered to award their own degrees by royal charter. In 1992 polytechnics were given university status and the power to award their own degrees
2. For an analysis of the tensions that arise from and methods of allocating research funds among institutions in a number of European countries see Geuna (2001)
3. An earlier version of this chapter included an ordered probit that excluded failures and dropouts, and in neither the male nor the female equations was the TQA variable significant (see McNabb *et al.*, 2001). Therefore teaching-quality assessment seems to improve performance solely in terms of reducing the number of students who either drop out or fail.

References

Adams, J. (2000) 'The Role of Selectivity and the Characteristics of Excellence', report to the Higher Education Funding Council for England, Higher Education Policy Unit, University of Leeds, October.

Arestis, P. and Young, A. (1994) 'The Economics of Assessment and the Assessment of Economics: The 1992–93 SHEFC Exercise', *Royal Economic Society Newsletter*, no. 87 (October), pp. 2–4.

Cave, M. (1994) 'Why Students Need (Consumer) Protection', *Royal Economic Society Newsletter*, no. 87 (October), pp. 18–20.

Cave, M. and Weale, M. (1992) 'The Assessment: Higher Education, the State of Play', *Oxford Review of Economic Policy*, vol. 8, no. 2 (Summer), pp. 1–18.

Cohn, E., Rhine, S. L. W. and Santos, M. C. (1989) 'Institutions of Higher Education as Multi-Product Firms: Economies of Scale and Scope', *Review of Economics and Statistics*, vol. 71 (May), pp. 284–90.

Dearing Report (1997), The National Committee into Higher Education, London, HMSO.

De Groot, H., McMahon, W. W. and Volkwein, J.F. (1991) 'The Cost Structure of American Research Universities', *Review of Economics and Statistics*, vol. 73, pp. 424–31.

Euwals, R. and Ward, M. (2000) 'What Matters Most: Teaching or Research? Empirical Evidence on the Remuneration of British Academics', IZA working paper (Bonn: IZA, August).

Geuna, A. (2001) 'The Changing Rationale for European University Research Funding: Are there Negative Unintended Consequences?', *Journal of Economic Issues*, vol. xxxv, no. 3 (September), pp. 607–32.

Hare, P. and Wyatt, G. (1992) 'Economics of Academic Research and its Implications for Higher Education', *Oxford Review of Economic Policy*, vol. 8, no. 2 (Summer), pp. 48–66.

Harrison, M. and Lockwood, B. (2001) 'What Price Teaching Quality?', *Royal Economic Society Newsletter*, no,. 113 (April), pp. 3–5.

HMSO (1987), *A Strategy for the Science Base*, London.

James, E. and Neuberger, E. (1981) 'The University Department as a Non-Profit Labour Co-operative', *Public Choice*, vol. 36, pp. 585–612.

Johnes, G. (1988) 'Research Performance Indicators in the University Sector', *Higher Education Quarterly*, vol. 42, no. 2 (Winter), pp. 54–71.

Johnes, G. (1990) 'Measures of Research Output: University Departments of Economics in the UK, 1984–88', *Economic Journal*, vol. 100, no. 401 (June), pp. 556–60.

Johnes, G. and Taylor, J. (1992) 'The 1989 Research Selectivity Exercise: A Statistical Analysis of Differences in Research Ratings Between Universities at the Cost Centre Level', *Higher Education Quarterly*, vol. 46, no. 1 (Winter), pp. 67–87.

Johnes, G., Taylor, J. and Francis, B. (1993) 'The Research Performance of UK Universities: A Statistical Analysis of the Results of the 1989 Research Selectivity Exercise', *Journal of the Royal Statistical Society*, series A, part 2, vol. 156, pp. 271–86.

McNabb, R. Pal, S. and Sloane, P. J. (2002) 'Gender Differences in Student Attainment: the Case of University Students in the UK', *Economica*, vol. 69, pp. 481–503.

McNay, I. (1997) *The Impact of the 1992 RAE on Institutional and Individual Behaviour in English Higher Education* (Bristol: HEFC, May).

Moore, W. J., Newman, R. J. and Sloane, P. J. (2001) 'Effects of Research Assessment Exercise in Research Productivity of UK Academic Economists', unpublished manuscript, Baton Rouge, Louisiana State University.

Nerlove, M. (1972) 'On Tuition and Costs of Higher Education: Prolegomena to a Conceptual Framework', *Journal of Political Economy*, vol. 80, pp. S178–218.

Talib, A. A. (1999) 'Simulations of the Submission Decision in the Research Assessment Exercise: The Who and Where Decision', *Education Economics*, vol. 7, no. 1 (April), pp. 39–52.

Taylor, J. (1995) 'A Statistical Analysis of the 1992 Research Assessment Exercise', *Journal of the Royal Statistical Society*, series A, vol. 158, part 2, pp. 241–62.

Taylor, J. and Izadi, H. (1998) 'The 1992 Research Assessment Exercise: Outcomes, Outputs and Impacts in Economics and Econometrics', *Bulletin of Economic Research*, vol. 48, no. 1 (January), pp. 1–26.

Williams, B. (1991) *University Responses to Research Selectivity* (London: CHES).

Part II

Education, Training and Labour Market Outcomes in Europe

6
Graduates and Graduate Labour Markets in the UK and Italy

Gianna Boero, Abigail McKnight, Robin Naylor and Jeremy Smith[1]

Introduction

Education, and not least higher education, has been at the forefront of public policy discussion and government policy making in the UK in recent years. A large number of educational reforms have already been implemented and others are pending. Similarly, in Italy significant reform packages have been proposed. In the context of the ongoing higher education debates in these two countries, this chapter addresses a number of empirical questions pertaining to the UK and Italy. When relevant to policy discussions, and when the data permit, we draw conclusions about similarities and differences between the two cases.

Our main findings are as follows. First, with respect to the academic performance of Italian university students, we find that on average, as in the UK, university performance by male students is weaker than that of females and varies considerably across degree subject areas and by university region. Also consistent with evidence for the UK, degree performance in Italy is strongly influenced by the nature of prior educational attainment, such as score in the *Maturità* (high school diploma) and type of *Maturità* taken. Unlike in the UK, graduation in Italy is a lengthy process: the mean period of study for successful graduates in 1995 was about 7.5 years, which is thought to have a significant negative effect on performance.

With regard to the determinants of graduate earnings, the results for Italy suggest that neither the *Maturità* score nor the degree score influence graduate earnings: only graduating *con lode* distinction generates a small graduate pay premium for Italian students. This is in sharp contrast to the result for the UK, which show that graduate earnings depend strongly on the level of educational attainment both prior to and at university. In both Italy the UK there are large pay differences according to the degree subject studied, but in Italy, unlike in the UK, pay is affected little by the university attended (as measured by university region). It is also interesting to note that Italian university students who take longer to graduate earn significantly less than those who graduate more quickly. Similarly there is a pay penalty for those who are overqualified for their job.

The UK policy context

In the UK, one of the main themes on the higher education agenda over the last 20 years has been increasing the participation rate of young people in higher education. Until the 1980s only about 10 per cent of each cohort of 18 year-olds entered higher education, one of the lowest participation rates in the industrialised world. Successive Conservative governments implemented a variety of policies that raised the figure to 30 per cent by the early 1990s, taking the entry rate close to that for Italy. The drop-out rate, however, was much higher in Italy. In more recent years the Labour government set a target of a 50 per cent participation in higher education. Hence there has been a consistent attempt to transform status of UK universities as elite institutions into institutions of mass participation.

The expansion of higher education is, of course, expensive and in the UK it has been accompanied by a substantial programme of compensatory reforms. The first concerned the methods of student funding. Until the start of expansion, full-time university students paid no tuition fees and received maintenance grants to cover term-time accommodation expenses and other subsistence costs. The full maintenance grant was generally sufficient to cover the basic costs of living and studying. It was, however, related to parental income, and with the rule changes in the 1980s an increasing percentage of students became dependent on parental contributions towards their living and studying costs. In this manner the maintenance grants were phased out, to be replaced from 1988 by student loans. This shift in policy was associated with a dramatic rise in student debt, exacerbated by the introduction in 1998 of university tuition fees. This was the first time that full-time UK undergraduates had been required to contribute towards their tuition costs. Overseas students, part-time students and postgraduates, *inter alia*, had been liable to pay tuition fees for a longer time.

Higher education in the UK is expensive for two reasons: the unit of resource per student is traditionally high; and the fact that so many UK students leave home to study renders the university experience an expensive one.

The introduction of tuition fees caused outrage in many quarters, and in Scotland the newly instituted parliament overturned the policy for Scottish students. The issue was also prominent in the subsequent general election, and at the annual Labour Party conference in 2001 the prime minister announced a review of student finance and funding. It was estimated that the average student graduated with a debt of around £120 00. Against the growing concern about student debt it was pointed out that tuition fees had been introduced following the Dearing Committee's (1997) inquiry into higher education, which had taken evidence on the estimated private rates of return on university degrees. One of the pieces of evidence had been provided by Blundell *et al.* (1997), who estimated that the *ceteris paribus* earnings premium for an undergraduate degree would be around 17 per cent for men and 37 per cent for women. Essentially the UK government defended its introduction of tuition fees on this basis. (In contrast, in Italy the rate of return to a degree is low.)

In part, the expansion of the university participation rate was due to the abolition of the binary divide that had separated the university sector from the polytechnic sector. Paradoxically, the increased participation rate and abolition of the binary divide have been followed by growing concern about equality of access to higher education. There are two obvious sources of this concern. First, it is feared that the size of student debt combined with the requirement to make up-front payments, (as opposed to, say, a graduate tax system) will have a particularly strong disincentive effect on poorer students. This could be manifested either in a reduced rate of university registration or in an increased drop-out rate. The drop-out rate has actually increased over the last ten years, although there is no conclusive evidence that this is the result of funding changes or that the effect has been disproportionate among students from less advantaged backgrounds. The second source of concern is the attention paid by the more traditional and prestigious universities to the social background of prospective students. The widely-reported remarks by the chancellor of the exchequer during the academic year 1999–2000 on the fairness or otherwise of the admissions procedure implemented by the University of Oxford were associated with criticism of other universities at which over 50 per cent of students had come from private schools. This was substantially disproportionate to the percentage of pupils educated in private schools in the UK – less than 10 per cent.

Just as evidence on the average earnings premium associated with a degree has been used to justify the transfer of more of the burden of costs to students and their families and away from the general tax-payer, so too have there been strong suggestions that the extent of this transfer should vary according to the extent of the premium for a degree (see for example the Greenaway Report, 2000). Dolton *et al.* (1997) have called for research into how estimates of the rate of return to a degree are likely to vary according to factors such as the degree course taken and the institution attended. The secretary of state for education has announced official opposition to the introduction of differential fees across courses and institutions, but has not ruled out their introduction in the future. Nor is it impossible that individual universities will autonomously introduce differential – or 'top-up' – fees. In the context of concern about equality of access to university, it is feared that institutions and courses associated with the greatest rates of return will become closed to students from poorer backgrounds is top-up fees are introduced, with adverse consequences for the improvement of intergenerational social mobility.

Although the binary divide between universities and polytechnics has been abolished, the expanded sector has remained heterogeneous. The expansion in student numbers has been accompanied by a decrease in resources from central government and a consequent increase in the incentive for universities to attract private funding. Official league-table rankings of universities has added to the pressure. Among the ranking exercises conducted on behalf of the government are the four-yearly national research assessment exercises, which evaluate the quality of academic research in each university department (see chapter 5). The results are widely published and are feed into the university funding formulae. This has affected the academic labour market in two particular ways: there has been a growing threat to the employment security of 'underperforming' research staff; and something of a 'suppliers' market' has developed for high-performance academics. The latter has had an impact on the national system of pay scales negotiated during the annual centralised bargaining between the national trade union of university staff (the AUT for the pre-1992 universities) and the national committee that represents university employers (Universities UK, formerly the CVCP). Moreover the powerful shift towards decentralisation and the competition between universities induced by the ranking exercises and the need for increased financial independence has stimulated calls by some for the privatisation of universities. Indeed this was an explicit policy proposal by the main opposition party at the general election in 2000.

In the absence of privatisation, the UK higher education sector is increasingly resembling a quasimarket. Deprived of the ultimate price mechanism, efficiency in the sector is encouraged by the prominence of published performance measures that affect both direct central funding and each institution's status and reputation in the sector. In line with one of the recommendations of the Dearing Report (1997), the government established performance indicators for all higher education institutions. In addition to the long-established performance indicator (PI) based on the research assessment exercises' evaluation of research output, there are newly introduced PIs based on criteria such as teaching quality, student withdrawal (and its converse, progression), access and graduate employment outcomes.

The performance indicator based on teaching quality is very intrusive at the level of the individual university department, consisting as it does of a week-long visit by the members of an expert panel who examine all aspects of the delivery and quality assurance mechanisms associated with the department's teaching programmes. PIs based on student access and student withdrawal are based on the centralised annual records of each student registered at each institution. These records are very comprehensive and contain information on:

- The student's personal details (age, gender, marital status, nationality, ethnicity, social class of family, family address and postcode, and fee status).
- The student's pre-university educational background. This information is based on the data contained in the student's formal university application and typically has been monitored by the applicant's previous educational institution. The information includes the identity of the previous school and the student's scores for each of the subjects studied (typically the A-level subject scores). Knowledge of which school the student attended prior to university enables the researcher to merge into the data information on the characteristics of the school obtained from official school-level data sets, which are themselves rich in information on average academic performance at the school and the socioeconomic characteristics of the school population and neighbourhood. Furthermore knowledge of the postcode of the student's family enables the addition of information

on the geodemographic, economic and social characteristics of the neighbourhood, as obtained from, *inter alia.*, the offical census.
- Details of the student's time at university, such as course taken, annual performance, accommodation arrangements, withdrawal/completion and reason for leaving/final degree classification.

All universities are required to submit detailed individual records to the Higher Education Statistics Agency (HESA), which acts as the central depository for student records. The universities are also required to provide information on the destinations of university leavers for six months after the end of the academic year in which they leave. This provides information on the first destinations of students, which can then be matched to their full student records. This enables quite precise statistical modelling of the determinants of students' first destination outcomes, for example to analyse how these vary by academic performance, personal characteristics and institution of study. Government-produced indicators of institutional performance are based on these data.

Reform of higher education in Italy

Higher education in Italy is currently undergoing a significant transformation that will affect many aspects of the sector, including the length of undergraduate degree programmes, the content and structure of degrees (including a 3+2 model that distinguishes between ordinary and specialist degrees), the prerequisites and objectives of programmes, the administration of university admissions and the extent of university autonomy and independence, both educationally and financially. One reason for these changes is concern about students' transition from university to the labour market.

In view of these significant changes it seems appropriate to investigate the determinants of student progress through university and into the labour market. An extensive research agenda would include the following questions (each of which begs the question of how the results for Italy would compare with experiences in other countries):

1. What factors cause students to apply for a university place, and in particular for specific courses and universities? What personal characteristics influence whether they choose to study at a university distant from their family home?

2. What determines whether students will complete their course, and over what time horizon?
3. What determines the academic performance of students? Does family background play an important part in this? To what extent is previous educational performance – as indicated, for example, by the *voto* (score) in the *Maturitā* – important?
4. What would be the optimal university admissions process?
5. What determines the speed and success of a graduate's entry to the labour market? How important are sociogeographical mobility factors?
6. Do each of the above vary according to the course studied and the institution attended?
7. What issues are involved in measuring institutional performance?

This chapter addresses questions 2, 5 and 6. With regard to question 7, league tables of Italian universities – by general faculty – are widely published in newspaper, and by Censis (Centre for research in Social Science). The Censis rankings of university faculties (see for example *La Repubblica*, 16 June 2001 are based on data from various sources, such as the Ministry for Universities and its statistical office, the Committee for the Evaluation of the University System, Cineca (Network universitario per l'ettronica e l'informatica) and the offices of the European Committee and the Agency for the Socrates Programme. The league table rankings are based on five sets of criteria:

1. Student success and failure, based on student numbers and student progress.
2. Attractiveness and reputation, based on student quality (the capacity to attract high-calibre students and students from other regions) and the reputation of the faculty within the university sector.
3. Learning, based on factors such as the variety of courses offered to students.
4. Research, based on factors such as the amount of research funding attracted.
5. International activities, based on the degree of participation in student exchanges and international research collaboration.

Given this, it is clear that both the methodology and the data used to produce university league tables differ substantially between the UK and Italy. A major difference is that the rankings in Italy are not adjusted to account for differences in university characteristics and circumstances. It would be interesting to conduct an analysis to test the sensitivity of Italian rankings to the inclusion of differing characteristics and adjusting for some of the possible differences in economic conditions. Moreover the Italian data do not enable us to identify individual universities, merely universities grouped into nine university regions, so an analysis of individual university performance is not possible here.

Selective survey of recent evidence for the UK

The various policy initiatives in the UK have stimulated a variety of studies of student behaviour and institutional performance. This section presents a brief and highly selective survey of some recent work, plus some results and conclusions from our own studies. Such work has been facilitated by the release to the academic community of anonymised) student records – including first-destination data – for students leaving UK universities at the close of the 1993 academic year. This release occurred with the closure of the HESA's predecessor: the Universities Statistical Record (USR). Equivalent records for the period since then are not available.

The work conducted to date focuses on four aspects of student outcomes or university performance: student drop-out behaviour, student degree performance, student first-destination outcomes and derived performance indicators for individual universities. We shall look briefly at the key findings in each of these areas before going on to consider the issues of access to and elitism in UK universities.

Student withdrawal

Given the argument stated above that the changes to student funding in the UK are likely to have a particularly adverse effect on students from relatively poor backgrounds in terms of entry to and/or withdrawal from university, Smith and Naylor (2001a) have analysed the impact of, *inter alia*, social class background on the probability of dropping out. The cohort studied was a group of students who entered university in autumn 1989 (this was the most recent cohort for which relevant data were available). As the USR data set used for the analysis contained no information on individuals who had decided not to enter university there could be no analysis of such decision'. Hence the results apply only to students who actually attended university. This is true of nearly all the analyses conducted on the basis of USR data, but more recent researchers have used external data to model the probability of university entrance and applied the results to correct for selection bias in the analysis of student outcomes.

The student drop-out or withdrawal rate has been the focus of much more analysis in the US than in the UK. This may in part reflect the fact that the withdrawal rate is much higher in the US (at almost 40 per cent). Before 1992 the university withdrawal rate in the UK was less than 10 per cent, but it is currently estimated to be approaching 20 per cent. One of the most influential theoretical explanations of student attrition is the path analysis model by Tinto (1975, 1987). According to this model the student's social and academic integration into the educational institution is the major determinant of completion, and this in turn can depend on the student's family background, personal characteristics, previous schooling, prior academic performance and interactions between students and with academic staff. To capture the effects of social integration, Smith and Naylor (2001a) included control variables for whether the student lived on campus, off campus or in the parental home, as well as various measures of the social mix in the university department in which the student studied, such as the male–female ratio. The results provided evidence of externality effects for a number of particular subgroups.

Following Tinto's (1997) suggestion that the effects of classroom activity and interactions might be important, Smith and Naylor (2001a) also included proxies for teaching quality, as embodied in the university's teaching quality assessment (TQA) scores, as these should reflect the effectiveness of the teaching relationship. The results suggest that departmental and university characteristics have a significant effect on individual students' performance.

There is a widespread belief that, unlike in much of continental Europe, only a very small proportion of UK students continue to live in the parental home during their university careers, but there is little hard evidence of this. In an examination of the association between place of residence and the probability of drop-out, Smith and Naylor (ibid.) found that students who lived with their parents were about 2–2.5 percentage points more likely to drop out, and students who lived off campus were about 5 percentage points more likely to drop out than students who lived on campus. These findings are consistent with the hypothesis of Tinto and others on the importance of social integration at university and suggest that, in the UK system at leat, campus accommodation has a positive effect on student progression.

Family background is likely to influence the probability of withdrawal for a number of reasons. First, it may govern students' financial capacity to complete their studies – in their study Smith and Naylor found that UK students from professional backgrounds are less likely to drop out of university. Second, it is likely to condition students' social preparedness for and commitment to higher education. Third, students' postgraduate occupational aspirations are likely to be influenced by their parents' experiences and circumstances, and there is an important link between postgraduate career prospects and drop-out probability. This offers the prospect of a virtuous circle. If university reforms are able to improve graduates' career prospects, this will increase the incentive for university registration and completion.

Smith and Naylor (ibid.) show that the student drop-out rate is influenced by labour market conditions, and particularly by unemployment in the county of prior residence. Students from counties with higher unemployment rates are more likely to drop out of university, especially those from poorer backgrounds. One inference that might be drawn from this is that such students are more likely to want to stay in their home region after graduating. The higher the unemployment in that region the less rewarding the investment in university seems to be and the more marginal the attachment of such students to their university studies. In contrast students from more advantaged family backgrounds are more likely to pursue a career in the national labour market for university graduates, and are therefore less concerned about the local labour market conditions. This is of relevance to the Italian case, where the geographical mobility of students, or at least prior to graduation, is more limited than in the UK. The extent to which the graduate labour market in Italy is a national one is an interesting question and one to which we shall return below.

Finally, from the point of view of higher education reform in Italy, Smith and Naylor (ibid.) have found that students who take a four-year degree course are more likely to drop out than students on a three-year course, and that the probability of dropping out begins in the first year. This finding provides backing for the suggestion that reducing the required and/or permitted period of study for a degree will have a positive effect on the completion rate, all other things remaining equal.

Student performance

Admission to university in the UK is based on a national system of supply and demand. The implicit 'price' in this quasimarket clearing system is the score achieved by the applicants in their final secondary school exams: usually A-levels for applicants from England and Wales and Highers for Scottish and Irish applicants. All prospective students are required to complete a national application form administered by a central agency (the Universities and colleges Admissions Service, or UCAS), and each applicant is restricted to a maximum of six university course applications. For many courses there are particular subjects that applicants must have taken in their A-level or Higher studies. For the courses in greatest demand it is not uncommon for university departments to restrict their placement offers to a select group of applicants. Departments filter applicants on the basis of the information contained in the completed UCAS application form. This includes details of the candidate's performance (or predicted performance) in public examinations at the ages of 16 and 18, a personal statement by the candidate, and a reference from the school or other educational establishment. In addition some departments conduct interviews and a very small number set entrance examinations. Many departments set very high requirements for the A-level (or Higher) scores that applicants must achieve in order to secure a place. These are often close to or equal to the maximum scores obtainable under the A-level/Higher marking schemes. In short, competition for places on the more popular university courses can be extremely fierce. As noted elsewhere in this chapter, higher education in the UK is very much a national provision and this explains to a significant extent the competitive nature of the university application process.

On the demand side, students have a number of incentives to win a place at one of the most prestigious universities. Apart from the kudos associated with attending these universities, it is likely that their reputation reflects the educational advantages to be had from studying there. Moreover future employment opportunities are likely to be advantaged by attendance at a highly regarded institution. On the supply side, universities have to equate demand with a fixed supply of places. One of the fairest and cheapest ways of doing this is to use the A-level/Higher scoring system. This amounts to a policy of constrained maximisation of the scores of the admitted student population and hence, in the absence of a systematic bias in these scores, of the academic potential of the students. In this way the more popular – arguably the 'better' – universities succeed in recruiting the 'better' students. Universities have had an added incentive to attract the best possible students since the introduction by the UK government of official indicators of university performance. Better students can be expected to have a lower drop-out rate, a better academic performance and consequently greater success in the postgraduate labour market.

The nature of the university application and clearing system, as described above, raises a number of questions, including the extent to which performance in prior examinations, such as A-level, is associated with subsequent success at university (and indeed in the postgraduate labour market). Typically, estimates of the correlation between A-level scores and degree classification in the UK are about 0.3. Smith and Naylor (2001b), in an ordered probit model of degree class outcome, have found that degree performance is very sensitive both to A-level scores and to the A-level subjects studied. For the purposes of a comparison between the UK and Italy, it would be interesting to examine the correlation between scores in the Maturità and in the university *laurea* (see the section on 'New evidence for Italy').

Smith and Naylor (ibid.) have also examined the effects exerted on university degree class outcomes by gender, family background and type of school attended prior to university. Gender is an interesting case not least because of policy discussions in the UK on the issue of gender differences in students' performance at school and in public examinations. It is a cause of considerable concern that at many age levels the performance of boys is falling below that of girls. Smith and Naylor have found that on average the same is true, at university, with the exception that male students are more likely than females to obtain first-class degrees, *ceteris paribus*. With regard to family background, the evidence is that students from professional and non-manual backgrounds perform much better at university, even after controlling for prior education and other influence on performance.

In the context of the debate on schooling effects (see for example Card and Krueger, 1992; Moffitt, 1996), it is interesting to note that a statistically significant effect on academic performance at university is associated with the type of school attended prior to university. Smith and Naylor (2001b) show that performance is significantly and substantially worse for students who attended a private rather than a state school prior to university (this result was also obtained by McNabb *et al.* 2001). In the section on 'New evidence for Italy' we shall examine how performance in Italian universities varies according to the characteristics of the school previously attended and the student's prior educational attainment.

First-destination outcomes

Smith *et al.* (2000) used a binomial probit model to examine the determinants of the first-destination outcome of university leavers six months after graduation. Again the data used covered the full population of 1993 leavers. In related work Naylor *et al.* (2001b) analysed the occupational earnings of employed graduates in their first destinations. Smith *et al.* (2000) distinguish between the following types of outcome: employment, further study, unemployment and seeking work or further study, and inactivity (unavailable for work or further study). The analysis revealed that the probability of unemployment or inactivity six months after graduation is strongly influenced by various factors including the individual's degree performance (that is, the class of degree obtained), the degree subject, pre-university qualifications and academic performance, gender and family background. (Later we shall examine the effects of these factors on the quality of labour market outcomes for Italian university graduates.)

With regard to occupational earnings, Naylor *et al.* (2001b) found very large differences according to the degree subject studied (the situation in Italy will be considered below). Their focus on this issue was prompted by the debate on the extent to which students could afford to pay more towards their higher education costs. As we have seen, estimates of the average earnings premium for a degree in the UK are large. But if there is considerable variation around the average, then increasing the cost to students will risk discouraging participation, especially by school leavers from poorer families. Naylor *et al.* also found a clear social gradient in the occupational earnings of graduates, even after controlling for the other observable factors. Moreover there is a sizeable and significant premium for students who previously attended a private school (for a more detailed discussion of the private school premium see Naylor *et al.*, 2001a).

University performance indicators

As noted above, the UK government now publishes a set of indicators of university performance (PIs). Before the introduction of these official PIs, prospective students and other stakeholders in the higher education sector – such as potential employers – had access only to unofficial league tables collated and published by various media. In many respects the official PIs can be thought of as an attempt to provide more sophisticated league tables of university performance than those previously disseminated through unofficial channels. (The use of league tables in quasimarket sectors such as health and primary and secondary education is well-established – if controversial – in the UK.) The universities themselves have justifiably criticised the unofficial league tables for not taking account of important differences among universities that are likely to affect their performance ratings against the imposed criteria. The main point about the construction of valid indicators is to take proper account of such differences in order to compare universities on a like-for-like basis.

In the context of graduates' postuniversity outcomes, Smith *et al.* (2000) extended Johnes and Taylor's (1990) framework to include individual student-level data in order to produce a methodology for the construction of university PIs and league tables. They produced a league table based on data on leavers in 1993 and examined the statistical properties of the ranking. In their conclusions they emphasise the importance of adjusting for relevant differences in university characteristics, as failure to do so can result in very different and potentially misleading institutional rankings. As we shall discuss below, the Italian data we use in our study not only conceal the identity of the university attended by each student, but also aggregate university affiliation to a nine-region university grouping. Consequently we cannot make interuniversity comparisons, even on an anonymous basis.

A second conclusion is that the ranking of universities is not well-determined statistically. Of the 60 or so universities in the analysis, three quarters were ranked close to the median in terms of their effect on the probability of graduate unemployment. Very similar conclusions emerged from an analysis of university performance in the context of student drop-out and the probability of withdrawal conducted by Smith and Naylor (2001) and (in the case of medical students) by Arulampalam *et al.* (2001).

Policy implications

The issues discussed above have a number of policy implications. The most obvious concerns the choice of methodology to construct performance indicators for higher education institutions. Analysing data on individual university students is one possible method of extracting measures of university effects. The work surveyed shows that derived measures differ substantially from measures calculated simply from raw data, which fail to take account of differences among universities in terms of the characteristics of students or other factors and circumstances.

A second policy implication concerns university access. Performance at university has been shown to depend not only on individuals' educational achievement prior to university but also on the type of school they attended. For example students who have attended fee-paying private schools perform substantially worse at university than most other students, *ceteris paribus*. This suggests that university admissions procedures that fail to allow for the possibility that the recorded achievements of students educated in private schools may have been artificially inflated will fail to recruit the most able students.

The focal point of the recent debate on elitism at UK universities has been the percentage of university students educated at (fee-paying) independent schools. Only 7–10 per cent of school children attend an independent school, but the overall percentage of university students from independent schools is disproportionately high at about 25 per cent. In six of the leading universities the proportion is more than 40 per cent, and in 15 others the figure is at least 30 per cent. It has been suggested that the fact that these figures are so much higher than the 7–10 per cent figure for the entire school population is proof of unfair discrimination against university applicants from the non-independent sector, but it is not obvious that this figure is an appropriate benchmark. University applicants are awarded a place on the basis of their A-level performance, and for the top universities it is necessary to achieve very high scores. Hence one could suggest that an appropriate benchmark would be the proportion of independent school students within the total population of students who obtain a sufficiently high score to merit a place at a top university. Setting this score at 28 out of 30 and using the individual-level USR data set, we calculate that the proportion of university students from independent schools would be 36 per cent. Against this benchmark these students would still be over-represented at the top UK universities, but less disproportionately than implied by the 7–10 per cent benchmark.

We should point out, however, that A-level performance figures are likely to produce an upwardly biased estimate of future performance as independent school students tend to obtain better A-level results than equally able students from state schools. For a detailed discussion and evidence of this, see Smith and Naylor (2001a).

Data and evidence for Italy

In recent years there have been a number of studies of the transition from university to the labour market in Italy, including Vitale (1999), Ghirardini and Pellinghelli (2000), Checchi (2001), Puggioni (2001), and Staffolani (2001) and Staffolani and Sterlacchini (2001). Each of these have analysed data on individual students from particular universities (or university regions). In addition ISTAT has analysed samples of graduates from all universities (see for example ISTAT, 1999). Finally, the recent work by Censis Servizi is a further example of the degree of interest in this issue.

These studies have focused mainly on the ease and speed of transition into employment, the process of looking for work, the relationship between degree course taken and the skills needed for the jobs held, and the determinants of graduates' pay. Checchi (2001) has examined a number of issues relating to the studies and labour market outcomes of political science graduates from the University of Milan. He has estimated both an earnings equation and an equation for the determinants of the period of time between graduation and labour market entry. Among other findings, it seems that the type of school attended prior to university, the faculty attended and the specific skills acquired have a significant effect on earnings. Interestingly the score gained in the Maturità does not appear to have a significant effect. This finding is very different from that for the UK, where A-level scores can be related both to performance at university and to labour market outcomes, even after controlling for university degree class. Degree score was significant in some of Checchi's calculations, but ceased to be so when controls for workplace characteristics were included.

Bratti and Staffolani (2001) have analysed factors that influence academic performance and the choice of faculty attended, using data from an IPLAM (Inserimento Professionale Laureati Atenei Marchigiani) survey of all students who had graduated in 1992 from the four universities in the region of Marche (Ancona, Camerino, Macerata and Urbino). As well as finding that individuals' social background has a strong bearing on academic performance, the authors point to a number of 'inertial' factors that strongly influence the choice of degree course, including the type of secondary school attended prior to university. They also found that 'rational' factors such as expected performance play a significant part in individuals' choice of faculty. Puggioni (2001) has examined a number of issues related to the performance of students at the University of Cagliari, including the effective input (effort – measured in terms of hours of study and translated into credits – required for students to pass each exam.

Staffolani and Sterlacchini (2001), using the same data set as Bratti and Staffolani (2001) for the four universities in the region of Marche, have examined graduates' transition into employment and the determinants of their earnings. Unlike the finding by Checchi (2001) but in line with results for the UK, Staffolani and Sterlacchini (2001) found that the score in the Maturità has a significant effect on earnings (and on the probability of being employed). In particular earnings seem to be positively correlated with the score in the Maturità and negatively correlated with the time needed to achieve the *laurea* (university degree). Among other important determinants of earnings are faculty, gender, family, social and educational background, and work experience during the period of university study, and the period of time between graduation and employment (on average women take three months more than men to obtain their first job). Among other policy proposals, Staffolani and Sterlacchini highlight the potential value and importance of reducing the length of university courses (which is a major part of the current university reform) and the need for students to establish more links with industrial schemes during their period of study.

In 1998 ISTAT conducted the fourth and most recent survey on the transition of Italian graduates to the labour market (see ISTAT, 1999). The objective was to analyse the occupational position of graduates three years after completion of their university studies. Accordingly the survey concentrated on people who had graduated in 1995. The total number of graduates that year had amounted to 105 097 (49 393 males and 55 704 females). ISTAT contacted 25 per cent of these students, stratified according to university attended, degree course taken and gender. The response rate was about 67 per cent, yielding data on 17 326 graduates. The data contained details of the subjects studied at university, occupational status and related work details in 1998, the job-search processes used between 1995 and 1998, and family background and other personal characteristics.

ISTAT's annual report of 2000 provides an analysis of various aspects of the transition from university to the labour market, largely based on an examination of the summary statistics of the 1998 survey. There is also a logit model analysis of the probability that an individual worker will find a job and a linear regression analysis of monthly earnings. The results indicate that the faculty chosen significantly influences the probability of graduates being in employment three years after graduation. Graduates in economics/statistics and engineering have the highest employment probability. The type of school attended also exerts an influence, but the degree score (as measured by the average score for all courses taken) does not. Family background, as indicated by the father's occupation, has only a weak effect. Marital status and gender are both significant, with married men most likely to be in employment. There are enormous differences according to region of residence. With regard to monthly salary, again there are large and significant differences across faculties, and here degree score does have a significant positive effect. The father's occupational background is also a significant factor. Again there are large regional differences, with earnings in the north-west being over 20 per cent higher than in the Mezzogiorno, *ceteris paribus*. Men tend to earn about 10 per cent more than women, once occupational status is controlled for.

New evidence for Italy

This section presents the results of econometric analyses of data from the 1998 ISTAT survey of people who had (graduated in 1995. It examines the determinants of academic success, as indicated by the score (*voto*) in the *laurea*, and than the determinants of the log of net monthly pay of employed graduates. Table A6.1 in the appendix presents relevant summary statistics for the population of students who studied for their first degree, where that degree was marked out of a maximum score of 110. Forty-two per cent of respondents were male, 30 per cent were married, 2 per cent were non-Italian (mostly from other EU countries) and the average age was 26 years and 8 months. About one third of the male respondents had carried out their compulsory military service while at university and 7 per cent had completed it prior to university. With regard to educational performance, the mean reported degree score was 104 out of 110. This seems somewhat high, but there are a number of factors that might explain it. First, unlike the UK data used by Smith and Naylor (2001a) and others, all the information in the Italian data set was provided by the respondents, rather than being derived from matched administrative data. Hence there was likely to be an upward bias in the reported level of educational achievement. Second, the survey response rate was about two thirds, so it is likely that the sample was not random but contained disproportionately more individuals who had performed well at university. In contrast, however, the score (out of 60) in the Maturità seems reasonable at an average of 49 points, especially since the sample consisted exclusively of individuals who had successfully completed their university degree: again this is likely to have been an unrepresentatively well-qualified group.

Table A6.1 also shows that 32 per cent of the respondents had moved from the parental home in order to attend university. Compared with the UK this was a remarkably low figure. In the UK about 92 per cent of university students live away from home, and only about 12 per cent attend a university in the region in which the parental home is situated. From the table we can see that 56 per cent of respondents engaged in some form of paid employment during their time at university and that the mean number of years taken to complete a degree was 7.4 – considerably higher than in the UK, where the overwhelming majority finish within the three- or four-year period specified in most course regulations. With regard to satisfaction with teaching quality, on a scale in which 1, 2, 3 and 4 represent high, average, low and very low levels of satisfaction respectively, the average score awarded by the respondents was close to 2 against five criteria: competence, clarity, punctuality, presence and engagement with students in the academic relationship.

Table A6.1 also provides a breakdown of respondents by type of Maturità, university (by regional group), broad degree subject area and region of (residence in 1998. Of the 16 370 individvals in the sample, 72 per cent were in employment in 1998. Of these 16 per cent worked part-time. For those who provided details of net monthly pay, the average pay was just over 1.8 million lire. Approximately two thirds were employed in the private sector.

Finally, Table A6.1 shows the average Maturità score by university region. Here there is a remarkable degree of homogeneity, but it is likely that this partly reflects the aggregation of data at the regional level – within each region the Maturità score was likely to have varied among universities. It would be interesting to examine this variation, but it is not possible with our data set. Nonetheless this finding provides convincing support for the view that Italian universities are far more homogeneous in terms of intake than are UK universities. Of course if the rationing of student numbers in degree programmes becomes more prevalent in Italy, this homogeneity might lessen, or at least in the absence of a strategy to address the issue of fairness and efficiency in the allocation of students across the university sector.

Determinants of degree performance

The following analysis focuses on the determinants of the score in the *laurea*, where for most of the respondents the score is represented by a continuous variable with an upper limit of 110. The top-performing students received the additional award of *con lode*. We should reiterate here the point made earlier that the sample consisted of students who had obtained their degree and thus omited individuals who had failed or dropped out of university. Thus our measure of performance is conditional on successful graduation. Following Smith and Naylor (2001a, 2001b), we hypothesise that students' performance at university is influenced by various factors, including academic preparedness, personal characteristics, and characteristics of the subject studied and the processes and location of study

Table A6.2 in the appendix presents the results of an OLS regression of degree score against the selected characteristics. Males performed significantly worse than females. All other things remaining constant, males scored over half a point less than female students. A similar result was obtained for the UK. Individuals who had married by 1998 and non-Italian graduates also performed less well than their unmarried and Italian counterparts respectively. Performance significantly and monotonically deteriorated with age, but was surprisingly uninfluenced by family background. Only a small number of family background factors appear to be significant, which is a very different finding from that reported for the UK by Smith and Naylor (2001a). Students did better if (when they were aged 14) their father had a professional qualification or was either a university academic or a teacher. Table A6.2 reports only the significant estimated coefficients. A wide range of other family background characteristics were included in the regression.

After controlling for the effects of all the other regressors, there is strong evidence that degree score varied substantially across the broad subject area of study. Relative to the default cases of politics and social studies, the degree score was significantly different at the 1 per cent significance level in all but four of the other 14 subject areas, with a range of over six points between the highest and lowest. Similarly, relative to students at university in Emilia-Romagna, performance was significantly different for students in all but one of the other university regions – with a span of over three points – even after controlling for factors such as subject area and prior qualifications. Whether this indicates use of differential standards across the different institutions or genuine institutional differences in value-added cannot be ascertained from the data.

There is evidence of a highly significant (and quadratic) correlation between score in the Maturità and degree score. On average a three-point increase in the score in the Maturità was associated with a one-point rise in degree score. The type of Maturità taken prior to university also had a statistically significant effect on degree performance. Relative to students who had taken a classical Maturità, the degree score was lower for all other types of students, although by varying amounts according to the exact type of Maturità taken. For example students who had taken a scientific Maturità attained a degree score that on average was only one quarter of a point below that of former classical Maturità students. We also calculated that the correlation between degree score and score in the Maturità was about 0.36:

much higher than that between A-level scores and the degree outcome of UK university students.

Table A6.2 shows that students who moved away from the parental home typically performed less well at university than did students who stayed at home, irrespective of accommodation type. Students on longer courses tended to score more highly than others, but given the official course length, the longer students took to complete their degree the lower the degree score. For example relative to students who finished after five years, degree score was lower by 0.6 (1.3, 1.8, 2.1, 2.9, 3.7) points for students who completed after six (seven, eight, nine, 10, 11 or more) years. Students who attended lectures frequently tended to perform better than students with poor attendance records. Moreover students who paid for private extra tuition scored one degree point higher on average. Level of satisfaction with teaching quality seems to have had relatively little bearing on degree performance, although those who reported that their lecturers were readily available and committed to their students performed significantly better than those who were less satisfied with their lecturers on this criterion.

In sum the degree performance of students who graduated from Italian universities in 1995 was significantly influenced by various factors, including personal characteristics (age, gender, nationality, status of military service obligation), prior educational attainment (Maturità score and type), degree subject area, university (by regional group) and factors pertaining to the students' studies (such as accommodation, time registered, intensity of study, satisfaction with teaching). This is very different from the findings for UK university students, for whom surprisingly few of the estimated parameters on an extensive array of family background characteristics were found to be significant. Finally, we note that the estimated equation shows a reasonably good measure of fit, with an R^2 of 0.36.

Determinants of graduates' net monthly pay

This section presents the results of an OLS regression of the log of net monthly pay of employed graduates. In future work we propose to address the question of what determines the probability of employment. For now, our results for graduates' pay should be interpreted as conditional on employment.

As stated earlier, the average net monthly pay of the respondents who had graduated in 1995 was just over 1.8 million lire in 1998. Table A6.3 in the appendix presents the results of an OLS regression of the log of net monthly pay against similar groups of variables as those used in the analysis of degree performance above. We also included measures of degree performance and used information on the experiences of the respondents in the three years after graduation. This information included data on post-university training – both on and off the job – and job tenure, plus attitudinal information on issues such as the relevance of the degree obtained to the job undertaken. The estimated equation shows a good measure of fit, with an R^2 of 0.46.

Ceteris paribus, employed male graduates earned about 3 per cent more than female graduates three years after graduation. There was a premium for being married of about 2 per cent and earnings increased with age. There is some evidence that family background influenced postuniversity earnings. Earnings were higher for those whose fathers were highly qualified and whose mothers were employed in a professional or highly skilled occupation. Male graduates' earnings were influenced significantly by whether or not they had completed their military service: earnings were highest for those who had either completed their military service prior to graduation or had been exempted from serving. There is evidence of a pay penalty for those who had to honour their military obligation after graduating. Students who had engaged in paid work while studying received a graduate pay premium of over 2.5 per cent. This might reflect employers' preference for graduates with work experience.

There were significant differences in pay according to subject studied at university, even using the highly aggregated set of 15 broad subject areas. Relative to graduates in politics or sociology, medical graduates were receiving a pay premium of over 20 per cent three years after graduating. The equivalent premium for engineering graduates was about 14 per cent and that for chemistry/pharmaceutical graduates was 12 per cent. There was a premium of about 6 per cent for economics/statistics graduates relative to their politics/sociology contemporaries. Literature graduates were paid about 6 per cent less than the latter and negative premia were associated with the study of education, law and architecture. In the latter two cases it is likely that the early career earnings were not representative of future earnings.

In contrast there was surprisingly little correlation between graduate pay and region of university attendance. This was true both with and without the inclusion of controls for region of residence. Relative to students who had studied in Emilia-Romagna, graduates of universities in Lazio and Lombardia respectively earned about 10 per cent and 5 per cent more three years after graduation, *ceteris paribus*. There were no other significant correlations.

With regard to the impact of pre-university qualifications on graduate pay, we saw earlier that UK graduates' first-destination earnings are influenced significantly by their pre-university A-level performance. In contrast Maturità scores have no effect on graduate pay. One possible reason for this difference is that UK university students often receive job offers prior to graduation, with employers basing their offers on A-level results. In Italy degree scores are often known – or accurately predictable – at the point when pregraduation job offers are made, and therefore pre-university educational performance is likely to be less important. Furthermore there is a higher correlation between Maturità and degree scores in Italy than between A-level results and degree outcomes in the UK. The type of Maturità taken has almost no bearing on graduate earnings, although a small pay premium may be paid to those who have taken a technical/industrial Maturità, and those who graduate *con lode* may receive about 2 per cent extra. In our study the effect of degree and Maturità score was insignificant even when control variables for contract type, occupation and industry were excluded from the regression equation.

Whilst geographical transfer and accommodation type influenced the degree performance of those in our sample, these variables seem to have had no effect on graduate pay. This is perhaps surprising as one might have expected the more mobile graduates to have commanded higher pay. On average students who took more than seven years to graduate received lower earnings. Respondents who reported a high level of attendance at university lectures and consequently obtained a better degree score in earned less than other graduates, *ceteris paribus*. In general these individuals may have been less able than other students and hence the sign of the estimated effect on earnings. In contrast, paying for extra tuition while at university seems to have had no effect on earnings.

With regard to employment characteristics, graduate pay varied according to contract type and hours of work: the net monthly earnings of part-time workers were about 30 per cent lower but there was a pay premium of about 8 per cent for those who worked more than 40 hours per week. No significant effects were associated with tenure three years after graduation. The amount of training received since employment began, however, did have a significant effect. Relative to respondents who had undergone no training since starting work, those who had received more than four months of training earned about 7 per cent more. Respondents who were working in jobs in which a non-specialist degree was a prerequisite earned about 8 per cent more than those in jobs with no degree requirement. The more specialist the degree requirement, however, the smaller the pay premium over jobs with no degree requirement.

As is usually the case, the analysis revealed that establishment size had a well-determined and monotonic effect on earnings. For example pay was about 16 per cent higher for those working in establishments with more than 100 workers than for those in firms with two to five workers. Controlling for industry and occupation, private sector employees earned about 3 per cent less than public sector workers. Finally, region of residence had surprisingly little bearing on graduate pay, with the striking exception of the Lazio region, where there was a pay penalty of over 9 per cent relative to that in Emilia-Romagna. This almost exactly offset the positive pay premium associated with having attended university in the Lazio region.

In summary, graduate pay in Italy is influenced by a variety of factors, including personal characteristics (age, gender, marital status, status of military obligation), broad subject area studied, years of study prior to graduation, and employment characteristics such as training and size of establishment. Most surprisingly, and in stark contrast to the finding for the UK, educational achievement appears to have little effect on graduate pay. Maturità scores have an insignificant effect, as does the type of Maturità taken. Furthermore, higher degree scores do not have a possitive effect on graduate earnings. Only graduating *con lode* results in a pay premium.

Conclusions

This chapter has provided a selective review of recent empirical analyses of higher education outcomes in the UK and Italy. It has focused on the outcomes and characteristics that are most pertinent to the current policy debates in the two countries. In the case of the UK it has presented new findings on the issue of elitism in the higher education. In the case of Italy it has analysed the determinants of degree performance and graduate earnings. The contrasts and similarities between the findings for Italy and the UK have been highlighted. For example, on average university performance by male students in both the UK and Italy is weaker than that of females and varies considerably according to subject area and university region. Also consistent with the finding for the UK, degree performance in Italy is strongly correlated with prior educational factors, such as score in the Maturità and type of Maturità taken. However, unlike in the UK, graduation in Italy is a lengthy process and this is associated with a significantly negative effect on performance. Moreover students in Italy who transfer to a university outside their home region perform less well than other students. In the UK far more students move away from the parental home in order to study.

With regard to the determinants of graduate earnings, the results for the UK show a strong dependence on the level of educational attainment both prior to and at university. In Italy, in contrast, neither the Maturità score nor the degree score appear to influence graduate earnings: only graduating *con lode* generates a pay premium for Italian graduates. As in the UK there are large pay differences according to subject studied, but unlike in the UK pay is little affected by which university is attended (as measured by university region). Those students who take a long time to graduate in Italy – especially those who study for more than seven years – earn significantly less than those who graduate more quickly.

However it should be noted that the data used for the analysis of Italian university graduates differed substantially in nature from those used for the UK studies discussed in this chapter, although each of the two data sets had its own merits. We believe that analysis in this general area would be greatly facilitated and its policy usefulness enhanced if those responsible for data collection and dissemination in the two countries were to borrow ideas from each other. For example in the UK there are no data on graduates' actual earnings, so this has to be estimated from occupational averages. Moreover survey data on the first destination of graduates only provides information on the labour market outcomes of UK graduates for six months after graduation. In contrast the Italian data set used in our analysis has (banded) individual earnings information on graduates' labour market status three years after graduation. On the other hand the UK data set has a number of features that, could significantly enhance the power of the Italian data. First, the UK survey-based information on the labour market characteristics of graduates is matched to data from individuals' university records (for all students in each cohort). These include reliable information on the performance and other characteristics of students while at university, plus pre-university details recorded on the university application form, such as performance in public examinations (for example A-level subjects and results). Second, because of this matching approach the UK data contains information not only on students who graduated but also on students who failed to complete their courses. This enables an analysis of drop-out probability, which is not possible with the Italian data set. Consequently our findings for Italy are restricted to successful graduates.

154

Appendix 6.1 Results of the econometric analyses of the Italian data

Table A6.1 Summary statistics

	No. obs.	Mean	Std dev.
Personal characteristics:			
Male (%)	13517	0.4249	0.4943
Married (%)	16370	0.3002	0.4584
Non-Italian (%)	16370	0.0195	0.1384
Rest of EU (%)	16370	0.0159	0.1250
Non-EU (%)	16370	0.0037	0.0604
Age	13694	26.6634	1.9820
Military service:			
Completed before university	5743	0.0688	0.2531
Completed during university	5743	0.3235	0.4679
Completed after university	5743	0.3005	0.4585
Under way	5743	0.0068	0.0821
Not yet started	5743	0.0075	0.0862
Exempt	5743	0.2929	0.4551
Degree study:			
Degree score (out of 110)	16370	104.0285	6.7094
Maturità score (out of 60)	16370	48.6595	7.3436
Percentage who changed course	16370	0.1039	0.3052
Percentage who move from home			
to attend university	16370	0.3200	0.4665
To owned accommodation	16370	0.0239	0.1529
To rented accommodation	16370	0.2298	0.4207
To hostel	16370	0.0192	0.1374
To student hostel	16370	0.0283	0.1658
To friends/relatives	16370	0.0125	0.1109
Other	16370	0.0063	0.0791
Percentage of students employed			
while at university	16370	0.5629	0.4960
Years registered for degree	16370	7.4158	3.0149
Satisfaction with studies:			
Competence	14403	1.5689	0.6801
Clarity	14271	1.9753	0.8174
Punctuality	14180	1.8764	0.8891
Presence	14043	2.3326	0.9786
Availability/commitment	14263	2.3086	0.9946
Students with private tuition (%)	16370	0.9339	0.2485
Postgraduate employment:			
Graduates in employment (%)	16370	0.7173	0.4503
Employed part-time (%)	10964	0.1614	0.3680
Net monthly pay	10392	1815295	664011
Employed in private sector (%)	7019	0.6595	0.4739

	No. obs.	Mean	Std dev.
Year employment began:			
1995	9371	0.1397	0.3467
1996	9371	0.2898	0.4537
1997	9371	0.3077	0.4615
1998	9371	0.2628	0.4402

	Freq.	Per cent	Cum.
Type of maturità:			
Science	6402	39.11	39.11
Classical	3517	21.48	60.59
Tech./industrial	970	5.93	66.52
Tech./geometry	501	3.06	69.58
Tech./commercial	2025	12.37	81.95
Other technical	376	2.3	84.25
Educational certificate	1197	7.31	91.56
Languages	632	3.86	95.42
Professional	413	2.52	97.94
Arts	116	0.71	98.65
Other	221	1.35	100
University region:			
Piedmont/Liguria	1455	9.52	9.52
Lombardy	2156	14.1	23.62
Trentino/Veneto/Giulia	1741	11.39	35.01
Emilia-Romagna	2018	13.2	48.21
Tuscany/Umbria/Marche	1947	12.74	60.94
Lazio	1490	9.75	70.69
Abruzzi/Molise/Campania	1705	11.15	81.84
Puglia/Basilicata/Calabria	1147	7.5	89.34
Sicily/Sardinia	1629	10.66	100
Broad degree subject area:			
Science	1019	6.42	6.42
Chemistry/pharmaceutics	1009	6.36	12.78
Geology/biology	1091	6.87	19.65
Medicine	1158	7.3	26.95
Engineering	1558	9.82	36.76
Architecture	433	2.73	39.49
Agriculture	478	3.01	42.5
Economics/statistics	2800	17.64	60.14
Politics/sociology	996	6.28	66.42
Law	1946	12.26	78.68
Literature	1592	10.03	88.71
Languages	1090	6.87	95.58
Teaching	471	2.97	98.54
Psychology	231	1.46	100

	Freq.	Per cent	Cum.
Region of residence:			
Piedmont/Liguria	1688	10.68	10.68
Lombardy	2134	13.51	24.19
Trentino/Veneto/Giulia	1949	12.34	36.53
Emilia-Romagna	1687	10.68	47.2
Tuscany/Umbria/Marche	1784	11.29	58.49
Lazio	1376	8.71	67.2
Abuzzi/Molise/Campania	1801	11.4	78.6
Puglia/Basilicata/Calabria	1776	11.24	89.84
Sicily/Sardinia	1605	10.16	100

	Obs.	Mean	Std Dev.
Maturità score:			
Piedmont/Liguria	1455	48.8117	7.0276
Lombardy	2156	48.4777	7.1368
Trentino/Veneto/Giulia	1741	48.2539	7.3304
Emilia-Romagna	2018	48.5292	7.2503
Tuscany/Umbria Marche	1947	49.1171	7.5098
Lazio	1490	49.6181	7.4961
Abruzzi/Molise/Campania	1705	48.4745	7.3712
Puglia/Basilicata/Calabria	1147	48.6722	7.0614
Sicily/Sardinia	1629	48.0700	7.5318

Table A6.2 Dependent variable: degree score

	Coeff.	standard error	T-stat	P-value
Constant	79.1494	2.1509	36.798	0.000
Personal characteristics:				
Male	–0.5663	0.1185	–4.777	0.000
Married	–0.5035	0.0954	–5.279	0.000
Non-Italian	–0.5622	0.3055	–1.840	0.066
Age 25	–0.2420	0.1790	–1.352	0.176
Age 26	–0.5511	0.2006	–2.747	0.006
Age 27	–0.6985	0.2316	–3.016	0.003
Age 28–9	–0.9575	0.2336	–4.098	0.000
Age 30+	–1.0872	0.2493	–4.361	0.000
At age 14, educational attainment of father:				
Professional qualification	0.5351	0.1903	2.812	0.005
At age 14, employment status of father:				
Employed	0.1876	0.2045	0.918	0.359
Father's occupation:				
University academic	1.0250	0.3966	2.584	0.010
Teacher	3.5461	1.3540	2.619	0.009
At age 14, educational attainment of mother:				
Professional qualification	–0.0809	0.1905	–0.425	0.671
At age 14, employment status of mother:				
Employed	0.1189	0.0942	1.262	0.207
Mother's occupation:				
University academic	0.8682	0.8176	1.062	0.288
Teacher	–1.8043	0.8383	–2.152	0.031
Military service:				
Completed during university	–0.8773	0.1594	–5.503	0.000
Student employed	0.0097	0.0928	0.105	0.916
Broad university subject area:				
Science	–2.1253	0.2554	–8.321	0.000
Chemistry pharmeutics	–2.4182	0.2710	–8.924	0.000
Geology biology	0.4501	0.2465	1.826	0.068
Medicine	–0.5913	0.3795	–1.558	0.119
Engineering	–2.7506	0.2873	–9.575	0.000
Architecture	1.9920	0.3698	5.387	0.000
Agriculture	–0.4022	0.3432	–1.172	0.241
Economics/statistics	–2.3414	0.2078	–11.267	0.000
Law	–3.3996	0.2180	–15.595	0.000
Literature	3.4347	0.2251	15.260	0.000
Languages	2.3514	0.2450	9.599	0.000
Teaching	4.4577	0.3175	14.038	0.000

158

	Coeff.	standard error	T-stat	P-value
Psychology	–0.0563	0.4304	–0.131	0.896
Course change	0.6304	0.1445	4.363	0.000
University (grouped by region):				
Piedmont/Liguria	–0.6162	0.1902	–3.239	0.001
Lombardy	–1.4232	0.1696	–8.392	0.000
Trentino Veneto Giulia	–0.0739	0.1814	–0.407	0.684
Tuscany Umbria/Marche	1.9295	0.1745	11.059	0.000
Lazio	1.5609	0.1886	8.275	0.000
Abruzzi/Molise Campania	0.4894	0.1828	2.677	0.007
Puglia/Basilicata/Calabria	1.2474	0.2050	6.085	0.000
Siciliy/Sardinia	0.8606	0.1853	4.643	0.000
Prior qualifications:				
Maturità score	0.4702	0.0821	5.726	0.000
Maturità score squared	–0.0019	0.0008	–2.313	0.021
Maturità type:				
Science	–0.2697	0.1213	–2.224	0.026
Tech./industrial	–0.8871	0.2125	–4.174	0.000
Tech./geometry	–1.7174	0.2789	–6.157	0.000
Tech./commercial	–1.6510	0.1666	–9.908	0.000
Other technical	–1.6374	0.3014	–5.432	0.000
Educational certificate	–1.2121	0.1958	–6.191	0.000
Language	–0.9619	0.2500	–3.848	0.000
Professional	–2.1836	0.2884	–7.572	0.000
Arts	–1.1310	0.5248	–2.155	0.031
Other	–1.5055	0.3790	–3.973	0.000
Residence type after geographical transfer:				
Owned accommodation	–0.4514	0.2798	–1.613	0.107
Rented accommodation	–0.7870	0.1073	–7.336	0.000
Hostel	–1.2854	0.3115	–4.126	0.000
Student hostel	–1.2079	0.2611	–4.626	0.000
Friends/relatives	–0.8967	0.3827	–2.343	0.019
Other	–1.3971	0.5362	–2.605	0.009
Length of study:				
Course length	1.8793	0.1679	11.191	0.000
Actual years taken to complete				
4 years	0.1018	0.2155	0.472	0.637
6 years	–0.6141	0.1426	–4.307	0.000
7 years	–1.3045	0.1684	–7.745	0.000
8 years	–1.7538	0.1983	–8.844	0.000
9 years	–2.1373	0.2252	–9.490	0.000
10 years	–2.8888	0.2374	–12.171	0.000
11 + years	–3.6590	0.2375	–15.405	0.000

	Coeff.	standard error	T-stat	P-value
Intensity of study:				
Median attendance	0.5151	0.2961	1.739	0.082
High attendance	0.9246	0.3551	2.604	0.009
Private tuition	1.1445	0.1748	6.546	0.000
Satisfaction with academic staff:				
Competence				
High	0.0099	0.1091	0.091	0.928
Low	0.6864	0.2013	3.410	0.001
Very low	0.5836	0.4144	1.409	0.159
Clarity				
High	0.1927	0.1184	1.628	0.104
Low	−0.2658	0.1343	−1.980	0.048
Very low	−0.0894	0.2488	−0.359	0.719
Presence				
High	0.1318	0.1363	0.967	0.333
Low	0.0566	0.1244	0.455	0.649
Very low	0.2927	0.1646	1.778	0.075
Availability/commitment				
High	0.5053	0.1342	3.766	0.000
Low	−0.4273	0.1248	−3.424	0.001
Very low	−1.1372	0.1666	−6.828	0.000

Table A6.3 Dependent variable: log of net monthly pay

	Coeff.	S.e.	T-stat	P-value
Constant	14.2146	0.5972	23.802	0.000
Personal characteristics:				
Male	0.0275	0.0105	2.621	0.009
Married	0.0218	0.0064	3.409	0.001
Non-Italian	−0.0135	0.0200	−0.674	0.500
Age 27	0.0075	0.0114	0.653	0.514
Age 28–9	0.0255	0.0121	2.101	0.036
Age 30+	0.0412	0.0139	2.957	0.003
At age 14, educational attainment of father:				
No qualification	0.0023	0.0274	0.083	0.934
Medium qualification	0.0088	0.0086	1.016	0.309
Professional qualification	0.0051	0.0134	0.378	0.705
Diploma (Junior high School)	0.0358	0.0094	3.797	0.000
University diploma	0.0887	0.0277	3.204	0.001
University degree or higher	0.0426	0.0110	3.865	0.000
At age 14, employment status of father:				
Job-seeker	−0.0160	0.0441	−0.364	0.716
Inactive	−0.0372	0.0528	−0.704	0.481
Retired	0.0084	0.0200	0.417	0.677
Other non-employed	−0.0354	0.0223	−1.584	0.113
Father's occupation:				
Entrepreneur	0.0314	0.0123	2.555	0.011
Professional	0.0239	0.0276	0.864	0.388
Self-employed	0.0225	0.0085	2.651	0.008
Manager	0.0175	0.0104	1.687	0.092
Middle manager	0.0065	0.0109	0.596	0.551
Teacher (Junior high school)	−0.0195	0.0171	−1.146	0.252
Teacher (Primary school)	0.0351	0.0292	1.202	0.229
Military	−0.0207	0.0159	−1.300	0.194
Unskilled worker	0.0188	0.0142	1.325	0.185
Home worker	0.1911	0.1171	1.632	0.103
Other	0.0632	0.0256	2.468	0.014
Mother's occupation:				
Professional worker	−0.0344	0.0276	−1.246	0.213
Professional	0.0754	0.0370	2.038	0.042
University academic	0.1075	0.0645	1.667	0.096
Skilled worker/supervisor	0.0473	0.0203	2.330	0.020
Military service:				
Completed before university	0.0402	0.0195	2.058	0.040
Completed during university	0.0426	0.0124	3.439	0.001
Under way	−0.0386	0.0635	−0.607	0.544
Not yet started	−0.0034	0.0704	−0.049	0.961

	Coeff.	S.e.	T-stat	P-value
Exempted	0.0392	0.0123	3.176	0.001
Student or employed	0.0256	0.0065	3.910	0.000
Broad university subject area:				
Science	0.0431	0.0175	2.460	0.014
Chemistry/pharmeutics	0.1203	0.0203	5.935	0.000
Geology/biology	−0.0246	0.0181	−1.362	0.173
Medicine	0.2027	0.0283	7.158	0.000
Engineering	0.1421	0.0205	6.921	0.000
Architecture	−0.0454	0.0257	−1.765	0.078
Agriculture	0.0057	0.0247	0.231	0.817
Economics/Statistic	0.0561	0.0136	4.123	0.000
Law	−0.0297	0.0161	−1.846	0.065
Literature	−0.0561	0.0158	−3.547	0.000
Languages	−0.0277	0.0165	−1.679	0.093
Teaching	−0.0378	0.0209	−1.813	0.070
Psychology	0.0405	0.0308	1.316	0.188
Course change	0.0114	0.0096	1.179	0.238
University (grouped by region):				
Piedmont/Liguria	0.0238	0.0264	0.900	0.368
Lombardy	0.0476	0.0193	2.461	0.014
Trentino/Veneto/Giulia	0.0177	0.0213	0.834	0.404
Tuscany/Umbria/Marche	0.0009	0.0219	0.040	0.968
Lazio	0.1005	0.0289	3.482	0.001
Abruzzi/Molise/Campania	0.0151	0.0273	0.552	0.581
Puglia/Basilicata/Calabria	−0.225	0.0265	−0.848	0.396
Sicily/Sardinia	−0.0278	0.0333	−0.836	0.403
Educational qualifications:				
Degree score (out of 110)	0.0001	0.0118	0.007	0.994
Degree score squared	0.0000	0.0001	0.122	0.903
Con lode	0.0182	0.0088	2.078	0.038
Maturità score	0.0001	0.0056	0.010	0.992
Maturità score squared	0.0000	0.0001	0.166	0.868
Maturità type:				
Science	0.0063	0.0086	0.731	0.464
Tech./industrial	0.0300	0.0137	2.192	0.028
Tech./geometry	−0.0016	0.0180	−0.090	0.928
Tech./commercial	0.0047	0.0114	0.415	0.678
Other technical	0.0040	0.0196	0.204	0.839
Educational certificate	0.0130	0.0143	0.914	0.361
Languages	0.0023	0.0171	0.135	0.892
Professional	0.0234	0.0195	1.202	0.230
Arts	−0.0130	0.0374	−0.348	0.728
Other	0.0094	0.0244	0.385	0.700

	Coeff.	S.e.	T-stat	P-value
Residence type after geographical transfer:				
Owned accommodation	0.0158	0.0190	0.830	0.407
Rented accommodation	0.0033	0.0076	0.439	0.660
Hostel	−0.0227	0.0215	−1.059	0.290
Student hostel	−0.0060	0.0185	−0.323	0.746
Friends/relatives	0.0133	0.0266	0.498	0.618
Other	−0.0316	0.0376	−0.841	0.400
Length of study:				
Course length	−0.0417	0.0115	−3.641	0.000
actual years taken to complete				
4 years	0.0095	0.0140	0.677	0.499
6 years	0.0003	0.0142	0.019	0.985
7 years	0.0013	0.0150	0.088	0.930
8 years	−0.0295	0.0168	−1.753	0.080
9 years	−0.0262	0.0185	−1.416	0.157
10 years	−0.0482	0.0192	−2.514	0.012
11+ years	−0.0272	0.0191	−1.424	0.154
Intensity of study:				
Median attendance	−0.0250	0.0198	−1.263	0.207
High attendance	−0.0313	0.0182	−1.721	0.085
Private tuition	−0.0052	0.0114	−0.458	0.647
Post-degree training:				
Professional state exam	−0.0052	0.0093	−0.561	0.575
Further specialisation	−0.0334	0.0090	−3.707	0.000
Further degree/diploma	−0.0087	0.0188	−0.464	0.643
University study grant	−0.0179	0.0113	−1.580	0.114
training, apprenticeship	−0.0271	0.0074	−3.667	0.000
volunteering activities	−0.0292	0.0110	−2.642	0.008
Other	−0.0137	0.0081	−1.693	0.091
Type of contract:				
Self-employed	−0.1451	0.0114	−12.676	0.000
Contract: finite	−0.0947	0.0083	−11.356	0.000
Contract: seasonal casual	0.2888	0.1350	2.139	0.032
Non-contract: indefinite	−0.1753	0.0255	−6.873	0.000
Non-contract: finite	−0.2671	0.0263	−10.163	0.000
Non-contract: seasonal/casual	0.3705	0.1338	2.769	0.006
Part-time	−0.2920	0.0089	−32.962	0.000
Exceeds 40 hours per week	0.0780	0.0076	10.201	0.000
Year employment began:				
1996	0.0115	0.0102	1.125	0.260
1997	0.0033	0.0104	0.321	0.748
1998	0.0073	0.0108	0.675	0.500
Degree requirement:				
Any degree	0.0825	0.0214	3.863	0.000

	Coeff.	S.e.	T-stat	P-value
Degree in general area	0.0482	0.0093	5.206	0.000
Specific degree	0.0041	0.0096	0.426	0.670
On the job training:				
Less than one month	0.0272	0.0102	2.656	0.008
One month	0.0327	0.0128	2.545	0.011
Two months	0.0472	0.0128	3.690	0.000
Three months	0.0449	0.0161	2.789	0.005
Four months	0.0710	0.0166	4.288	0.000
Five months or more	0.0537	0.0085	6.349	0.000
Overqualified for job	−0.0492	0.0078	−6.319	0.000
Underqualified for job	−0.0118	0.0132	−0.893	0.372
Size of establishment:				
Sole worker	−0.0293	0.0137	−2.145	0.032
6–14 workers	0.0666	0.0112	5.933	0.000
15–49 workers	0.0871	0.0116	7.536	0.000
50–99 workers	0.1119	0.0138	8.113	0.000
100+ workers	0.1597	0.0107	14.926	0.000
Private sector	−0.0276	0.0100	−2.760	0.006
Region of residence:				
Piedmont/Liguria	−0.0235	0.0257	−0.916	0.360
Lombardy	0.0132	0.0198	0.667	0.505
Trentino/Veneto/Giulia	−0.0017	0.0212	−0.082	0.935
Tuscany/Umbria/Marche	−0.0265	0.0228	−1.164	0.244
Lazio	−0.0916	0.0295	−3.104	0.002
Abruzzi/Molise/Campania	−0.0494	0.0274	−1.802	0.072
Puglia/Basilicata/Calabria	−0.0358	0.0246	−1.456	0.145
Sicily/Sardinia	−0.0271	0.0338	−0.802	0.422
Industry controls	Included			
Occupation controls	Included			

Note

1. We acknowledge the USR, as the original depositor, and the UK Data Archive for the use of the data set SN:3456 Universities' Statistical Record. We also acknowledge ISTAT for the use of the data 'Inserimento professionale dei laureati dell'anno 1995, Indagine 1998'. None of these individuals or organisations bears any responsibility for any of the analysis or interpretations presented in this chapter.

References

Arulampalam, W., Naylor, R. A. and Smith, J. (2001) 'A hazard model of the probability of medical school dropout in the United Kingdom', mimeo, University of Warwick.

Blundell, R., Dearden, L., Goodman, A. and Reed, H. (1997) *Higher Education, Employment and Earnings in Britain* (London: Institute of Fiscal Studies).

Bratti, M. and Staffolani, S. (2001) 'Performance accademica e scelta della facoltà universitaria: aspetti teorici e evidenza empirica', *Quaderni di ricerca, Università degli studi di Ancona, Dipartimento di Economia*, April.

Card, D. (1999) 'The causal effect of education on earnings', in Asheutelter, O. and Cord, D. (eds) in *Handbook of Labor Economics* (Amsterdam: North-Holland).

Card, D. and Krueger, A. (1992) 'Does school quality matter: returns to education and the characteristics of public schools in the United States', *Journal of Political Economy*, vol. 100, pp. 1–40.

Censis – La Repubblica (Centro Studi Investimenti Sociali) (2001) *La grande guida all'università*, La Repubblica, Roma.

Checchi, D. (2001) 'Primi risultati dell'indagine sui percorsi lavorativi dei laureati dell'Ateneo di Milano: Facolta di Scienze Politiche', mimeo, University of Milan.

Dearing, R. (1997) *Higher Education in the Learning Society* (London: HMSO).

Dolton, P., Greenaway, D. and Vignoles, A. (1997) 'Whither higher education? An economic perspective for the Dearing Committee of Enquiry', *Economic Journal* vol. 107 pp. 710–26.

Ghirardini, P. G. and Pellinghelli, M. (2000) *I non disoccupati – Laureati e diplomati nell'Italia della piena occupazione* (Bologna: Il Mulino).

Greenaway Report (2000), *Funding Higher Education in the UK*, Department of Education London.

ISTAT (1999) *Inserimento professionale dei laureati dell'anno 1995: Indagine 1998.* Istat, Rome.

ISTAT (2000) *Annual Report*, Istat, Rome.

Johnes, J. and Taylor, J. (1990) *Performance Indicators in Higher Education* (Oxford: SRHE Oxford University Press).

Mc. Nabb, T., Pal, J. and Sloane, P. J. (2002) 'Gender differences in student attainment: The case of university students in the UK,' *Economica* vol. 69, pp. 481–503.

Moffitt, R. (1996) 'Symposium on school quality and educational outcomes: introduction', *Review of Economics and Statistics*, vol. 78, pp. 559–61.

Naylor, R., Smith, J. and McKnight, A. (2002) 'The impact of schooling on graduate earnings', special issue of *Bulletin of Economic Research* vol. 54, no. 4, pp. 315–40.

Naylor, R. Smith, J. and McKnight, A. (2001b) 'Determinants of graduate occupational earnings in the UK', mimeo, University of Warwick.

Puggioni, G. (2001) 'Una valutazione dell'impegno di studio degli studenti universitari – Il caso della facoltà di Scienze Politiche di Cagliari', in *Quaderni del Dipartimento di Ricerche Economiche e Sociali Sezione Statistica* (Cagliari: Università di Cagliari).

Smith J. and Naylor, R. (2001a) 'Dropping out of university: a statistical analysis of the probability of withdrawal of UK university students', *Journal of the Royal Statistical Society*, series A, vol. 164, no. 2, pp. 389–405.

Smith J. and Naylor, R. (2001b) 'Determinants of individual degree performance', *Oxford Bulletin of Economics and Statistics*, vol. 63, no.1, pp. 29–60.

Smith J., Naylor, R. and McKnight, A. (2000) 'Graduate employment outcomes and university performance measures', *Economic Journal*, vol. 110, no. 464, pp. F382–411.

Staffolani, S. and Sterlacchini, A. (2001) *Istruzione universitaria, occupazione e reddito. Un'analisi empirica sui laureati degli atenei marchigiani* (Milan: F. Angeli).

Tinto, V. (1975) 'Dropout from higher education: a theoretical synthesis of recent research', *Review of Educational Research*, vol. 45, pp. 89–125.

Tinto, V (1987) *Leaving College: Rethinking the Causes and Cures of Student Attrition* (Chicago, Ill.: University of Chicago Press).

Vitale, C. (1999) 'Indagine sugli sbocchi dei laureati dell'Università di Salerno', mimeo, Università di Salerno.

7
The Pay-Off from Education: A North–South Comparison

Paolo Barbieri and Stefani Scherer

Young people's transition to adulthood is of interest to sociologists and economists alike. Their entry into the labour market is regarded as of crucial importance, given its capacity to structure life history and occupational outcomes. Marked changes in the Italian labour market have included the arrived of 'atypical',[1] 'contingent' and 'partial guarantee' jobs, as opposed to traditional Fordist employment relations, with lifelong employment and institutional protection. Taking it as given that these types of job are largely restricted to new labour market entrants (Barbieri *et al.*, 1999; Schizzerotto, Pisati 2003),[2] and given the partial and selective deregulation of the Italian labour market in recent years (Esping-Andersen and Regini 2000), the question that arises is whether such jobs should be viewed as traps or stepping stones.

Another point to consider is the pronounced geographical dualism that has always characterised the Italian labour market. This dualism will be treated here as an essential dimension of analysis, not only because of the well-known macroeconomic differences between the north and south of Italy, but also because recent empirical research has found profound differences between the behaviour of young workers and would be workers in northern and southern Italy (Bentolila and Ichino, 1998; Barbieri, 2000). These differences are especially significant in respect of job-search behaviour, with longer waiting times for labour market entry and significantly higher reservation wages in the south, despite the very different levels of youth unemployment in the two regions.

This chapter analyses patterns of first labour-market entry, and in particular the consequences of two different types of job that offer access to employment:

- *Atypical* jobs (fixed-term contracts).
- Jobs that are *downgraded* with regard to the educational qualifications possessed, regardless of the type of work contract.

Fixed-term contracts are perhaps the most striking example of the new forms of 'flexible' employment introduced in Italy, and are increasing quite rapidly. Downgraded jobs – irrespective of the type of contract – reflect the situation of first-time job seekers who are sufficiently aware of the difficulties of labour market entry to accept a job for which they are overqualified purely in order to start work. Accepting a downgraded job is therefore for removed from the hypothetical 'idleness' of the labour supply.

Our results will show that labour-market entry via an atypical job does not constitute a trap that is bound to have a deleterious effect on the rest of the worker's career. By contrast, accepting a downgraded first job that does not match the initial investment in human capital does indeed penalise career development. Our results will also show that downgrading carries much more of a stigma in the south than it does in the north. This finding may shed new light on the behaviour of young workers in southern Italy. Given the lesser degree of intragenerational social mobility in the south and the greater stigma attached to downgraded entry into the labour market, one can understand the preference to wait, even for a considerable time, and to obtain a higher reservation wage – that is, there are greater expectations in the south with regard to the first job.[3]

Data and methods

Our analysis is based on data from the first Italian Longitudinal Household Survey (*Indagine Longitudinale sulle Famiglie Italiane*, ILFI) conducted by the University of Trento in collaboration with ISTAT on a national sample of 9874 individuals from 4457 households. The survey collected retrospective longitudinal information on various aspects of the respondents' lives, of which career was explored in great detail.

Because unemployment only became a serious social problem (although not an economically serious one, despite claims to the contrary at the end of the 1970s, we shall consider only those who have entered the labour market in the past two decades, that is, those individuals who left the education system in the 1980s and 1990s (up until 1997, the year of the survey). We believe this to be the period of greatest interest not only because it saw the onset of the problems studied below, but also because these problems have get to be solved. Moreover by focusing only on young first-time entrants we can avoid the recall problems that often afflict retrospective longitudinal surveys (Elias, 1996; Gershuny and Hannan, 1997).

Preliminary remarks

This section briefly reviews the issues of greatest interest to us: regulation of the Italian labour market, differences in the behaviour of the labour supply, and the 'flexible' new jobs.

A distinctive feature of the Italian occupational pattern is the length of time required to enter the labour market. The literature refers to this phenomenon as 'pre-entry unemployment' in order to emphasise that it mainly affects young people, who are often forced to spend long periods 'queuing' for a job (Reyneri, 2002). Various authors, especially labour economists, tend to regard this as a consequence of the high degree of protection afforded to the regular labour force, the so-called insiders, to the detriment of outsiders, most of whom are young and educated.

Although labour market regulation has changed in recent decades – especially during the 1990s – its insider/outsider nature does not seem to have been greatly affected by Italy's partial and targeted deregulation (Esping-Andersen and Regini, 2000). Making the employment conditions of new entrants more flexible has done almost nothing to eliminate the insider/outsider dichotomy – if anything it has exacerbated the problem by adding cohort segmentation to the already segmented labour market.[4]

A number of recent studies have pointed to the behaviour of young job seekers as a cause of pre-entry unemployment. With the average reservation wage already significantly higher in the south, it has been found that an upward push on the reservation wage is exerted by the job-seeking behaviour of young unemployed people who live with their parents. In fact when the main, breadwinner becomes unemployed, the reservation wages do not substantially differ between north and south, while family circumstances (position in the household and number of dependants) reduce the reservation wage and increase the propensity for geographical mobility (Bentolila and Ichino, 1998; Barbieri, 2000). It has also been shown that if subjects who are exclusively in search of a public sector job are analysed, all the variables that support the hypothesis of a 'lengthy wait for a public sector job in the shelter of the family' are of the expected sign and statistically significant. Young unemployed people who live with their families in southern areas are not only at greatest risk of remaining trapped in unemployment, but also adopt apparently irrational job-seeking behaviour in that they cling on to their high-wage, high-job-status expectations and thereby reinforce the queue for public sector jobs (Barbieri, 2000). In this regard Bettio and Villa (1993, 1998) point to an intergenerational exchange in which parents provide their children with the protection that they themselves received from their parents. They therefore act as a substitute for (non-existent) public and market welfare and enable their children to wait for long periods to find a job that matches their high-status (rather than high-wage) expectations.

Finally, a crucial issue in the debate on the evolution of the labour market is the effect of the recently introduced measures for partial and targeted deregulation: 'atypical' contracts are becoming the prevalent – if not the only – way in which young labour can be regulated. It is probably too early to reach firm conclusions about the effect of atypical contracts on the rest of individuals' careers, although some evidence is emerging. Acting in counterpoint to the substantial pessimism prompted by the ISTAT labour force survey data and by international experiences of labour market deregulation (Barker and Christensen 1998; Kalleberg *et al.*, 2000) are the first longitudinal analyses on individual careers, which suggest that atypical and temporary jobs do not necessarily constitute 'traps' for young people (Contini *et al.*, 1999; Booth *et al.*, 2000; Ghirardini and Pellinghelli, 2000; Korpi and Levin, 2001; Schizzerotto and Pisati, 2003).

'Atypicality' need not in itself constitute a stigma or a particularly severe hindrance to an individual's career or professional growth. We know that the Fordist-Keynesian model of a life-long job in the same profession, or even in the same firm, is bound to become increasingly obsolete. Instead what matters is not so much the 'stability' of the job (which in the Fordist organisational and productive model almost invariably corresponded to unskilled and deskilled work) as the opportunities afforded by the job for continuousing training and upskilling. More than the job, therefore, today it is skill that is the crucial determinant in the labour market. And obviously in a situation of almost full employment – or at least in the industrialised regions of northern Italy – we may reasonably expect that even an atypical first job will not prove to be a trap and have harmful effects on the rest of an individual's career.

However matters are rather different when we consider that prolonged and repeated fragmentation of careers can result in failure to achieve the minimum eligibility threshold for social benefits, which today are available almost only to individuals with a long-standing and uninterrupted record of contributions to the welfare system. A further consideration is that in capacity to work has potentially much more serious consequences for those whose careers have been punctuated by episodes of unemployment.

These are real problems that relate to the manner in which a welfare regime protects its citizens against widespread social risks. However they are first and foremost problems to do with welfare, and not directly with the labour market. A reformed welfare system – one that would be less insurance-based and more universal – should not only be able to handle the new kinds of risk arising from the post-Fordist mode of production and labour market, but also facilitate flexibility in the labour market (Atkinson, 2001).

Labour market entry

We begin by examining – for the north and south of Italy – the pay-off from education in respect of the rapidity of labour market entry and the quality (prestige) of the jobs taken by young people who left full-time education in the 1980s and 1990s. The levels of formal education reached by individuals before entering the labour market are distinguished according to the extended version of the Casmin international classification of educational levels (Brauns *et al.*, 2003; see also the appendix to this chapter). Continuous time, piecewise constant exponential models were used to analyse the transition from school to work, and simple OLS regressions to determine the quality of entry. The units of analysis were individual episodes.

Table 7.1 shows that education in the south has less marked effects on the acceleration of work entry than it does in the north, where basic vocational training (Casmin 1c and 2a) and academic tertiary education (Casmin 3a and 3b) are the educational qualifications that are most appreciated in the labour market. In the south university education (Casmin 3b) may accelerate work entry, but it is of less importance than in the north. The differences are slight however. Education has a clearer and more linear acceleration effect in the north, but disaggregation by broad disciplinary group does not yield particularly illuminating results.

The returns from education measured in terms of the status (DLS score – see De Lillo and Schizzerotto, 1985) of the first job are also relatively similar in the north and south (Table 7.2). Although intermediate vocational education and university education are somewhat better rewarded in the south – again in terms of the prestige of the occupation entered – when tertiary education is broken down by faculty there are only small differences between the north and south.

Overall the data presented in Tables 7.1 and 7.2 give the impression that education (especially tertiary education) is slightly more appreciated in the south in terms of the social status of jobs entered, but slightly less efficacious in accelerating work entry than it is in the north. However the differences are relatively small if they are interpreted in terms of the pay-off from education in the labour market. So they appear to be insufficient to account for the differences in young people's job-seeking behaviour in the north and south of the country.

Thus far we have examined the speed and quality of first job entry. But the type of formal regulation to which these first jobs are subject may differ substantially. Table 7.3 shows the types of contract that regulated the first jobs of the respondents, divided by area, gender and entry cohort, while Table 7.4 shows fixed-term first jobs by educational qualification.

The figures show that during the 1980s and 1990s these was a general increase in fixed-term first jobs, work and training contracts and cash-in-hand work (especially in the south). This was matched by a decrease in permanent jobs, which in the south fell by half. Fixed-term contracts increased to a particularly marked extent among more highly educated respondents, reducing the strong(er) educational differences in the south. However, given that these results add nothing substantially new to what is already known from other sources, we shall not comment on them further. Instead, we shall discuss the consequences of the means of entry. These consequences will be are investigated as effects on subsequent employment positions (measured as prestige scores). This obviously is just one of a number of possibilities, but it serves to complement the unemployment-centred approach. Usually studies focus on the risk of unemployment that is connected with atypical or contingent jobs, compared with standard jobs.

Before proceeding further a brief explanation of the models used in our analysis is required. When analysing the effects of entering the labour market via specific employment situations (temporary or educationally downgraded jobs in our case) we are confronted by the fact that entry is not evenly distributed across the population but concentrated among

Table 7.1 Transition to first job. Constant time, piecewise constant exponential model

		North			South	
	Full Casmin	*Casmin + faculty*	*Tertiary education only*	*Full Casmin*	*Casmin + faculty*	*Tertiary education only*
Period 1	−0.84	−0.93	−1.77	−1.23***	−1.24***	−2.37**
Period 2	−1.51	−1.61	−2.65	−1.90***	−1.91***	−3.20***
Period 3	−1.66	−1.77	−2.99	−2.02***	−2.03***	−3.19***
Period 4	−2.16**	−2.28**	–	−2.80***	−2.80***	–
Period 5	−2.19**	−2.34**	–	−2.37***	−2.38***	–
Gender: female	−0.38***	−0.39***	−0.55**	−0.90***	−0.92***	−0.49*
Cohort: 1990s	−0.23*	−0.23*	–	−0.14	−0.18	–
Married (time varying)	0.29***	0.26**	–	0.61***	0.64***	–
Additional vocational training (0/1)	−0.41***	−0.40***	–	−0.01	0.02	–
Education		†			†	
Casmin 1c	0.65***	–	–	0.69***	–	–
Casmin 2a	0.68***	–	–	−0.02	–	–
Casmin 2cg	0.36***	0.13	–	−0.01	−0.08	–
Casmin 2cv	0.60***	0.32***	–	0.03	−0.05	–
Casmin 3a	0.91**	–	–	−0.31	–	–
Casmin 3b	0.69***	–	–	0.56***	–	–
Dropout	0.35***	0.20**	–	0.36***	0.30***	–
Faculty						
Medical science	–	0.60**		–	0.84***	
Law	–	−0.10	−1.04*	–	0.28	−0.75*
Economics	–	0.21*	−0.45	–	0.68**	−0.44
Technical science	–	0.70***	0.01	–	0.47	−0.81

Human science	–	0.27	–0.58*	–	0.58	–0.90*
Social science	–	0.35	–0.50	–	1.37***	0.16
Other	–	0.42*	–0.45	–	–0.01	–0.88**
Missing	–	2.66***	2.32**	–	–0.33	–1.51***
Social background						
Father self-employed	0.14	0.11	–	–0.04	–0.07	–
Father professional	0.48***	0.48***	–	–0.33	–0.26	–
Father white collar	0.14	0.12	–	–0.14	–0.11	–
Father unskilled	–0.12	–0.10	–	–0.20	–0.23	–
Missing	–0.29	–0.31	–	–1.13***	–1.16***	–
Parents' education: high	–0.57***	–0.59***	–	–0.04	0.02	–
Regional unemployment Rate (time var.)	–0.33*	–0.25	–	–0.09***	–0.08***	–

*Notes:*** = significant at the 1 per cent level; ** = significant at the 5 per cent level; * = significant at the 10 per cent level.
+ reference category is Casmin 1ab except when indicated otherwise († reference case is Casmin 2c).
Source: ILFI 1997.

Table 7.2 Determinants of first job status (OLS regression)

| | North | | South | |
	Full Casmin	Casmin + faculty	Full Casmin	Casmin + faculty
Constant	15.03	20.90	26.78	31.34
Gender: female	–2.65**	–1.85	–3.27*	–1.75
Education				
Casmin 1c	5.15**	(*Ref:* 2c)	8.29**	(*Ref:* 2c)
Casmin 2a	13.30***		20.98***	
Casmin 2cg	15.86***	13.18***	15.01***	10.08***
Casmin 2cv	15.08***	10.54***	18.13***	14.72***
Casmin 3a	21.98**	–	28.35***	
Casmin 3b	37.48***	–	43.75***	
Faculty				
Medical science	–	42.85***	–	49.22***
Law	–	42.47***	–	52.67***
Economics	–	37.33***	–	46.11***
Technical science	–	34.90***	–	38.18***
Human science	–	22.22***	–	29.47***
Social science	–	21.46***	–	5.36
Other	–	29.44***	–	30.59***
Dropout	2.38	–0.24	3.79*	2.93
Social background				
Father self-employed	2.06	3.04*	5.75**	3.49
Father professional	3.83	3.04	5.62	2.44
Father white Collar	2.75	2.88	2.99	3.41
Father unskilled	–1.46	–1.09	–1.13	–2.71
Entry Cohort: 1990	2.77*	2.12*	–0.90	–1.61
Regional unemployment rate	1.61	1.18	–0.11	–0.09
R^2	39.8	38.6	49.6	48.4
N	646	672	374	395

Notes *** = significant at the 1 per cent level; ** = significant at the 5 per cent level; *= significant at the 10 per cent level.
Source: ILFI.

certain subgroups or categories of individuals (young people, the more highly educated and so on). Recent works on causal estimation argue that this results in a bias of the coefficients of conventional OLS estimates due to the uneven distribution of the observed covariates for subsamples who do or who do not experience the event in question. In our case, moreover, this selection bias might interact with the effects of education on the dependent variable.

Table 7.3 Description of first jobs by type of work contract and labour-market entry cohort (per cent)

	Male		Female	
	1980s	*1990s*	*1980s*	*1990s*
North:				
Work and training contract (*Contratti di Formazione-Lavora*) CFL	12.1	17.3	12.1	10.8
Fixed-term	8.1	12.7	17.4	19.6
Permanent	71.8	64.5	59.7	52.9
None (irregular/cash-in-hand work)	8.1	5.5	10.7	16.7
South:				
Work and training contract (CFL)	7.2	13.7	6.5	8.7
Fixed-term	13.3	16.4	21.7	32.6
Permanent	50.6	26.0	42.4	21.7
None (irregular/cash-in-hand work)	28.9	43.8	29.3	37.0

Table 7.4 Fixed-term first jobs by labour-market entry cohort and level of education (per cent)

	1980s			*1990s*		
	Lower secondary	*Upper secondary*	*Tertiary*	*Lower secondary*	*Upper secondary*	*Tertiary*
North	37.0	31.1	37.1	32.1	45.8	48.6
South	61.7	50.0	28.6	77.8	75.0	71.4

The standard econometric procedure to control for this is based on the Heckman correction of treatment effects, which in turn uses the 'inverse of Mills' ratio' (Heckman's two step method for estimating selection models), so that the means to control for this bias is included in the regression model (Greene, 2000). We use this procedure to correct possible bias in the estimate of the likelihood of a particular risk occurring (for example entering the labour market as an atypical worker rather than as an insider, and so on), so that the effect of the variable in question can be estimated independently of the possible effect of selection on the cases (selection bias). In the following paragraphs we present models using this control procedure together with a conventional model that does not include this correction.

Model 1 in Table 7.5 shows only the effects of entry into fixed-term jobs and of the correction, model 2 excludes the correction but includes control variables, and model 3 combines the two. In all three models in both north and south, and with and without control for

Table 7.5 Consequences of a first job with a fixed-term contract on the status of subsequent jobs (OLS regression).

	North			*South*		
	M1	*M2*	*M3*	*M1*	*M2*	*M3*
Entry position: fixed-term job	–3.05	–1.27	–1.83	4.31	1.97	1.98
Correction variable	4.08**		90.22**	–20.37***		24.97
Labour market experience		0.16	0.19		1.42	1.43
LM Exp.^{2}		–0.00	–0.00		–0.10	–0.11
Education						
Casmin 1c		3.58	29.29***		4.94	21.76
Casmin 2a		12.56***	75.65***		11.21***	20.87
Casmin 2cg		14.13***	11.88***		10.61***	23.62**
Casmin 2cv		14.94***	47.53***		14.64***	28.05**
Casmin 3a		18.47***	71.21***		24.16***	43.61***
Casmin 3b		37.88***	38.65***		39.87***	56.91***
Dropped out		6.62**	–11.61***		2.68	7.43
Gender: female		–3.72***	44.78***		–1.71	–4.99
Social background						
Father self-employed		0.51	–17.24**		2.10	2.06
Father professional		–0.73	5.22		4.54	–9.97
Father white collar		0.06*	16.17*		4.27	7.99
Father unskilled		–1.18	7.35		–3.36	–6.21
Regional unemployment rate		–2.48	–2.53*		0.27	0.28
Entry cohort: 1990s		–2.97**	15.71*		–4.63*	–2.11
Intercept	33.28	42.64	–151.6	70.64	19.09	–33.18
R^2	1.5	38.3	38.8	17.0	56.2	56.1
N	658	658	658	209	209	209

Notes: *** = significant at the 1 per cent level; ** = significant at the 5 per cent level; * = significant at the 10 per cent level. M1: model with treatment effect and control variable only; M2: model without correction for the treatment effect; M3: model with correction for the treatment effect.
Source: ILFI.

possible selection bias, entering the labour market by means of an atypical contract has little effect on the prestige of subsequent occupations in people's careers, that is on their subsequent chance of career mobility.[5]

Fixed-term contracts therefore do not seem to constitute entry-traps for the development of individuals' professional careers. One should be aware, however, that this result might be specific to the early labour market experience. It might very well be the case that non-permanent jobs at later stages of individuals' careers have negative effects on occupational positions. We should also stress that we are focusing on the occupational position only. From other research (DiPrete *et al.*, 2002; Scherer *et al.*, 2003, Bernardi, 2003) we know that temporary contracts tend to reproduce unemployment risks, and by construction to expose individuals to higher unemployment risks.

But what happens in the case of labour-market entry to positions for which individuals are overqualified with regard to the educational qualifications they possess? Such jobs are defined as 'downgraded' by observing the average social prestige scores (De Lillo and Schizzerotto, 1985) – by region and educational qualification (The extended Casmin scale) – , of the occupations entered by individuals in their first job and considering as 'downgraded' those individuals who accept, as their first job, occupations with a status score that is inferior to one standard deviation from the average occupational status value for that region and for the particular educational qualification. We believe that this procedure is suitably robust, and that establishing (regional standards, as well as considering educational level, allows account to be taken not only of possible differences in occupational structures across geographical areas but also of regional differences in the returns from education. Above all we believe that operationalising the concept of 'downgrading' in objective and verifiable terms, rather than relating it to the subjective assessment of interviewees, as often happens, provides a methodological guarantee that the consequences of the various labour market entry channels will be accurately assessed.

Table 7.6 provides an overview of 'downgraded' individuals by region, gender, labour market entry cohort and educational level. Although the regional differences are not marked, it is notable that whereas entry to downgraded positions increased in the north during the 1980s and 1990s, it decreased in the south.

The OLS regression reported in Table 7.7 analyses the consequences on the subsequent career of individuals of taking a downgraded first job. The models follow the same logic as those in Table 7.5, but their articulation, because of the covariates introduced, is slightly more complex.

The first model (M1) considers the pure effect of downgraded entry, labour market experience in years and the usual control covariates (education, gender, social origin, regional unemployment rate and the period of labour market entry – these covariates are the same in all the

Table 7.6 First jobs in 'downgraded' positions by gender, labour-market entry cohort and educational level (per cent)

	North	South
Gender		
Male	13.2	12.8
Female	21.0	21.9
Labour market entry Cohort		
1980s	15.0	18.0
1990s	19.4	15.3
Educational level		
Secondary (2a)	11.3	13.8
Upper secondary (*licei*)	26.6	26.7
Tertiary	8.8	6.2

models.) It shows that a bad mismatch at the moment of labour market entry has a negative effect on the rest of an individual's career. Including the treatment control variable does not alter the parameter in question (see the second model, M2), influencing only, by construction, the control variables, and education in particular. The stigma of beginning one's career in an overly downgraded position seems to be more severe in the south: the value of the parameter for the south is three to four times higher than that for the north (see models M1 and M2).

However it should be pointed out that various other factors structure the course of individuals' personal and working lives. As reported in a large number of sociological studies, social closure mechanisms regulate the intragenerational social and labour market mobility of individuals (Erikson and Goldthorpe, 1992). Social mobility (relative and inter- and intragenerational) is particularly low in Italy, and especially in the south (Cobalti and Schizzerotto, 1994). We can therefore expect social rigidity to be of particular importance in structuring the individual careers analysed here, and that it also exerts an influence on our models.

The simplest and most direct way of controlling for the possibility that the status of the first occupation has a 'stickiness' effect on the chance of social mobility is to introduce a measure of the social status of the respondents' first jobs to the covariates. In this case the socioeconomic status of their occupations will act as a proxy for social closure mechanisms, and the relative parameter will be more closely correlated with the dependent variable (the social status scores of subsequent occupations) the greater the degree of social closure, thereby removing the effect of social structure (operationalised with a continuous variable) from the effect of the mismatch (operationalised with a dummy variable).

Models M3 and M4 include this control. Unsurprisingly, the social position occupied when entering the first job is strongly and significantly correlated with subsequent social positions. As well as being high, the value of the parameter is stable and statistically significant both in the two models considered (M4 also includes the control for possible selection bias used in M2) and between the north and south of Italy. This is indicative of the strong effect exerted by the first occupation on subsequent ones, or in other words the scant career mobility that generally characterises the Italian labour market.

With regard to the parameter that registers the effect on an individual's career of initial downgrading, 'purged' of the effects of social closure, models 2 and 3 the north and south assume opposite signs. This reflects the substantial differences between the two regions' labour markets. In the north, beginning one's career in an occupation for which one is over qualified no longer has a bearing on the prestige of subsequent occupations,[6] but in the south such downgrading maintains its negative effects and imposes a severe social stigma that has a negative effect on one's entire career.[7] This emphasises the importance of achieving a good match between job and qualifications up on entry into the labour market.

This dualism in the consequences of entering the labour market entry via a downgraded position is an extremely interesting finding as it enables us to consider the social structuring phenomena and dynamics that operate at the broad social level, together with actors' behaviours, expectations and choices. That is, it provides an interpretative key – in terms of methodological individualism – to action by individuals within the context defined by social structuring factors. From this point of view, the markedly negative effect of downgrading in the south provides an understanding of labour supply behaviour that to date has been interpreted solely in terms of family network effects, rather than of idleness or a southern approach to work, in contrast to the 'Protestant' work ethic or approach that is more characteristic of the northern regions.

We may therefore offer an interpretation in terms of rational action theory, applied in this case to the job search behaviour of young southern people. For young first-job seekers in the south, mindful of the fact that their educational qualifications may give them access to a slightly better

Table 7.7 Consequences of a first job in a downgraded position on the status of subsequent occupational positions (OLS regression)

	North				South			
	M1	M2	M3	M4	M1	M2	M3	M4
Entry position too low job for the given								
level of education	–4.65**	–5.46**	5.67**	5.40**	–14.93***	–21.88***	–0.73**	–7.63**
Prestige of first job (standardised)	–	–	0.44***	0.44***	–	–	0.49***	0.48***
Correction variable	–	–33.55	–	–39.91	–	36.80	–	30.32
Labour market experience	–0.01	–0.09	0.10	0.08	0.58	–0.32	0.61	–0.20
LM Exp.^{2}	0.01	–0.01	0.01	0.01	–0.05	0.00	–0.04	–0.00
LM Exp *entry too low position	–	0.34	–	0.17	–	2.62**	–	2.51**
Education								
Casmin 1c	2.62	26.41	2.95	31.28	2.78	–16.87	2.38	–13.74
Casmin 2a	11.89***	13.41***	6.07**	7.90*	11.84**	11.00*	1.52	0.90
Casmin 2cg	15.73**	–3.53	8.96**	–13.91	14.28***	28.31	7.66**	19.13
Casmin 2cv	15.57***	3.30	8.46***	–6.12	18.74***	37.94	9.92**	25.97
Casmin 3a	17.92**	14.69*	8.66	4.77	21.72**		12.57*	
Casmin 3b	37.48***	43.05***	21.86***	28.50***	40.26***	28.84	21.79***	12.74
Drop-out	6.40***	7.94**	5.24***	7.10**	0.01	–16.76	–1.42	–15.16
Gender: female	–3.63**	–10.86	–3.82**	–12.44	–0.24	7.54	–1.33	5.26
Social background								
Father self-employed	0.22	11.42	0.82	14.16	1.52	0.15	1.71	0.67
Father professional	–0.61	7.93	–0.38	9.75	1.45	1.43	–0.73	–0.68
Father white collar	0.42	–0.93	0.30	–1.27	3.41	1.91	2.76	1.56
Father unskilled	–0.62	–8.01	–1.05	–9.81	–5.78**	–15.27	–2.54	–10.36
Regional unemployment rate	–1.97	–1.97	–3.80*	–3.84*	0.29	0.46	0.07	0.23
Entry cohort: 1990s	–2.99*	–4.72*	–2.17	–4.19	–6.44**	–11.87	–4.48*	–9.04
Intercept	40.60**	94.99	38.93	103.56	24.62**	–28.41	15.14	–28.63

R^2	0.39	0.39	0.45	C.45	0.63	0.65	0.70	0.70
N	658	658	658	€58	209	205	209	205

Notes: *** = significant at the 1 percent level; ** = significant at the 5 per cent level; * = significant at the 10 per cent level. M1: model without correction for the treatment effect; M2: model with correction for the treatment effect; M3: model without correction for the treatment effect, controlling for the prestige of the first job; M4: model with correction for the treatment effect, controlling for the prestige of the first job.
Source: ILFl.

job than would be available to them in the north, but also very well aware that a lower-status one will put an indelible stain on their *curriculum vitae*, it is extremely logical (in the Paretian sense) as well as rational (in the Weberian sense) to wait for a job that matches their human capital endowment. This is an outright strategy of 'downgrading resistance' (d'Iribarne, 1990), implemented through the instrumental[8] use of the family and unemployment by young southern first-job seekers, who – aware of the few chances they will have to better themselves in the labour market – seek to maximise the initial result of their job search efforts, thus prolonging or maintaining their high-status expectations.

From a sociological point of view, assuming that actors' choices are guided by absolute rationality may appear rash. However we maintain that this behaviour is based at least in part on widespread customs in the local community, and as such can also be interpreted in terms of shared culture. In other words the rationality of actors is a bounded rationality structured by the cognitive cultural context in which it arises and developes. Obviously, irrespective of whether or not it is rational and/or cultural, this strategy depends on the existence of a broad network of social and familial support, which enables individuals drastically to reduce their reproduction costs (Campiglio, 1996) while maintaining a standard of living that is better from a social point of view, and not worse from an economic one, than that which would be available to them if they were to move to another region to work.

Concluding remarks

The results presented in this chapter show that a professionally rewarding first job that offers opportunities for further growth can be an atypical one without this necessarily proving detrimental to the individual's subsequent career. By contrast, in certain circumstances the chance of career mobility may be reduced by downgrading, that is, accepting a job with a lower status (albeit one that is permanent and endows the status of 'insider') than the educational qualification possessed.

However this stigma effect is only present in the southern Italian labour market. In the north, such jobs are viewed as a means to gain experience and thereby secure a better job in the future. For this reason even a relatively low-status first job is a good point of entry and does not have negative consequences on intragenerational career mobility.

The differing reactions to initial downgrading in the two Italian labour markets can be linked to the findings of previous studies (Reyneri and Barbieri 1996; Barbieri, 2000). These argued for the utility of a labour market analysis that considers the relationships between intragenerational social mobility and the labour markets in the north and south of Italy, based on the hypothesis that different occupational strategies correspond to the different chances of social mobility in the two labour markets – more open and dynamic in the north, static and closed in the south. It is widely recognised that the south lacks good opportunities for regular and secure employment in the private sector, in that there is a dearth of 'guaranteed' jobs outside the public sector. If we add to this the stigma of accepting a downgraded job – a stigma that cannot be shed in the course of a career – one can understand in the light of a methodological individualism approach) why young southerners prefer to wait for the right job for their qualifications. This often means a secure job in the public sector, which is a conveyor of higher social status for the mass of young southerners with above average human capital,[9] for whom the solidarity of the extended family takes the place of the benefit system in other welfare regimes. This behaviour also generates a higher reservation wage, because the reference group is the guaranteed occupational group in the public or semipublic sector, which in the south enjoys more positive pay differentials than in the rest of the country (Capparucci and Macri, quoted in Ghignoni, 1997). Hence the longer wait times in the south can be viewed as an investment in stable employment in the future.

In summary, for individuals who intend to optimise their human capital and are mindful of the severe stigma attached to initial downgrading, it is logical and rational to wait for the best possible job to come along, given that once they have entered the labour market the chances of changing jobs will be few and far between. The family is the crucial resource for this occupational strategy to be viable.

Appendix 7.1 Variables and implemented measures

Table A7.1 Prestige of job: DeLillo–Schizzerotto prestige score

---

Social background
    Father's employment position when student aged 14
    Educational background of parents; 1 = highly educated (*laurea*), 0 otherwise

Education
    Measured via CASMIN educational classification: see Table A1 for details
    Dropout: 1 = exiting the education system without degree, 0 = otherwise
    Faculty: Detailed faculty information for those with tertiary education and degree
Labour market experience in years since first job entry
Regional unemployment rate: time varying

Table A7.2 The CASMIN educational classification, as applied to Italy

1ab	Lower secondary, primary and below
1c	Vocational training schools (until 1963), vocational institutes (2–3 year)/lower-secondary diploma and vocational training courses of more than six months' duration
2b	Secondary – general
2a	Secondary – vocational institutes (4–5 years)/four-year diploma
2cvoc	Higher secondary – vocational track: technical institutes (5 years), teacher training school (5 years), art school, supplementary year
2cgen	Higher secondary – general track: *licei* (classics, languages, science, arts), conservatory, upper-secondary diploma
3a	Lower tertiary: university diploma or school for special purposes, school for social workers
3b.1	Higher tertiary: university degree course, academy of fine arts
3b.2	Higher tertiary plus doctorate: PhD programme

Notes

1. The Italian Census Bureau (ISTAT) uses the term 'atypical jobs' to denote all contractual forms that differ from full-time, open-ended, guaranteed employment. On this definition part-time work is also 'atypical', even voluntary part-time work in the secure public and semiprivate sectors. ISTAT's definition illustrates the changes that have recently taken place in the regulation of employment relations in Italy, and as such it is uncontroversial. However, through no fault of ISTAT, many commentators interpret 'atypical' work as *ipso facto* relating to 'precarious and marginal' workers who are condemned to increasingly insecure careers. Not only is this interpretation vaguely ideological but it is also wrong, because it shifts attention from the problem of the professionalism and quality of the work performed to formal job guarantees alone.

2. Barbieri *et al.* (1999) report marked gender discrimination, as well as cohort differences, with regards to job insecurity.

3. Of course first labour market entry can depend on many unobservable factors that may well affect career progress including the individual's choice of a low-prestige position (incidentily sociological prestige scores do not consider income – or at least not directly). We assume that actors are behaving rationally when they choose to wait longer for a suitable job, and do not consider the opposite option – the voluntary choice of a downgraded position.

4. Boeri (1999) states that those who are at greatest risk of exclusion from the labour market are unemployed ex-workers squeezed between protected insiders and young outsiders with 'flexibilised' labour-market entry.

5. Obviously the 'sociological' model (M2, without control for possible selection bias) magnifies the value of the educational qualification, a covariate that is more 'penalised' in the econometric models (M1 and M3) because the control variable bias is constructed by estimation the likelihood of indi-

viduals having an unprotected' first job and including education among the regressors (the same variables later contained in the final model are inserted). The change in the sign and value of the coefficient for gender is very probably due to the fact that there is a marked gender effect on the risk of having a temporary and unprotected first job. We would point out, however, that although the coefficient changes direction, it is of low significance.
6. That is, it does not affect the chance of intragenerational mobility.
7. No matter how much positive work experience is gained, it is never enough to close the gap caused by the initial downgrading.
8. We use the term 'instrumental' in an absolutely non-judgemental sense.
9. In 1995, graduates everywhere were overrepresented in the civil service entrance examinations. This overrepresentation amounted to 18 per cent in the north and more than 27 per cent in the south.

References

Atkinson, A. (2001) 'The Implications of Labour Market Flexibility for the Welfare State', paper presented to the LABOR Conference on The Costs of Labour Market Flexibility, Moncalieri, 2 3 February 2001.

Barbagli, M. (1996) *Sotto lo stesso tetto: mutamenti della famiglia in Italia dal XV al XX secolo* (Bologna: Il Mulino).

Barbieri, P. (2000) 'Salari di riserva, famiglia e ricerca di lavoro. La lunga attesa del "posto" pubblico in Italia', *Economia e Lavoro*, no. 1.

Barbieri, P. (2001) 'Self-employment in Italy: Does Labor Market Rigidity Matter?', *International Journal of Sociology*, vol. 31, no. 1.

Barbieri P., Bison, I. and Esping-Andersen, G. (1999) 'Italy: The Great U-Turn or an Historical Laggard?', paper presented to the ECSR workshop, Mannheim, 7–9 September 1999.

Barker, K. and Christensen K. (eds) (1998) *Contingent Work. American employment relations in transition* (Chicago: ILR Press).

Bentolila, S. and Ichino, A. (1998) *How Painful is Unemployment? Household Consumption and Job Losses in Four European Countries* (London: CEPR).

Bernardi, F. (2003) 'Globalisierung, Vermarktung der Arbeit und soziale Schichtung: Wandel der Erwerbskarrieren in Italien', in Walter Mueller and Stefani Scherer (eds), *Mehr Risiken- mehr Ungleichheit. Abbau des Wohlfahrsstaates, Flexibilisierung des Arbeitsmarktes und die Folgen*, (Frankfurt: Campus) (earlier English version at www.mzes.uni-mannheim.de/rc28).

Bettio, F. and Villa, P. (1993) 'Strutture familiari e mercati del lavoro nei paesi sviluppati. L'emergere di un percorso mediterraneo per l'integrazione delle donne nel mercato del lavoro', *Economia & Lavoro*, no. 2.

Bettio, F. and Villa, P. (1998) 'A Mediterranean perspective on the break-down of the relationship between participation and fertility', *Cambridge Journal of Economics*, vol. 22, no. 2.

Bettio, F. and Villa, P. (1999) 'To what extent does it pay to be better educated? Education and market work for women in Italy', *South European Society and Politics*, vol. 4, no. 2.

Boeri, T. (1999) 'Enforcement of employment security regulations, on-the-job search and unemployment duration', *European Economic Review*, vol. 43.

Booth, A. L., Francesconi, M. and Frank, J. (2000) 'Temporary Jobs: Stepping Stones or Dead Ends?' ISER, University of Essex, Discussion Paper no. 205, October.

Brauns, H., Scherer, S. and Steinmann, S. (2003) 'The CASMIN Educational Classification in International Comparative Research', in J. Hoffmeyer-Zlotnik, and Ch. Wolf (eds), *Advances in Cross-national Comparison. A European Working Book for Demographic and Socio-Economic Variables* (New York: Kluwer and Plenum Publishers), pp. 221–44.

Campiglio, L. (1996) *Il costo del vivere: Nord e Sud a confronto* (Bologna: Il Mulino).

Checchi, D. (1997) *La diseguaglianza: istruzione e mercato del lavoro* (Milan: Laterza).

Checchi, D. (1999) *Istruzione e mercato: per una analisi economica della formazione scolastica* (Bologna: Il Mulino).

Cobalti, A. and Schizzerotto, A. (1994) *La mobilità sociale in Italia* (Bologna: Il Mulino).

Contini, B., Pacelli, L. and Villosio, C. (1999) 'Short Employment Spells in Italy, Germany and Great Britain: Testing the "Port-of-Entry" Hypothesis' (CEP/LSE paper: CEP/LSE, June) London.

De Lillo, A. and Schizzerotto, A. (1985) 'La valutazione sociale delle occupazioni: una scala di stratificazione occupazionale per l'Italia contemporanea' (Bologna: Il Mulino).

DiPrete, T., Goux, D., Maurin, E. and Quesnel-Vallee, A. (2002) 'Insecure Employment Relationships in Flexible and Regulated Labor Markets: Trend, Distribution, and Consequences in the United States and France', paper presented at the April 2002 meeting of Research Committee 28 (Social Stratification) of the International Sociological Association, Oxford, England.

d'Iribarne, P. (1990) *Le Chômage Paradoxal* (Paris: PUF).

Elias, P. (1996) 'Who forgot they were unemployed?', Working papers of the ESRC Research Centre on Micro-social Change, Paper 97–19, University of Essex.

Erikson, R. and Goldthorpe, J. H. (1992) *The Constant Flux: A Study of Class Mobility in Industrial Societies*, (Oxford: Clarendon Press).

Esping-Andersen, G. and Regini M. (2000) *Why Deregulate Labour Markets?* (Oxford: Oxford University Press).

Gershuny, J. and Hannan, C. (1997) 'Unemployment: blame the victim?', Working papers of the ESRC Research Centre on Micro-social Change, Paper 97–23, University of Essex.

Ghignoni E. (1997) 'I differenziali territoriali nei salari minimi di accettazione in Italia', *Quaderni di Economia del Lavoro*, no. 59.

Ghirardini, P. G. and Pellinghelli, M. (2000) *I non disoccupati. Laureati e diplomati nell'Italia della piena occupazione* (Bologna: Il Mulino).

Greene, W. H. (2000) *Econometric Analysis*, 4th edn (Englewood Cliffs, NJ: Prentice-Hall).

Kalleberg, A., Reskin, B. and Hudson, K. (2000) 'Bad Jobs in America: Standard and Nonstandard Employment Relations and Job Quality in the United States', *American Sociological Review*, vol. 65.

Korpi, T. and Levin, H. (2001) 'Precarious footing: temporary employment as a stepping-stone out of unemployment in Sweden', *Work, Employment and Society*, vol. 15.

Monducci, R. (1992) 'Disoccupazione e intensità della ricerca: prime evidenze empiriche sulla base della nuova indagine sulle forze di lavoro', *Politiche del lavoro*, nos 22–3.

Reyneri, E. (2002) *Sociologia del mercato del lavoro* (Bologna: Il Mulino).

Reyneri, E. and Barbieri, P. (1996) 'La tipologia della disoccupazione in Italia', Progetto.

Scherer, S. (2001) 'Early Career Patterns: A comparison between Great Britain and West Germany', *European Sociological Review*, vol. 17, no. 2.

Scherer, S. (2003) 'Sprungbrett oder Falle? Konsequenzen der Position des Erwerbseintritts auf den Karriereverlauf in Westdeutschland, Großbritannien und Italien', in Walter Mueller and Stefani Scherer (eds), *Mehr Risiken- mehr Ungleichheit. Abbau des Wohlfahrsstaates, Flexibilisierung des Arbeitsmarktes und die Folgen* (Frankfurt: Campus).

Schizzerotto, A. and Pisati, M. (2003) 'Befristete Verträge in Italien: Ausgangspunkt für stabile Beschäftigung oder Falle?', in Walter Mueller and Stefani Scherer (eds), *Mehr Risiken- mehr Ungleichheit. Abbau des Wohlfahrsstaates, Flexibilisierung des Arbeitsmarktes und die Folgen* (Frankfurt: Campus) [Italian translation in A. Schizzerotto, *Vite Ineguali*, Bologna: Il Mulino, 2002]

Shavit, Y. and Müller, W. (eds) (1998) *From School to Work. A Comparative Study of Educational Qualifications and Occupational Destinations* (Oxford: Clarendon Press).

Stata 7 (2000) *User's Manual* (College Station, Texas: Stata Press).

8
Labour Market Institutions and the Complementarity between Education and Training in Europe

Giorgio Brunello[1]

Introduction

Since training is generally considered to be necessary for productivity and competitiveness, an important research question is what economic factors cause a greater incidence of training in the labour force? While there is a large body of empirical literature on this question (see the reviews in OECD 1991, Lynch, 1994, and Booth and Snower, (1995), most of these works are based on national data and comparative work is scarce (Pischke, 2000).

One obstacle faced by researchers in this area is that different national surveys often define training in different ways, which makes it difficult to make cross-country comparisons. This obstacle has been partially removed by the European Community Household Panel (ECHP), a large household survey that covers 14 EU member countries. For this, rather than trying to harmonise the findings from national surveys the European statistical agency (Eurostat) has adopted an input-oriented approach and uses a standard EU questionnaire. The data are collected by the National Collection Units and checked by Eurostat (European Commission, 1999). However, although the definitions of and questions on training, the reference period and the survey methods used in the ECHP are common across countries, this has not eliminated all comparability problems as interpretation of the questions can vary across countries because of country-specific practices and customs (OECD, 1991).

In this chapter ECHP data sets are used to compare training incidence in a large number of European countries, to investigate which features of their labour markets lead to a higher incidence of training and to determine how these features affect the relationship between

188

education and training. The chapter exploits well-documented details of cross-country variations in institutionalised employment practices across Europe to identify the relationship between these and the incidence of training. This approach is similar to those used to study the effects of differing minimum wages on the provision of training in the US, as reviewed in Acemoglu and Pischke (1998b).

The present investigation is based on the following three questions:

- Is training more common among the better educated?
- Does a larger supply of educated workers in a country increase the incidence of training in the presence of externalities?
- Do wage compression and other labour market institutions, such as employment protection and the minimum wage, affect the incidence of training?

The chapter is organised as follows. The following section briefly discusses the theoretical economic background of the subject, and the subsequent sections present the data, the empirical evidence and the conclusions.

Education, training and labour market institutions

The idea that education and training are complementary goes back at least to Thurow (1975) and Rosen (1976). According to Thurow (1975), employers rank workers in accordance with their personal characteristics, including education, which they use as indirect indicators of the costs needed to produce a standard work performance. These costs are usually expected to be lower for individuals with higher education. In his theory of lifetime earnings, Rosen (1976) argues that education improves job-related learning skills, thereby reducing training costs. Both these views suggest that, *ceteris paribus*, individuals with more education will receive more training. As Heckman (1999, p. 6) puts it, 'human capital has fundamental dynamic complementarity features. Learning begets learning. Skills acquired early on make later learning easier.'

One justification for government training policies is the presence of externalities. As discussed by Soskice (1994), Snower (1994), Acemoglu (2000), and Brunello and Medio (2001), a training supply externality occurs when an increase in the supply of educated workers raises the probability that firms will successfully fill their training vacancies for skilled jobs, thereby raising the expected return from opening these vacancies. In these circumstances training incidence should increase not only with individual educational attainment but also with the share of educated individuals in the labour force.

The standard economic theory of training developed by Becker (1975) assumes competitive labour markets. When labour markets are non-competitive, however, institutionalized employment practices that influence wage compression can affect training incidence. Acemoglu and Pischke (1998a) show that a more compressed wage structure, induced by a minimum wage, by the presence of unions or by other sources, is likely to increase the provision of training when firms bear the training cost. When both firms and workers contribute to training investment, however, wage compression may increase or decrease the total provision of training. The sign of this relationship is an empirical matter.

The data

The data used in this chapter are drawn from the 1994 and 1996 waves of the European Community Household Panel. As pointed out in the introduction to this chapter, the main advantage of these data is that the same questionnaire is used for each participating country, which increases comparability. Each survey gathers household and personal details, and the same households and individuals are interviewed over time. In the 1996 survey some 60 500 nationally representative households and approximately 130 000 individuals from 14 countries were interviewed. Austria and Finland did not participate in the 1994 survey.[2]

The key question on training was whether the interviewees had engaged in vocational education or training during the reference period, which ran from January of the year before the survey to the time of the survey.[3] Since the reference period of the second survey (1995) partially overlapped the reference period of the most recent survey for which details are available (1996), only the 1994 and 1996 data will be used in this chapter.

Interviewees who had received vocational education or training were asked to specify whether this involved a third-level qualification from, for example, a technical college, specific vocational training at a vocational school or college, specific vocational training in a programme that provided both work experience and complementary instruction elsewhere, or specific vocational training in the workplace without complementary instruction elsewhere. They were then asked whether the training had been paid for or organised by the employer (only for individuals employed in 1996) and the duration of the course. There was also a question on the highest level of general education completed. The replies were coded into three categories: less than second-stage or lower secondary education (ISCED 0–2), second-stage or upper secondary education (ISCED3) and recognised third-level education (ISCED 5–7).

This chapter will consider only individuals who were aged 16 to 58 in 1994, were interviewed in both 1994 and 1996 and did not change their educational attainment in the interim.[4] Hence individuals from Austria and Finland will be excluded from the analysis as they were interviewed only in 1996, and the sample will include slightly less than 89 per cent of the interviewees in the remaining 11 countries. These individuals can be divided into the following employment categories: employed for at least 15 hours per week (64.2 per cent); employed for fewer than 15 hours per week (2.7 per cent); unemployed (7.1 per cent); discouraged workers (i.e. workers not actively searching for a job because of slack economic conditions) (0.9 per cent) and inactive (i.e. workers not participating to the labour market) (25.1 per cent).

Table 8.1 shows training incidence in 1996 (defined as the percentage of individuals in the sample who had received vocational education or training in the reference period) by country and gender. Training incidence was generally higher among males than females. Based on these data the countries in question can be classified into three groups: a 'high incidence' group (Denmark, Germany and the

Table 8.1 Training incidence by country and gender, 1996 (per cent)

	All	*Males*	*Females*	*No. in sample*
Denmark	0.426	0.448	0.404	3 140
Germany	0.209	0.242	0.177	5 936
Netherlands	0.134	0.138	0.130	5 387
Belgium	0.140	0.169	0.116	3 316
France	0.135	0.139	0.132	7 387
UK	0.315	0.343	0.289	4 477
Ireland	0.090	0.100	0.080	4 446
Italy	0.055	0.056	0.054	11 698
Greece	0.034	0.037	0.031	6 486
Spain	0.125	0.127	0.124	9 647
Portugal	0.022	0.023	0.021	6 749
Average	0.128	0.137	0.119	68 669

Table 8.2 Training incidence in 1996 by country and number of hours per week in paid employment in 1994 (per cent, n = 68 669)

	> 15 hours	*< 15 hours*	*Unemployed*	*Inactive*
Denmark	0.493	0.233	0.286	0.105
Germany	0.251	0.082	0.202	0.075
Netherlands	0.110	0.243	0.195	0.139
Belgium	0.171	0.076	0.120	0.028
France	0.155	0.113	0.183	0.040
UK	0.394	0.213	0.170	0.087
Ireland	0.108	0.067	0.089	0.056
Italy	0.074	0.038	0.055	0.022
Greece	0.035	0.000	0.036	0.032
Spain	0.123	0.109	0.159	0.113
Portugal	0.023	0.010	0.017	0.021
Average	0.156	0.138	0.121	0.060

UK), a 'low incidence' group (Ireland, Italy, Greece and Portugal) and an intermediate group (France, Belgium, the Netherlands and Spain). This grouping is broadly consistent with the comparative evidence produced by the OECD and national surveys, which show that training incidence in Germany and the UK is higher than in France and Spain (OECD, 1991).

As shown in Table 8.2, training incidence in 1996 varied significantly according to the number of hours worked by the respondents in 1994. On average the incidence was highest among those employed for at least 15 hours a week and lowest among those who were inactive in 1994. In some countries (France, the Netherlands and Spain), however, individuals who were unemployed in 1994 had the highest training incidence in 1996. Not documented in the table, and limited to those employed for at least 15 hours a week, is the fact that training incidence was highest among manages, professionals, technicians, financial intermediaries and employees in the public sector.

Training in the workplace was the most common form of training (47.2 per cent), followed by specific vocational training at a vocational school or college (31.2 per cent), training in a dual programme (14.0 per cent) and a third-level qualification course at a technical college (5.7 per cent).[5] In principle one could use this classification to distinguish between general and firm-specific training, but unfortunately the response rate to this question was significantly below the percentage of trained individuals in the UK, Denmark and Belgium,

Table 8.3 Training incidence by country and educational attainment, 1996
(per cent, n = 68 669)

	Lower secondary	Upper secondary	Tertiary
Denmark	0.269	0.368	0.600
Germany	0.161	0.186	0.328
Netherlands	0.175	0.126	0.113
Belgium	0.062	0.124	0.226
France	0.072	0.136	0.229
UK	0.181	0.304	0.538
Ireland	0.048	0.119	0.151
Italy	0.021	0.081	0.178
Greece	0.013	0.038	0.084
Spain	0.064	0.197	0.247
Portugal	0.013	0.053	0.099
Average	0.061	0.147	0.270

so this useful distinction will not be pursued here and training is
defined as including both general and firm-specific.

Employers paid for or organised close to 66 per cent of training in
1996. This percentage was higher than average in the UK, Denmark
and Germany – the 'high-incidence' countries – and lower than
average in Southern Europe, where most of the 'low-incidence' countries are located. Close to 35 per cent of training programmes lasted
more than nine weeks. Interestingly the duration was longer in the
low-incidence countries.[6]

The relationship between educational attainment in 1994 and training in 1996 is explored in Table 8.3. With the notable exception of the
Netherlands, training incidence was higher among the more educated.
On average, more than a quarter of the individuals with college education received training in 1996, compared with less than 15 per cent of
those with a high school diploma and 6 per cent with lower-secondary
education.

Training incidence: the empirical evidence

The empirical investigation of the factors that affect training incidence
in Europe is based on the following probit model:

$$\text{Prob } [T96 = 1] = \Phi (Z' \beta) \qquad\qquad (8.1)$$

where T96 is a dummy equal to 1 if training occurred during the reference period (January 1995 to the start of the 1996 survey), Z is a vector of explanatory variables, β is a vector of parameters and Φ is the standard normal distribution. Most of the variables included in the vector Z are drawn from the 1994 survey, before the reference period of T96. This avoids the problems associated with the potential endogeneity of explanatory variables.

In the baseline regression Z includes a gender dummy (Gender = 1 for males, 0 for females); two education dummies – one for tertiary education in 1994 (College 94) and the other for upper-secondary education in 1994 (High school 94); age (Age); degree of experience in 1994 (Experience 94); measured as present age minus age at labour market entry; marital status in 1994 (Married 94); health status in 1994 (Health 94 = 1 if health was good or fair, 0 otherwise); satisfaction with leisure time in 1994 (Happy 94 = 1 if satisfied, 0 otherwise); job search in 1994 (Search 94 = 1 if searched for a new job, 0 otherwise); training in 1994 (T94 = 1 if training took place during the period 1993–94, 0 otherwise); total net personal income in 1994 (Y94), including social assistance and insurance; and measured in 10 000 ECU;[7] main activity in 1994 (E94 > 15 = 1 if employed for at least 15 hours per week, 0 otherwise; E94 < 15 = 1 if employed for fewer than 15 hours per week, 0 otherwise; U94 = 1 if unemployed or discouraged workers in 1994, 0 otherwise); and long-term unemployment (ULT = 1 if at least one spell of unemployment lasted longer than one year in the five years prior to 1994, 0 otherwise).

Personal income, Y94, is expected to capture finer differences in economic circumstances after controlling for the main economic activity in 1994. If training was financed totally or partially by an individual, this variable also measures ability to pay. The dummies Health 94, Happy 94 and Search 94 are indicators of fitness and of satisfaction with the main employment activity in 1994. Training in 1994 (T94) is designed to measure persistence in training episodes. Since information on this is not available for the Netherlands, this country has been dropped from the sample.[8]

The summary statistics of the variables used in the probit regression are shown in Table A8.1 in the appendix. It turns out that the percentage of individuals undergoing training was significantly higher in 1996 (12.7 per cent) than in 1994 (8.9 per cent). Average age and average experience were about 40 and 22 years respectively. Nearly 51 per cent of the sample were males and about 66 per cent were married. The large majority were in good or fair health, but only 15.7 per cent were

Table 8.4 Training probit (marginal effects) and linear probability model (dependent variable T96, n = 58 453)

	Coef. probit	*P-value*	*Coef.* LPM	*P-value*
Gender	–0.004	0.044	–0.009	0.002
College 94	0.129	0.000	0.129	0.000
High school 94	0.045	0.000	0.032	0.000
Age	–0.003	0.000	–0.003	0.000
Experience 94	0.0006	0.003	0.0008	0.000
Married 94	–0.011	0.000	–0.011	0.000
Health 94	0.027	0.000	0.009	0.016
Happy 94	–0.008	0.008	–0.016	0.000
Income 94	0.009	0.000	0.015	0.000
T94	0.149	0.000	0.201	0.000
Search 94	–0.0002	0.953	0.005	0.326
LTU 94	–0.020	0.000	–0.028	0.000
E94 > 15	0.046	0.000	0.038	0.000
E94 ≤ 15	–0.002	0.800	–0.017	0.025
U94	0.053	0.000	0.029	0.000
Pseudo R^2	0.22		0.18	

Notes: Robust standard errors. Coefficients are significant at the 5 per cent level of confidence when the P-value is less than 0.050. Each regression includes a constant and country dummies. LTU = a spell of unemployment of at least one year during the five years prior to joining the 1994 survey.

happy with their leisure time. Furthermore 17.5 per cent of the sample were searching for a new job in 1994 and 9.4 per cent were unemployed or discouraged workers. Finally, close to 12 per cent of the individuals in the sample had experienced at least one spell of long-term unemployment in the five years prior to 1994.

Table 8.4 presents the results on training incidence. To facilitate the interpretation, the first two columns of the table show the marginal effects of the estimated probit model (Equation 8.1) and the last two columns show the estimated coefficients of a linear probability model. 'Marginal effects' mean the changes in probability for an infinitesimal change in each independent, continuous variable, and discrete changes in the probability for dummy variables.

The analysis revealed that training incidence was higher among younger individuals who were male, single, healthy, more experienced and less satisfied with their leisure time, asked who had experienced no long-term unemployment and had a higher personal income. There is also evidence of persistence in training, in that individuals who had engaged in training in 1994 were more likely to do so again in 1996. Conditional on income in 1994, training was more likely for those who had been working for at least 15 hours a week and for the unemployed.

Finally, *ceteris paribus*, individuals with a college education had the highest probability of investing in training. Individuals with upper-secondary education did better than individuals with less education (in the constant term), but not as well as college graduates. The increases in the probability of training associated with an upper-secondary education and a college degree were 0.045 and 0.129 respectively.

Cross-country differences in the complementarity between education and training

The relationship between educational attainment and training incidence varied significantly across countries, as shown in the first two columns of Table 8.5, which presents the results of a probit regression that included among the regressors the interactions between each education dummy and the country dummies. The degree of complementarity between education and training, measured by the estimated coefficients of these interactions, was lowest in Germany and Ireland and highest in Italy and the UK.

The cross-country differences in the relationship between education and training incidence might be due, or at least in part, to the way in which schools are organised in European countries. One important dimension is the degree of differentiation between vocational, academic tracks. In some countries (for instance Germany), differentiation is high and starts early on. In other countries, secondary schools are comprehensive and there is little differentiation between tracks (for instance Ireland). The systems in the remaining countries fall between these two extremes (Shavit and Muller, 1998).

The question of whether educational stratification is an important factor in the relationship between educational attainment and training incidence is addressed in the last two columns of Table 8.5, where the interactions between educational attainment and the country dummies have been replaced by the interactions between the education dummies and the dummy Tracking, which is equal to 3 for countries where secondary schools are very stratified (Germany), 2 for countries where stratification is important (Belgium), 1 where there is some degree of stratification (France, Italy, Greece, Spain and Portugal) and 0 where schools are mainly comprehensive (UK, Ireland and Denmark).[9] The results shown in the table suggest that the impact of

Table 8.5 Training probit (marginal effects) with interactions between educational attainment and country dummies, and between educational attainment and tracking (dependent variable T96, marginal effects, n = 58 453)

	Coeff.	*P-value*	*Coeff.*	*P-value*
Gender	−0.004	0.064	−0.004	0.063
Age	−0.003	0.000	−0.003	0.000
Experience 94	0.0006	0.004	.0006	0.003
Married 94	−0.010	0.000	−0.010	0.000
Health 94	0.026	0.000	0.027	0.000
Happy 94	−0.008	0.006	−0.008	0.008
Income 94	0.009	0.000	0.009	0.000
T94	0.146	0.000	0.149	0.000
Search 94	−0.0004	0.915	−0.0003	0.923
LTU 94	−0.019	0.000	−0.020	0.000
E94 > 15	0.047	0.000	0.045	0.000
E94 ≤ 15	0.0001	0.985	−0.002	0.786
U94	0.055	0.000	0.052	0.000
College 94	–	–	0.155	0.000
High school 94	–	–	0.057	0.000
College 94 * Tracking	–	–	−0.014	0.000
High school 94 * Tracking	–	–	−0.010	0.000
College 94 * D	0.078	0.000	–	–
College 94 * DK	0.159	0.000	–	–
College 94 * BE	0.131	0.000	–	–
College 94 * FR	0.100	0.000	–	–
College 94 * UK	0.215	0.000	–	–
College 94 * IR	0.078	0.000	–	–
College 94 * IT	0.232	0.000	–	–
College 94 * GR	0.135	0.000	–	–
College 94 * ES	0.127	0.000	–	–
College 94 * PO	0.153	0.000	–	–
High school 94 * D	0.006	0.000	–	–
High school 94 * DK	0.023	0.353	–	–
High school 94 * BE	0.041	0.022	–	–
High school 94 * FR	0.029	0.004	–	–
High school 94 * UK	0.050	0.002	–	–
High school 94 * IR	0.057	0.000	–	–
High school 94 * IT	0.087	0.000	–	–
High school 94 * GR	0.046	0.001	–	–
High school 94 * ES	0.091	0.000	–	–
High school 94 * PO	0.041	0.004	–	–
Pseudo R^2	0.22	–	0.22	

Notes: See notes for Table 8.4.

educational attainment on the incidence of training is significantly lower in countries with more stratified education systems. This is consistent with the view that stratified schools increase specialisation, thereby reducing the need to undertake additional training after labour market entry.[10]

Cohort effects in the complementarity between education and training

To investigate whether training incidence and the complementarity between educational attainment and training varied with the date of birth of individuals, individual age was replaced by three cohort dummies (Co1834 = 1 if the individual was aged 18–34 in 1996, 0 otherwise; Co3549 = 1 if the individual was aged 35–49 in 1996, 0 otherwise; Co50 = 1 if the individual was aged 50 or above in 1996, 0 otherwise) and the regression included the interactions between these dummies and the two educational dummies: College 94 and High school 94. Table 8.6 shows the results of the probit regression. With

Table 8.6 Training probit with cohort dummies (dependent variable T96, marginal effects, n = 58 453)

	Coef.	*P-value*
Gender	−0.003	0.155
C3549	−0.030	0.000
C50	−0.058	0.000
College 94 * C1834	0.090	0.000
College 94 * C3549	0.147	0.000
College 94 * C50	0.163	0.000
High school * C1834	0.032	0.002
High school * C3549	0.061	0.000
High school * C50	0.062	0.000
Experience 94	−0.0006	0.160
Married 94	−0.022	0.000
Health 94	0.031	0.000
Happy 94	−0.007	0.010
Income 94	0.008	0.000
T94	0.150	0.000
Search 94	0.0006	0.824
LTU 94	−0.023	0.000
E94 > 15	0.034	0.000
E94 ≤ 15	−0.008	0.253
U94	0.046	0.000
Pseudo R^2	0.22	

Notes: See notes for Table 8.4.

regard to individuals with at most lower-secondary education and those with upper-secondary education, the analysis shows that training incidence was lowest for the oldest age group. One possible reason for this was that the incentive to train was less for older workers because the time left to reap the rewards from training was shorter.

With regard to individuals with tertiary education, however, the analysis shows that training incidence was slightly higher, not lower, in the intermediate and oldest age groups than among younger workers with the same educational attainment. It might be that training incidence did not fall among more educated older workers because their human capital had depreciated faster than that of younger workers with the same education and needed to be maintained by additional training.[11]

Labour market institutions and the incidence of training

As discussed in the second section, in the presence of a training supply externality the incidence of training increases with the aggregate supply of educated workers. In this chapter, aggregate supply is measured by the percentage of individuals who had attained at least an upper-secondary education in 1992.[12]

The models of non-competitive labour markets reviewed by Acemoglu and Pischke (1998a) suggest that wage compression should lead to more firm-sponsored training and could increase the overall investment in skills. Sources of wage compression are transaction costs, such as matching and search frictions, and asymmetric information between the current employer of the worker and other firms in the labour market. The structure of wages can also be compressed by institution such as minimum wages, employment protection measures, the relative strength of unions in wage determination and the degree of centralisation of wage bargaining.

Traditionally, stronger unions have compressed wage differentials by skill and education.[13] In an imperfect labour market, stronger unions can also reduce turnover, thereby encouraging firms to sponsor training programmes (Acemoglu and Pischke, 1999; Booth *et al.*, 1999). The impact of minimum wages on training incidence is less straightforward. On the one hand minimum wages have a negative effect on training in the standard competitive model because they prevent workers from taking wage cuts and investing in training. On the other hand a high minimum wage relative to the average wage leads to wage compression and can favour firm-sponsored training in a non-competitive environment.

The relationship between the degree of centralisation of wage bargaining and wage compression is not clear-cut. Calmfors (1993), for instance, uses a simple two-sector model of a unionised economy to show that a higher degree of centralisation is associated with a less dispersed wage structure only if particular restrictions on union preferences are imposed. Relative compression of the wage structure is also associated with strict employment protection practices. As argued by Bertola and Rogerson (1997), firing restrictions can hardly be binding if wages are completely unrestrained and employers can reduce them in order to make stable employment profitable. Limiting the freedom allowed to employers and workers when setting wages gives force to these constraints. Higher employment protection can also favour investment in human capital by increasing turnover costs and discouraging involuntary separations, i.e. separations initiated by the employer.

The cross-country differences in institutionalised employment norms and in aggregate educational attainment are illustrated in Table 8.7. Greece has been excluded from this and the next table because of lack of data. The selected indicators for institutionalised norms relate mainly to the 1980s and early 1990s and include the OECD index of employment protection (EPL), which increased with the degree of protection and was highest in Italy (14.25) and lowest in the UK (2.25); average union density (U.dens) during the period 1975–95, which ranged from 14 per cent in France and Spain to 73 per cent in Denmark; the Kaitz index (the ratio between the minimum wage and the average wage), which was lowest in Spain (0.32) and highest in Italy (0.71); and the degree of centralisation of wage bargaining (Ranking), which ranged from 4 (high centralisation) in Denmark to 13 (low centralisation) in Italy.

Table 8.7 also shows the share of the active population with at least upper-secondary education in 1992 (E92). Educational attainment was highest in Germany, Denmark and the UK (the members of the 'high-incidence' group) and lowest in Italy, Spain and Portugal, where training incidence was lower. The last two columns of the table show the estimated country-specific 90–50 and 50–10 wage differentials, two standard measures of wage compression. One source of such measures is the OECD, which has computed these differentials for the early 1990s (see OECD, 1999). Two problems with this source for the present purposes are that it does not include Spain and Ireland and that it uses heterogeneous national sources. Both these problems have been overcome by computing the 90–50 (D95) and 50–10 (D51) differentials in 1994 using ECHP data. The definition of earnings used here is the net

Table 8.7 Educational attainment and institutionalised employment norms, by country

	EPL	U.dens	Kaitz	Ranking	E92	D95	D51
Germany	12.0	0.33	0.55	6	0.82	1.84	1.94
Denmark	3.25	0.73	0.54	4	0.59	1.46	1.35
Belgium	10.5	0.53	0.60	8	0.45	1.51	1.43
France	9.5	0.14	0.50	11	0.52	1.88	1.60
UK	2.25	0.43	0.40	12	0.68	1.79	1.80
Ireland	2.75	0.53	0.55	12	0.42	1.93	1.91
Italy	14.25	0.28	0.71	13	0.28	1.44	1.45
Spain	11.5	0.14	0.32	11	0.23	1.85	1.72
Portugal	12.5	0.44	0.45	11	0.14	2.14	1.56

Sources: OECD (1999); Nickell and Layard (1999); ECHP, 1994 survey.

monthly wages and salaries of individuals who work full-time for 30–50 hours per week and whose main income comes from paid employment. Reassuringly, these measures correlate well with the OECD measures. For instance the correlation between the OECD's and our measure of the 90–50 differential is 0.907. Moreover the analysis reveals that wage compression is highest in Denmark, Belgium and Italy, as in the OECD data.

Table 8.8 presents the estimates of the probit model of training incidence when the country dummies are replaced by the time-invariant institutional variables described in Table 8.7.[14] All these variables differ across countries but are constant among individuals in the same country. Therefore the standard errors are adjusted by allowing errors to be independent among countries and dependent within countries. The table shows the marginal effects based on the probit model (1), both without (columns 1 and 2) and with (columns 3 and 4) the two measures of wage compression. The key findings can be summarised as follows:

- The incidence of training is higher in countries with a greater supply of educated workers.
- Training incidence is higher in countries with a more compressed wage structure, as suggested by Acemoglu and Pischke (1999).
- Wage compression above median earnings (D95) reduces training incidence significantly more than wage compression below median earnings (D51);
- Irrespective of whether measures of wage compression are included or excluded, training is less frequent in countries with a higher

Table 8.8 Training probit with country-specific variables (dependent variable T96, marginal effects)

	Coef. (1)	P-value (2)	Coef. (3)	P-value (4)	Coef. (5)	P-value (6)
Kaitz index	–0.128	0.345	–0.371	0.000	–0.444	0.000
Union density	–0.058	0.609	–0.005	0.819	0.002	0.957
EPL	–0.008	0.094	–0.004	0.000	–0.007	0.001
E92	0.113	0.055	0.197	0.000	0.284	0.000
Ranking	–0.005	0.343	0.0005	0.653	0.001	0.544
D95	–	–	–0.170	0.000	–0.216	0.000
D51	–	–	–0.020	0.092	–0.052	0.007
Gender	–0.006	0.082	–0.005	0.116	0.011	0.024
College 94	0.151	0.000	0.138	0.000	0.072	0.000
High school 94	0.053	0.000	0.050	0.000	0.036	0.000
Age	–0.003	0.000	–0.003	0.000	–0.002	0.000
Experience 94	0.0005	0.391	0.0005	0.409	–0.0004	0.567
Married 94	–0.012	0.002	–0.010	0.013	–0.005	0.001
Health 94	0.032	0.007	0.030	0.015	0.019	0.320
Happy 94	–0.006	0.087	–0.007	0.036	–0.011	0.009
Income 94	0.010	0.001	0.010	0.000	0.007	0.002
T94	0.170	0.000	0.162	0.000	0.148	0.000
Search 94	0.002	0.707	0.0002	0.958	0.004	0.320
LTU 94	–0.018	0.000	–0.022	0.000	–0.022	0.000
E94 > 15	0.057	0.004	0.055	0.004	–	–
E94 < 15	0.004	0.728	0.002	0.813	–	–
U94	0.066	0.000	0.065	0.000	–	–
No. in sample	51 955		51 955		32 567	
Pseudo R^2	0.20		0.21		0.23	

Notes: See notes for Table 8.4. The last two columns refer to the subsample of individuals who worked at least 14 hours a week in 1994.

minimum wage to average wage ratio and with higher employment protection.

- Cross-country differences in union density and degree of centralisation of wage bargaining do not significantly affect training incidence.

It is tempting to interpret the first result as evidence of the presence of a training supply externality. One problem with this interpretation is that cross-country differences in the supply of educated workers could encompass composition effects. This is the case when training incidence varies with the occupation or sector of activity because of different skill requirements, and the allocation to occupations and sectors depends on education.

The data used in this chapter show that managers, professionals, technicians, financial intermediaries and workers in the public sector are on average better educated and are more likely to receive training. The cross-country correlation between E92 and the percentage of individuals who worked at least 15 hours a week in 1994 in the above capacities are 0.78 and 0.52 respectively. In these circumstances, the positive association between E92 and training incidence could simply mean that countries with a higher educational attainment also have a higher share of occupations and sectors with a high training incidence.

To try to control for composition effects the analysis focused on the subsample of individuals who worked at least 15 hours a week in 1994. Information on their occupation and sector of activity in 1994[15] was used to select four groups: professionals in the (public) education sector, skilled tradesmen in the construction industry, clerks in financial intermediation and service workers in the retail and wholesale sector.[16] For each group the probit model used for in Table 8.8 was estimated. This enabled a cross-country comparison of individuals with the same occupation in the same sector of activity. The results shown in Table 8.9 confirm that countries with a higher supply of educated individuals also had a higher training incidence. This can be seen as evidence of a positive externality in the relationship between education and training.

The (small) negative association between the degree of employment protection and training incidence revealed in the analysis is not consistent with the view that higher protection favours training by reducing turnover and increasing job security. Depending on wage compression, there is also no evidence that countries with stronger unions or more centralised bargaining systems have a higher training incidence. These results suggest that stronger unions can affect training positively only by increasing wage compression.

Variations in the minimum wage across countries, given wage compression, affect the probability of training significantly more than cross-country variations in employment protection. One can also see from Table 8.8 that inclusion in the probit model of the two measures of wage compression, D95 and D51, leads to an increase in both the size and the precision of the negative marginal effect of the Kaitz index on the probability of training. The increase in size may be induced by the negative correlation between the index and wage compression. In the current data, the correlation with measures D95 and D51 is –0.67 and –0.41 respectively. Therefore countries with a higher Kaitz index

Table 8.9 Training probit with country-specific variables (dependent variable T96, marginal effects, selected groups of workers)

	Coef. (1)	P-value (2)	Coef. (3)	P-value (4)	Coef. (5)	P-value (6)	Coef. (7)	P-value (8)
Kaitz index	−1.203	0.042	−0.072	0.030	−1.431	0.000	−0.156	0.000
Union density	−0.071	0.920	−0.054	0.309	0.063	0.786	−0.005	0.910
EPL	−0.008	0.746	−0.006	0.004	−0.0007	0.954	−0.002	0.179
E92	0.791	0.001	0.019	0.242	0.427	0.003	0.154	0.000
Ranking	0.008	0.731	−0.003	0.065	0.003	0.780	0.005	0.003
D95	−0.809	0.044	−0.163	0.000	−0.437	0.000	−0.087	0.000
D51	−0.117	0.752	0.086	0.001	−0.108	0.473	0.016	0.380
Gender	−0.011	0.626	−0.008	0.842	−0.009	0.721	0.013	0.099
College 94	0.137	0.172	0.038	0.039	−0.022	0.776	0.052	0.053
High school 94	0.161	0.200	0.008	0.477	0.017	0.824	0.006	0.542
Age	−0.002	0.728	−0.0004	0.605	0.009	0.238	−0.001	0.453
Experience 94	0.0006	0.909	−0.001	0.051	−0.015	0.056	0.0007	0.401
Married 94	−0.009	0.663	0.002	0.712	0.004	0.778	−0.028	0.121
Happy 94	−0.019	0.506	−0.011	0.307	0.067	0.318	−0.002	0.876
Income 94	−0.009	0.457	0.0004	0.855	0.092	0.007	0.027	0.009
T94	0.224	0.000	0.088	0.028	0.215	0.000	0.080	0.000
Search 94	−0.043	0.480	−0.004	0.658	0.016	0.780	−0.001	0.944
LTU 94	0.036	0.631	−0.009	0.668	−0.028	0.703	0.007	0.531
No. in sample	1491		1528		594		1271	
Pseudo R^2	0.15		0.26		0.14		0.13	

Notes: See notes for Table 8.4. The variable Health94 has been dropped because it rarely takes the value of 1 in smaller sample sizes. Columns 1–2: professionals in education; columns 3–4: trade workers in construction; columns 5–6: clerks in financial intermediation; columns 7–8: service workers in retail and wholesale trade.

have a more compressed wage structure and the minimum wage affects training both directly (a negative effect) and indirectly by influencing wage compression (a positive effect).

The cross-country evidence that, depending on wage compression, minimum wages are negatively correlated with training incidence is consistent with the findings of studies on the impact of differing minimum wages in the US (Leighton and Mincer, 1981, Neumark and Wascher, (1988 Acemoglu and Pischke, 1998b). One problem with cross-country (and cross-state) comparisons, however, is that the results can be confounded by the presence of other country or state effects. Whilst some of these effects are controlled for in this study by the inclusion of the country-specific variables shown in Table 8.7, other effects should also be considered. Acemoglu and Pischke (1998b), for instance, argue that the industrial and occupational composition of employment can vary substantially across countries and states, and that different industries and occupations have different skill requirements.

Here, cross-country differences in the composition of employment are controlled for in three ways. First, the last two columns of Table 8.8 show the results of a probit regression for the subsample of individuals' who worked at least 15 hours per week in 1994. Since information was available on these individuals occupations (nine categories) and sectors of activity (18 categories), both occupational and sectoral dummies could be included in the regression. These dummies were designed to capture the differences in training incidence due to industry and occupation. Second, Table 8.9 shows the results of probit regressions for subgroups of individuals in the same occupation and sector of activity. Finally (and not reported), included in the regressors in the last two columns of Table 8.8 are the country-specific percentage of managerial, technical and professional workers and the percentage of individuals who worked in financial intermediation and the public sector, where training incidence was higher. All these experiments reveal that minimum wages have a negative and significant marginal effect on training incidence. It can be concluded that countries with a similar degree of wage compression but with a higher Kaitz index have a lower incidence of training.

Overall the findings in Table 8.8 can be illustrated by comparing two of the countries in the sample, Denmark and Italy. The former country belongs to the 'high training incidence' group and the latter to the 'low training incidence' group. They have similar measures of wage compression, but Denmark has significantly less employment protection, a larger supply of educated workers and a lower Kaitz index than Italy. The bottom line is that these institutional factors are important to understanding the variations of training incidence observed in Europe.[17]

Conclusions

This chapter has used European Community Household Panel data to study in a comparative perspective training incidence and the relationship between training and educational attainment. These data are useful both because of their broad coverage and because their format enables cross-country comparisons. The analysis has revealed substantial differences in training incidence within Europe. In 1996 training incidence was higher than average in Germany, Denmark and the UK and lower than average in most Southern European countries. Using cross-country variations in institutionalised employment practices, cross-country differences in training incidence have been with correlated differences in educational attainment and in the relative importance of the minimum wage, employment protection, union density and wage compression. The results show that training incidence is higher in countries with a more educated labour force and a more compressed wage structure. Depending on wage compression, higher minimum wages and stronger employment protection are associated with lower training incidence. Cross-country differences in union density and wage bargaining rules do not significantly affect training incidence.

The analysis has also revealed that better educated individuals are more likely to invest in training. The complementarity between these two variables is stronger in countries with a comprehensive school system (the UK and Ireland) than in those with a stratified system (Germany), suggesting that training after school could be required to compensate for the relative lack of specialisation provided by the former system.

Appendix 8.1

Table A8.1 Summary statistics of the variables used in the training regressions

	Mean	Std deviation
T96	0.127	–
T94	0.089	–
Age	39.78	11.50
	Mean	Std deviation
Experience 94	22.32	12.44
Married 94	0.655	–
Health 94	0.945	4.258
ULT 94	0.123	–
Happy 94	0.157	–
Income 94	0.917	1.21
Search 94	0.175	–
Gender	0.490	–
E94 > 15	0.625	–
E94 ≤ 15	0.024	–
U94	0.094	–

Table A8.2 Training lasting longer than nine weeks (1) and employer financed training (2) by country, 1996, (per cent, n = 68 669)

	(1)	(2)
Denmark	0.175	0.860
Germany	0.389	0.736
Netherlands	–	0.357
Belgium	0.248	0.728
France	0.277	0.703
UK	0.251	0.862
Ireland	0.539	0.573
Italy	0.393	0.619
Greece	0.404	0.547
Spain	0.623	0.316
Portugal	0.430	0.586
Average	0.352	0.656

Notes

1. I am grateful to two anonymous referees for comments and suggestions and to Enrico Rettore for advice. The research was supported by the European Commission under the TSER program PL980182 for the PuRE project. The usual disclaimer applies.

2. The participating countries were Germany, Denmark, the Netherlands, Belgium, France, the UK, Ireland, Italy, Luxembourg, Greece, Spain and Portugal. Luxembourg is excluded from this study because of its small size.
3. The exact wording of the question in the 1996 survey was: 'Have you at any time since January 1995 been in vocational education or training, including part-time or short courses?'
4. Only 0.43 per cent of the interviewees had engaged in training during the period.
5. Other types of training account for the remainder (1.9 per cent).
6. See Table A8.2 in the appendix to this chapter for more details.
7. Income gross of taxes for France.
8. This and the presence of missing values in the explanatory variables serve to reduce the sample size to close to 58 000.
9. The values assigned to countries depend on the school age when differentiation begins. See OECD (1991), Hannah *et al.* (1996) and Lassibille and Navarro Gomez (1998) for details of school systems in Europe.
10. A possible objection is that education systems have changed over time in some countries. For example Italy and the UK shifted from a stratified to a more comprehensive system in the mid 1960s. The qualitative findings are robust, however, as the sample excludes individuals who were born before 1955 and went to a junior high school before these reforms took place.
11. As argued by Neuman and Weiss (1995, p. 946), 'it is reasonable to assume that an elementary school graduate's human capital does not suffer much from obsolescence since the material taught in elementary schools has not changed much over time. However, an electrical engineer who was trained 20 years ago learned vastly different material than one who just finished his schooling.'
12. Source: OECD (1995).
13. See Freeman (1993).
14. An alternative to replacing country dummies by institutional variables is to use a two-step method: in the first step one estimates the country dummies; in the second step weighted least-squares are used to regress these dummies on institutional variables. See Card and Krueger (1990).
15. The percentage of individuals who remained in the same occupation (sector) in 1994 and 1996 was greater than 0.87 (0.89).
16. I select the groups with the highest number of available observations.
17. An alternative approach, as followed by Bassanini and Brunello (2003), is to partition employees into clusters of relatively homogeneous workers and compare training participation rates with wage distributions for each of these clusters, controlling for country-specific effects. Although more rigorous as a test of the wage compression hypothesis, this approach does not shed light on the institutional factors that affect both training and wage compression.

References

Acemoglu, D. (2000) *Technical Change, Inequality and the Labor Market*, NBER Working Paper no. 7800 (Cambridge, Mass.: NBER).

Acemoglu, D. and Pischke, J. (1998a) *Beyond Becker: Training in Imperfect Labor Markets*, NBER Working Paper no. 6740 (Cambridge, Mass.: NBER).

Acemoglu, D. and Pischke, J. (1998b) 'Minimum Wages and On-the-Job Training, mimeo (Cambridge, Mass.: MIT).

Acemoglu, D. and Pischke, J. (1999) 'The Structure of Wages and Investment in General Training', *Journal of Political Economy*.

Bassanini, A. and Brunello, G. (2003) 'Is Training more frequent when wage compression is higher? Evidence from the ECHP', 17A Discussion Paper n. 839, Bonn.

Becker, G. (1975) *Human Capital* (Chicago: University of Chicago Press).

Bertola, G. and Rogerson, R. (1997) 'Institutions and Labor Reallocation, *The European Economic Review*, vol. 41, pp. 1147–71.

Booth, A., Francesconi, M. and Zoega, G. (1999) 'Training, rent sharing and unions', mimeo (Essex University).

Booth, A. and Snower, D. (eds) (1995) *Acquiring Skills* (Cambridge: Cambridge University Press).

Brunello, G. and Medio, A. (2001) 'An Explanation of international differences in education and workplace training', *European Economic Review*, vol. 45, n. 1, pp. 307–22.

Calmfors, L. (1993) *Centralization of Wage Bargaining and Macroeconomic Performance: a Survey*, IIES Discussion Paper no. 536 (Stockholm University).

Card, D. and Krueger, A. (1990) 'Does School Quality Matter?', *The Journal of Political Economy*, vol. 100, no. 1, pp. 1–40.

Card, D. and Krueger, A. (1995) *Myth and Measurement: The New Economics of the Minimum Wage* (Princeton, NJ: Princeton University Press).

European Commission (1999) *EHCP UDB Manual* (Brussels: European Commission).

Freeman, R. (1993) 'How Much has De-unionisation Contributed to the Rise in Male Earnings Inequality?', in S. Danziger and P. Gottschalk (eds), *Uneven Tides: Rising Inequality in America* (New York: Russell Sage Foundation).

Hannah, F., Raffe, K. and Smyth, J. (1996) 'Cross-National Research in School to Work Transition: an Analytical Framework', mimeo (Paris: OECD).

Heckman, J. (1999) *Policies to Foster Human Capital*, NBER Working Paper no. 7288 (Cambridge, Mass.: NBER).

Lassibille, G. and Navarro Gomez, M. (1998) *Organization and efficiency of education systems: some empirical findings*, LEO-CRESP Working Paper no. 4 (University of Orleans).

Leighton, L. and Mincer, J. (1981) 'The Effects of Minimum Wages on Human Capital Formation', in S. Rottemberg (ed.), *The Economics of Legal Minimum Wages* (Washington, DC).

Lynch, L. (ed.) (1994) *Training and the Private Sector: International Comparisons* (Chicago, Ill.: University of Chicago Press.)

Neuman, S., and Weiss, A. (1995) 'On the effects of schooling vintage on experience – earnings profiles: theory and evidence', *European Economic Review*, vol. 39, n. 4, pp. 943–55.

Neumark, D. and Wascher, W. (1998) *Minimum wages and training revisited*, NBER Working Paper no. 6651 (Cambridge, Mass.: NBER).

Nickell, S. and Layard, R. (1999) *Labour Market Institutions and Economic performance*, Centre for Economic Performance Discussion Paper no. 23 (Oxford: CEP).

OECD (1991) *Employment Outlook* (Paris: OECD).

OECD (1995) *Education at a Glance* (Paris: OECD).

OECD (1999) *Employment Outlook* (Paris: OECD).

Pischke, J. (2000) *Continuous training in Germany*, NBER Working Paper no. 137 (Cambridge, Mass.: NBER).

Rosen, S. (1976) 'A theory of life earnings', *Journal of Political Economy*, vol. 86, pp. S45–62.

Shavit, Y. and Muller, W. (1998) *From School to Work* (Oxford: Clarendon Press).

Snower, D. (1994) *The Low-Skill, Bad-Job Trap*, Discussion Paper no. 14 (London: Birbeck College).

Soskice, D. (1994) 'Reconciling Markets and Institutions: The German Apprenticeship System', in L. Lynch, *Training and the Private Sector* (Chicago, Ill.: University of Chicago Press).

Thurow, L. (1975) *Generating Inequality* (London: Macmillan).

Index